SCIENCE OF ENLIGHTENMENT

आत्मज्ञान का विज्ञान

Swami Maitreyanand

notionpress
.com

INDIA • SINGAPORE • MALAYSIA

ISBN 979-8-90392-257-4

Cover design: Mahendra Mistry

Images: Madhavi Erande & Mahesh Davadkar

Translation & Editing: Geeta Bedi

DISCLAIMER

The Science of Enlightenment (Atmagyan ka Vigyan) is a compilation of questions asked by sadhakas and wisdom shared by Sadguru Swami Maitreyanand Ji. The objective of this compilation is to help seekers understand the science of developing inner vision, self-reflection and self-observation for Ultimate Truth to dawn. Guruji started sharing his personal experiences and guidance in the form of deshanas with humanity, years after attainment of Nirvana.

His intention, in no way, is to criticize, judge, divide, look down upon or denounce any particular individual, any caste, culture, religion, rituals or rites being observed, nor is there any intention of judging, looking down upon, criticizing, dividing or denouncing any religious, political or societal mindset or mental impressions.

If at all, at any given point, any part of this text comes across as or seems hurtful, insulting, opposing any community, lineage, culture or tradition, we seek prior forgiveness for the same. Kindly accept our heartfelt apology. This text is being presented to you with an absolute good and sole intention of seekers' progress on the spiritual path, along with a feeling of utmost respect for all religions, systems of faith and education, all holy texts, different paths and traditions being followed across the globe. Any mention whatsoever of any particular tradition, custom or faith, if at all, has solely been made for the sake of self-reflection and learning and not with any intention of contradiction or a sense of judgement.

We sincerely hope that this Shower of Grace, these pearls of wisdom meant for leading us to the Ultimate Truth and Liberation, being given by Swamiji so selflessly and lovingly in the form of teachings, will be received by one and all in the right spirit with the right understanding.

DEDICATION

For all of us, getting an opportunity to soak in the sacred river of wisdom flowing through Sadgurudev Swami Maitreyanand Ji's words and his entire being, is a huge sign signifying that we are all under his divine canopy of infinite love and blessings.

We dedicate this sacred text, this Granth at Gurudev's holy feet.

Contents

Preface

'Science of Enlightenment' is a collection of a few chosen spiritual conversations out of more than fourteen hundred available online. These are in question & answer format - questions asked by the sãdhakas and the deshanas that flow through Guruji, Swami Maitreyanand. Sadhakas have been offered complete spiritual knowledge and wisdom in these deshanas, to overcome any obstacle or stopover they may be facing at any juncture in their journey of self-realisation. Every conversation has the power to break personal barriers that keep one stuck in the 'Wheel of Samsara'.

Capacity to receive and absorb this wisdom depends on the individual's capability and worthiness, which expands exponentially with repeated listening, reading and meditating upon these conversations. This is the beauty of these deshanas which are an Existential Grace being bestowed upon the spiritual seekers.

The heartfelt desire of many sãdhakas that Swamiji's deshanas be made available in a book format for reading, has been fulfilled today. This should not be regarded as any normal book but a sacred text, since Astitva's energy, Swamiji's energy is inherently present here in the form of divine and prophetic messages flowing endlessly through the pages. May all receive and absorb this energy, and free themselves from this illusory cycle of death and rebirth.

In the teachings and conversations present here, Swamiji has thrown light on various worldly and spiritual topics like the Soul, Supreme Soul, Self-Realisation(Nirvana), Supreme-Realisation or the Great Liberation upon death of the body (Mahaparinirvana), nature, subtle body, saints, gurus, diet to be consumed, dhyana, samadhi, karma-prarabdha and the chain of cause and effect.

It is absolutely possible that these deshanas, along with an unbroken and unshakeable faith in them, can become a tool and reason for someone's liberation, just as a falling leaf from a tree became one for Lao Tse's liberation and a star of dawn for that of Buddha's. Just as Totapuri Maharaj released Ramakrishna Paramahansa from his deep attachment to Maa Kali and just as being in the river for three days led to Guru Nanak Dev Ji's liberation, there is a very high possibility of these discourses being instrumental in the freedom of the sadhakas. The possibility of liberation, with utmost faith in the Guru and his vani, cannot be discounted at any cost. We bow down with reverence and extend our deep gratitude to Swamiji for his unending support and blessings present at every step of our life's journey.

This book is a translation of the Hindi version 'Atmagyan ka Vigyan'. It is important to mention that the flow of the text and its meaning have been maintained in the best possible way. Utmost care has been taken that the essence of Swamiji's deshanas does not get altered at any point. It is also vital to point out here that Astitva's energy, Guruji's energy is ever present and flowing endlessly through the pages and every printed word of this work.

His blessings are felt with every word being typed for this translation. It has been an absolutely transformative experience.

Nothing can be accomplished alone. It was a humble observation that it was not just a collective support from human beings, rather, all the divine energies from higher dimensions seemed to have come together to support this spiritual service meant for the higher good, transforming it into an existential happening.

A heartfelt gratitude to everyone whose contribution helped this sacred text to materialize.

A big thank you to Tejas Vaghela ji and Jignesh Varsani Ji for initiating the journey of Swamiji's books with 'Atmagyan ka Vigyan'. Their efforts will aways be remembered as instrumental in this journey going forward.

A special mention and thank you to the artists Madhavi Erande Ji and Mahesh Davadkar Ji, who have made a valuable contribution with their sketches.

A word of appreciation and thank you to Geeta Bedi Ji, for translating the Hindi version, 'Atmagyan ka Vigyan' into this English version, 'Science of Enlightenment'.

A sincere hope from the bottom of the heart that 'Science of Enlightenment' helps in the awakening and liberation of the sadhakas.

– Astu (so be it)

"The Guru removes you from everything, brings you to One, and then even dissolves the One"

Introduction

Swami Maitreyanand Ji

Born on 10th June 1972, Swami Maitreyanand Ji belongs to a small village situated amidst the forests of Madhya Pradesh, India. Since his early childhood his interests lay in spiritual practices and meditation. He loved spending time alone in the forests doing sadhana even at the age of six - seven. There were times when an entire night would pass with him meditating in the forest. His energy would attract wild animals and they would often be seen sitting close to him while he would be in meditation.

Swamiji has always had an affinity for nature. His association with the dense jungles continued even during his school and college years. That was his haven for sadhana. He graduated in the arts stream and holds a post graduation degree in English. Post his education, he worked for a government department. Under all circumstances, his priority was spirituality which was also the reason for him not to get married despite pressure from his family. He grew up mostly under his father's care after his mother passed away. He was still small when he lost his mother. The family being affiliated to politics saw some important dignitaries and influential politicians visiting their home. He once got an opportunity to take on some political responsibility which he politely refused so that he could pursue his spiritual calling. So much so, that to avoid any obstructions in his journey of self-realization, he left home, family and career, embracing a wanderer's life, a nomadic life. It was during this phase that he made the Himalayan Valleys his home.

His spiritual journey took him to the banks of the river Narmada where he spent quality time with many highly evolved sages and saints, ascetics and hermits. He also spent some time in the Osho Ashram and the Vipassana Institute, meditating and serving. His spiritual experiences began happening in his childhood. Once while bathing in the river, he experienced 'neti, neti' (not this, not this), leading to an experiential understanding of 'I am not this body, I am not this mind.' Later while still in his youth, he attained Self-Realization.

Swamiji is well versed in Ayurveda, Botany, Medicines, Economy and Politics. His suggestions provided to the state and central government for protection of the environment and forests were paid heed to and necessary actions were taken for the same, thereby making him instrumental in protecting the wildlife. Similarly, some wonderful suggestions he gave for economic welfare were also considered by the government, leading to certain policies being brought forth, which are helping in the advancement and progress of our nation. He stays away from taking credit for a lot of work that happened through him.

He does not have an ashram nor a permanent residence. Nomadic is his nature. Where so ever he stays, that he considers ashram for the time he spends there. He has not formed any cult or institution. He is moving towards building a spiritual community though, a sangha by the name of **'Siddha Kutumbakam'**, where he says peace must reign and issues whatsoever like, competition, rat race, jealousy, remain non-existent. A space where there's environmental growth, where everyone leads a simple life conducive to sadhana. A space where everything from farming to health arrangements are managed and sustained collectively by the community as a whole. The term 'Sustainable Model' suits the concept of Siddha Kutumbakam. It can be called a spiritual village based on a sustainable model.

There are a few You Tube channels by the names 'The Siddha Talks', 'Siddha Kriya', 'Divya Dhyanam' and 'Siddha Sangeet'. The channel 'The Siddha Talks' has more than 1400 audio and video recorded conversations and discourses in Q&A format, along with more than 115 methods for meditation which increases by one method every week. This channel has attracted thousands of followers till date. All the details pertaining to Siddha Kutumbakam can be found in the website 'Siddha kutumbakam.org'. The Siddha Talks is present on Facebook, Instagram and a mobile app as well.

Swamiji's one and only intent is to help every sadhaka progress on the path of self-realisation; every sadhaka who is stuck on this path for some reason and is not able to grow, or has deviated from his spiritual track in any manner. He is here to show the path and push each one towards attaining freedom from his/her suffering. His 'Sadhana Shivirs' (spiritual retreats) are not about collecting masses. They are about making each one who attends these retreats, feel special and loved like a parent. These retreats are all about going beyond body consciousness and experiencing 'The One'- The Mystical. Guruji has been gracious enough to allow seekers to contact him directly and resolve their queries first-hand. Each one who gets an opportunity to come into his energy field or gets associated with him in any manner is truly fortunate, for Swamiji is one of the very few Sadgurus present on this planet in this era.

– AUM

Chapter 1

If Dhyana Is Rama, Then Concentration Is Ravana

ARE YOU PRACTICING THE METHODS FOR MEDITATION THE RIGHT WAY?

Sadhak: Pranaam Swamiji! Is concentrating on the sahastrara (crown chakra), agya/ajna chakra (third eye chakra) or breath the right way of meditation? Is this practice right or wrong?

Swamiji: Defilements arise upon concentrating. All these defilements are an adverse consequence of concentration. Natural downfall of whosoever uses concentration in the name of sadhąna is inevitable. Bizarre mechanisms and actions get activated which their bodies experience, like the head going in different directions, frantic movements in the body, body turning upside down and then coming back etc. Such disturbances are born.

What is concentration? It is adharma which means unnatural (that which is against the Cosmic Law).

If dhyana is Rama, then concentration is Ravana. Based on this, if I may say so, all kinds of distortions are going on in the field of spirituality on this virtuous and sacred land. This sin of 'concentration' is taking place to a large extent and beyond control on this holy and sacred land of Bharat, where people are using concentration in the name of dhyana. Concentration is Ravana and this misguidance is a universal issue now, with most people speaking of increasing their power of concentration mistaking it for dhyana. This is going against 'Nature' and the Natural Order. People are 'doing' dhyana and making others 'do' it as well. Dhyana cannot be 'done' nor can it be asked or taught to 'do'. It is not a work or a job that needs to be done. Concentration is a work requiring effort. Concentration means you are doing something and in the process of doing, a 'doer' is born. What happens? A doer is born! 'Doer' is the problem, doer is the downfall. Doer once born keeps doing something or the other. It will move the body this way, that way. It will do this, do that. It'll dance. What is all this? A disease! In one way this is schizophrenia, a psychosomatic disorder. Glorifying such disorders and adorning them in the name of experiences is nothing short of a huge opportunity lost and a life wasted. This life is priceless and this opportunity is priceless. We must not waste it at any cost. So far you have wasted it. You've been in sadhana since years, haven't you? Let alone years, you may spend lifetimes doing sadhana involving concentration and nothing will come of it. Years have gone by and Enlightenment hasn't happened, Buddhattva hasn't happened. It won't. You've chosen the wrong path. You may walk thousands of kilometers, lakhs of kilometers or even travel endlessly, you're still on the wrong path leading nowhere. It'll only lead to an extended wandering and downfall. The schoolbag will keep getting heavier and fatter. You'll have to take many births. The bigger and fatter the schoolbag, that many births. The wandering will keep growing, this wandering which you yourself are responsible for because of the wrong techniques being embraced. This will take you astray. This sin, this evil happens maximum in this sacred and virtuous land. What is a greater sin than concentrating and focusing? Whatever you focus on, you strengthen that. If it's a particular name and form, you'll strengthen that name and form and strengthening the name and form in itself is a sin. Whatever you focus on, concentrate on, you're giving birth to that. Focusing on so called Paramatma (God or Supreme- Consciousness), you give birth to a God and that is the sin. You will give birth to a God by concentrating. Concentrating on some Paramatma means you're giving birth to one. You'll become Paramatma's father, mother. You will give birth to Paramatma, you!? What is a bigger sin than you giving birth to Paramatma? Understand that this is the basic mistake. When there's something wrong with the foundation, the palace will be shaky. That is the reason I keep repeating, "Dhyana yadi Rama hai toh concentration Ravana hai." (If dhyana is Rama, then concentration is Ravana).

One does not have to concentrate at all. 'Doing' is action. One who 'does' spoils everything; without 'doing' everything becomes alright. It is by constant 'doing' that you have spoilt everything. It is by repeatedly 'doing' that you have created this illusion (mayajaal), got yourself entangled in it and wasted lifetimes. How many births and lifetimes have you wasted? Look back and see. You'll find you've wasted this one as well. This life was an opportunity which has gone waste. Wake up now at least, wake up beloved Mohana (Krishna), wake up! The dawn is getting restless. In this Golden Era, the dawn is getting restless and urging you to wake up. You'll end up wasting this Golden Era too, this Golden Era of sadhana. Such an opportunity comes once in thousands of years. After cycles of two and half thousand years, the Golden Era comes and this particular one is slightly different. Calling this era a Diamond Era won't be wrong, since this one comes after seventeen and a half thousand years. You'll waste this one too by practicing the wrong way. Wrong practices where the head moves, body shakes and moves, a dance going on…you'll waste this opportunity in this dance.

You have to pause, halt, stop, "Nishchal tattvam jeevan mukti (Stillness is liberation)". Consciousness needs to rest. You attach Consciousness to your movements, your speed. What do you think the word 'concentration' means? You attaching the consciousness to your movements or to some name and form is concentration. Name and form are not something stable or unmoving. It is something that flows. Attaching consciousness to a thought is termed a concept… what else is a concept? It is a thought, a flow. When you concentrate, you attach the consciousness to a concept. It may be a concept of a God…which God? The God created by you, the one you've given birth to. You are small, petty and substantial and your God is even smaller and more substantial. Your God is born from you so he has to be smaller than you. The God, the Paramatma, the Supreme Consciousness that you are concentrating on, focusing on, is your creation. You may call your self-created Paramatma as Krishna or Shiva. Will Paramatma become Shiva or Krishna by your calling him so? You really think you have a status, standard or even the capacity to give birth to Shiva or Krishna and that too in your mind, through your intellect and imagination? You really think so? Your mind and intellect are so strong that whatever you create with your limitations and pettiness will be a very limited edition of that. Your Paramatma will also be very limited.

That what is dancing, is dancing to the mind's tunes. Your mind is deluding you and making you dance on its fingers. After having wasted so many life-times, you'll waste this one also and that too in this Golden Era. You are so fortunate for having taken birth in this era and so fortunate for having a longing for sadhana. You do have a longing for sadhana but your selection of the foundation on which sadhana has to deepen, is wrong. If you choose the wrong support system and a wrong path, you won't reach anywhere. However far you may travel, you'll keep getting distanced further from your longing.

Yesterday I was talking about the 'Bindu' (the point of Source). There is a Bindu and it is on a journey. There is one Bindu. It is not that upon completion of a journey, you're distanced from the Bindu. Bindu is the infinite, the endlessness which is inherent in the journey…an endlessness without a circumference. There is an endless expansion, unlimited, without qualities and attributes. In that Bindu is the attribute, the form, the manifested, the issue, the matrix. The Bindu is 'you' happening. You are the problem… you are the Bindu and you are the problem. You are the matrix and you are on a journey, okay? You are on an illusory journey and this journey is the cause for the Bindu to happen. Why else is the Bindu present? It is constantly being bruised and influenced and that influence is appearing as 'separate'. You per se, are not commanding this journey. You are just going along with the wind in whichever direction it blows. The wind is pushing you ahead. You claim to be on a journey but if any kind of influence pushes you and shifts you even one degree from your direction, it diverts you somewhat and your direction changes. As the Bindu travels in Anantata (endlessness), it will be endlessly distanced from the influences…those influences to which it had fallen prey to, even though the effect of the influence was just one degree. Your journey is a zig-zag if you observe it carefully, and it's not going to help you reach anywhere. Where do you want to reach is the question. Can you ever reach anywhere in the Endless? Can you ever reach anywhere by journeying in Ananta, in the infinite? You may journey as much as you want in Anant, you won't reach anywhere. You, along with your journeys, will go waste. Travel as much as you want in Anant, the value remains zero. 'Travel as much as you want' is something that needs understanding, since examples can never fully justify the concept being put across. You may travel crores and crores of light years - how much do you think you would have travelled? Nothing, zero. That's because any journey in endlessness remains zero. It doesn't hold any value at all. In endlessness, you can't reach anywhere, despite walking or travelling continuously. The moment you stop, you're already there. Here, stopping is reaching. When you stop, you are still, unmoving. When you are still and unmoving you are free from life and rebirth. The lesson you need to learn is of becoming still and resting, not running. You don't need to learn movement nor do you need to learn any calculative processes here--processes of multiplication and division. You've been running since eons, where have you reached? Just peep and see where you've reached. You've wasted your entire life walking, running, going somewhere. Where have you reached? Wake up now at least, shake yourself vigorously, come into awareness. You don't need to run. Just stop. Stopping is reaching. What happens when you stop? Stillness, quietude. That is 'Nishchal tattvam jeevan mukti'. It is here that liberation happens from life, from death.

Life is death and death is life. It's one and the same thing. Remove the veils of ignorance from your eyes and see that life is death and death is life. Just go beyond this web of life and death which you yourself have woven. Your 'doing' is the weaving of this web. Whatever you 'do' is the weaving and knitting of this web, this mesh and this mesh is called samsara; the samsara which you have created. Your created samsara, your created definitions of it. You are stuck in that very web which you have created yourself. The more you walk, the more the web expands. Hence, stop! The moment you stop, all problems end. In other words, 'you' as a separate entity remain no more upon stopping. It's the movement that creates an illusion of your separate self and that 'you' as a separate self is doing something. You are doing something means you are there. There is a 'you' who is doing something. Doing gives birth to you, doing gives birth to the doer but the instant you stop, 'you' the 'doer' vanishes, dies...it remains no more. You remain no more and your death is the most auspicious indication of a 'you' ending. Your death is sacred. That is the reason Guru Gorakhnath Ji urges, "Die hey yogi, die. Death is sweet. Die that death which Gorakh experienced." That is the reason Kabir Das Ji also says, "The death which the world fears, is bliss for me. I wait for that death, I wait for merging into absolute bliss."

When the 'I' dies (The death of the I, me, myself), only then meeting (merging) with the Supreme will happen. 'I' as a separate entity and complete bliss!? Not possible. Bliss is never incomplete, broken or dual. Supreme bliss would not exist if there was duality, if there were 'two' : one a complete supreme bliss (Purna Paramanand) and another an incomplete one (aadha-adhura). The speciality of bliss (ananda) is that it is never incomplete. Talking of receiving one percent, two percent or ten percent of bliss is rubbish. Bliss is complete and you won't get it without dying. You are the barrier. If you as a separate entity exists, how will you attain to Paramanand? How?

'Prem gali ati saankri, tame dui na samaaye'! The lane of unconditional love is very narrow where two cannot fit in. Where there is no space for two to fit in it, there 'you' are the problem, the issue. You are the other, you are the duality, you are the essence and the fragrance of Truth but still, you are not The Ultimate Truth. You are the perfume of Truth and your presence is Maya, a lie. You are a bundle of lies, a conglomeration of false concepts. 'You', the separate entity will have to go, you will have to die. When 'you' are no more, only then the entry into the lane of unconditional love happens.

'Prem gali ati saankri, taame dui na samaaye', a second cannot fit in and you are the other. Remember, a lot of people are deluded by these words sung by Kabir Das Ji, thinking "Only I, alone, will go, and no one else can accompany me". Listen, you yourself are that other. You cannot go there as a separate self. Understand that two cannot enter that lane and you are the other, the duality. It is your misunderstanding that some other relation, be it mother, father, friend etc. cannot go along with you and that you will go alone. You are the second, the other. If you are finished, then who else remains? Who then is the mother, father, friend, wife, husband, son? Everything is a chance happening just like a boat and river coming together (Nadi naav sanjog). You are the reason for the chance happenings. You as a separate self exists, hence everything else exists. The moment you die, no one remains. All diseases end once the root cause of the disease is cut. Destroy the root cause and you realize, you are 'The Self'. You being the issue, have to be immersed.

With the application of concentration, you are strengthening your own self. You have become very strong, a boulder. How do you think you're going to melt? By focusing and concentrating repeatedly, you have become as strong as rock and iron. How will you melt now? There's still time. Shake yourself hard out of this stupor. There's a furnace burning here which can melt you, so give your consent. Give up the madness you've been living till now...your insanity, your insane behaviour, your mad intellect. The furnace is burning. Just throw yourself into it, you'll melt. However hard as a boulder or iron you may have become, you'll melt. What is a retreat? It is a furnace, a burning kiln. Throw yourself into it. You'll melt completely, become smoke, finish completely, die. Enlightenment will not happen without dying. You have to die and that too the right way, not incompletely. Without death there is no liberation.

I'm not talking of the death of this body wherein you die here, cross over and then take birth again along with your school bag. Is this death, is it!? Who are you deceiving? Here you die and there you're born again! You pack your school bag with such great care, not leaving a single book behind before escaping. I see a dying person often making every effort to keep correcting the school bag so that no book is left behind. They fit in all the books so tight that none falls out. They do not want the big fat bag to fall down, so they run, escape as fast as they can. At first, they aren't ready to leave this torn costume which has now become useless. But when they're finally ready to leave, with great speed they fill up their school bag. They stuff it up tightly with such expertise that nothing falls out and then run. Later, looking to get admission in a school once again, they take birth. They take admission again in this school called life, carrying their school bag with utmost care. How can you learn the same 'A for apple, B for boy' again? You read the text but you don't study it properly enough to complete that text material. Instead, you keep adding new texts, new material while the old ones still haven't finished. I say study properly. This is a school, a Mystery School. This world is a mysterious educational institute where you have taken admission yourself; nobody else has given it to you. You take admission here (take birth) with the intention of studying properly. But then, upon reaching the higher dimension after death, you realize how foolish you were not to have studied properly while you were down here. You realize you had come here to do something else but ended up doing something different (Gaye thay Hari bhajan ko, autan lage kapaas).

You keep thinking, "What next should I do? What can I do for my children? Making a house is important. See, the neighbours have bought a car! I need to buy one too, or else I'll be viewed with disrespect. He has to see that we also own a car now and travel no more by a scooter." So much drama and fuss! Some are studious and they want to study everything left, right and center, irrespective of whether it comes of use or not. You came here to do one thing but have deviated and are doing something else. People are 'doing' politics. What will you learn from politics? Some are social reformers looking to improve the society. This world is a mess with many evils, all birthed by the social reformers. The society would have been very nice without them. They have spoilt everything by constantly doing and acting upon something or the other.

There used to be a small round lake in the village where my family home is. It was absolutely round and the water in it used to be crystal clear, so much so, that if a book was kept at the bottom of the lake, hypothetically speaking, it could be read clearly. It used to be so clean. One fine day, some social reformers appeared out of nowhere and started pointing out flaws. They said corrections needed to be done there, 'this needs to be done, that needs to be done, pull a drainage line from here, remove from there', so on and so forth. Now you go and see that place. It is so dirty. Nature knows, Astitva knows what needs to be kept and how, but the activists thought otherwise, "What does Astitva know" they thought. "We know better. How intelligent can the Existence or Astitva be!! It is foolish, we are more intelligent so we will improve it." In the process of improvising and beautifying it, the original circular shape of the lake was lost. It now looks crooked and shapeless at different places, not to mention how dirty the water has become. Nothing can be seen in it, not even the fish that could once be seen. The lake once pure is now absolutely dirty and impure, completely destroyed. They ruined the lake of the Gods. The doers have spoilt it. The doers have always spoilt things. Social reformers keep doing anything and with their actions, things tend to get worse.

Morality is the determining factor of down-fall, in fact it is the reason behind societal downfall and degradation. All ethics and morality degrade the society and all social reformers ruin the society in the name of reforming it. You also spoil yourself in the name of 'doing'; doing this and doing that. If meditation is Rama, then concentration is Ravana but if you see in the whole world now, people are being taught to 'do' meditation using concentration. 'Do dhyana, do dhyana' whereas you don't need to do anything. Dhyana means giving up 'doing'. It means leaving this madness of doing, withdrawing oneself from it. 'Nishchal tattvam jeevan mukti', just stop, stop! You've been running incessantly yet haven't gained anything. Despite running for lifetimes and doing so much, you haven't gained anything. Whatever you think you've gained or achieved, is all going to be left behind here. Your knowledge, your intellect, your concepts, your greatness is all going to take you down into a pit. Your greatness and your great knowledge will lead you into a great pit, a very deep ditch. Wake up! Come to your senses! Till when will you continue to deceive yourself? You think you can deceive others but no, you're deluded. You can do that only to yourself. It's not possible to deceive others. We can only deceive or cheat ourselves. It's a huge misconception that others can be cheated.

Wake up! Come to your senses. You can still wake up. This samsara is your creation. You haven woven this dream with your incessant 'doing' and are continuing to weave more in the name of dhyana by concentrating. Concentration is the needle(s) with which you knit sweaters. You hold on to the name and form with the needles of concentration and keep knitting the sweater, the samsara around yourself which keeps getting stronger and stronger and ultimately so strong a mesh it becomes that you struggle and scream 'I'm stuck in it'. "I'm stuck. I need to do something more now, to come out of it. I have to put in more effort to come out of this mesh." You now start knitting faster, using more concepts, more calculations and more intellect as a means to come out of this struggle but end up creating more matrix at a greater speed. The more you do, the stronger the web gets. Layer by layer, fold by fold, you keep knitting the sweater of samsara and keep screaming, "I'm further getting stuck. I need to do something about it, put in more effort. I need to concentrate more."

Kabir Das Ji made use of 'Ulatbansiyan (Paradoxical speech)'. Why did he use this mode of language? Now, understand everything. Your definitions, your intellect, your mind are all ulatbansi (paradoxical) and will never come of use. The world of mystery is an ulatbansi (a paradox). Here, the doers spoil everything but everything becomes fine and falls in place by non-doing. This is the ulatbansi I have been giving, isn't it? When I say that the doers ruin everything and everything becomes fine by non-doing, that's what I mean, that's the paradox. You've ruined everything by continuously doing something or the other. Till when do you plan to keep doing? You are doing in the name of dharma, doing in the name of sadhana and in the name of dhyana too. You 'do' dhyana! Can you ever do dhyana? There's a limit to a downfall too. If you fall so low, how will you come out? So much attachment to your degraded concepts, so much!? Please wake up, the dawn is approaching and you're still lost in your dreams. You are still creating the web in this Golden era! Stop 'doing'! It is so surprising that since so many days, non- doing is being spoken of over here and yet you continue to concentrate and focus. That is surprising! These words not penetrating inside you just shows how deep the hypnotism must be within! How often and how deeply you have hypnotized yourself!

Goebbel's principle suggests if a lie is repeated often, it starts appearing as the truth. You must have fed this lie of 'concentration' innumerable times, for it to have such a strong hold over you. That's the reason for you not understanding what's being put across. It has been spoken of during all the sessions and in all the methods for meditation that have been given, that nothing needs to be done, that doers spoil everything and that it is in non-doing that things become alright. Yet the hypnotism hasn't broken. It surely is a very dangerous one. This hypnotism isn't just from this life but from past lives as well. Certainly, these mistakes must have been made in past lives too. You must have made many mistakes since past lives and have made them stronger by continuing them in this life as well. It's been sixty-three, sixty-four years since you were born and you continue repeating the same mistake! That is the reason for these words and teachings not entering your system for the past twenty-five days.

It is clearly being said, "Don't concentrate" and people are sitting here 'doing' concentration, head going back, hand moving, different body movements happening...getting caught up in the body! What will happen by concentrating? You will get entangled in the body, get caught up in maya and body consciousness will become denser. Liberation from body consciousness happens in sadhana. You go beyond the body. With the body making different movements, you tend to get more entangled in the body, in maya. If sadhana goes even slightly deep, body consciousness goes away. First stage is 'I am not this body-I am not this body'. You have to go beyond the body. If you are caught up in the body, know that your school bag is getting stronger and heavier and liberation is impossible. You can still wake up. Wake up, the dawn has broken! There is something special about this dawn, something really special. Rub your eyes and stretch your body. Stretch your body and rubbing your eyes, open them properly. You'll wake up. You don't have to do much but you have to come out of your dream state. You'll have to come out of your sleep. Come on, break your sleep. Stretch, stretch yourself and rub your eyes and open them. Wake up, wake up, it's dawn! If you don't wake up in this dawn, when will you?

Upon awakening, you'll find everything that you had woven over lifetimes become invisible, all bondages fallen. The moment you wake up, all these bondages and all the created webs fall together. You'll come to know this in the very moment you awaken because everything is a dream and a dream doesn't break in installments but in an instant. Forgetting about the mistakes that happened in the past, pay attention to what's ahead. If you don't forget and let go of the mistakes done in the past, progressing ahead is impossible. The challenge is that you hold onto the past, thinking there must be some element of truth to it. You wonder, how can all that you've understood and picked up in the past from different teachers or great human beings be so wrong. "Were they all wrong in what they spoke? Am I a fool?" If you keep thinking this way, you won't progress and things won't work out for you.

It's an ongoing dream and dreams are all 'past'. If you carry the past baggage, dreams will continue. Carrying the past is the dream. What else is a dream? The dream will continue till you carry the past on your shoulders and you'll never wake up. If you say that you'll wake up while the dream continues, you're talking of the impossible. An ongoing dream means one is asleep, and it's impossible to wake up while still sleeping. You alone have to break your sleep, your dreams, your dream state. How will you break it? 'Beeti tahi bisaar de, aage ki sudhi le'...Forget whatever's happened in the past and move ahead wisely. Whatever you have collected and hoarded so far is all trash and it's stinking. You call them pearls and diamonds but just open your eyes and see it's all dirt, garbage and stink. At least open your eyes and see clearly. Seeing garbage as garbage, you'll promptly throw it away because now you know it is garbage. You now know that it is useless and that keeping it will only lead to its rotting and a bad stench, which will keep increasing with time. Your concepts are that garbage. You consider them to be valuables like gold, silver, diamonds and rubies but they're nothing more than garbage that's stinking.

It's only when you open your eyes that you'll be able to actually see. It's only when you wake up that all the senses will work. The nose will say 'this stinks', the eyes will say 'this is garbage'. So, wake up for the dawn is now getting anxious. Whenever you wake up, that is when it is morning. When is it considered morning? Whenever you wake up, it's morning! This is the Great Mystery. Dawn is eternally present but the mind and intellect say, "It's midnight and time to sleep...who wakes up at midnight! Morning is when one needs to wake up, so sleep." Come on, wake up and see! It's morning and the sun's glow is expanding in the east, the soft easterly wind is blowing, birds have started chirping, singing songs of the dawn. Listen! Only when you wake up will your ears be able to hear the sweet songs of dawn and the birds sing. All signs of the dawn having broken are present but you are under some misconception that it's not yet time to wake up, so you continue to make more dreams. This is the hypnotism. Why are you getting hypnotized? Your sleep will end once you stop weaving dreams and when that happens, you'll wake up to the visible brightness in the easter sky along with the soft winds embracing you. Leave your hypnotism. Why do you flow with your thoughts, your mind and the influences? It's the influences which say it's midnight, it's kaliyuga, all this talk about 5D, about portals opening up, twin flames etc. Where are you stuck? Just leave all influences.

Stories of all kinds are becoming the support system for your dreams and strengthening your sleep, your ignorance. Your dreams are getting stronger. Don't allow that, don't give any material to the dreams for them to flourish. Don't spice them up with stories, whether old or new, since they will keep creating more dreams. Be aware, do not get impressed by influences. To sleep and let the dreams go on is your decision and nobody else's. Influences are there but inviting them into your life is your decision. They do not come without your consent or invitation. Your reaction towards anything you see is the invitation…reaction is the invitation.

Who is a holy man, a sadhu? One who doesn't conclude, doesn't give a decision and does not react. Who is an unholy man? The one who gives decisions, concludes and reacts. You are the one reacting to influences which is why the chain of thoughts becomes a dream. You create your own dreams and result is that you continue to sleep. Sleeping is your decision, therefore waking up is your decision too. Wake up, it is dawn. How long will you delude yourself?

Look at your foundation, your roots. They're all baseless, false notions which you're carrying and everything false is Maya. All lies are a dream and dreams have no legs, you know that, right?

In a dream your wife becomes a horse with wings that starts flying or an ant stands up and starts talking. Haven't you seen such things in dreams? Dreams are baseless and fictional. They fly here and there at a fast pace without any logic. There's no logic to them and yet you justify them by trying to prove the stories correct, while considering those who do not agree to your dream-tales to be foolish. The flying horse you say was your wife and you proclaim it to be true. Just look at the fictional concepts you claim to be your reality, your truth. Reality is, you are hell-bent on calling your fictions and your concepts as the truth. Leave this stubbornness, this childishness and you'll find your dreams along with your school bag, getting immersed completely.

I'm asking you to put your schoolbag down so that I can burn it to ashes. What will you do by reading all those books? It's not a small bag you're carrying. There are too many lessons inside it. Contrary to your belief, this one lifetime is short for studying all those lessons. What's the guarantee that you'll be conscious enough in your next birth as you are in this one? The awareness in this birth is not the same as last birth so how will the awareness of this birth carry forward to the next one?

What had you decided? You had come here to do sadhana and free yourself from all the dreams and illusions but you lost your way, isn't it? You took birth to free yourself but then you took to concentration and focusing, thereby weaving the web again. "Aaye thay hari bhajan ko, autan lage kapaas" i.e. you came here for liberation but started creating a mesh. 'Upon waking up will bhajan happen!?' Awakening is liberation. Who are you to 'do' meditation (bhajan). Bhajan is happening, you conjoin with it. Wake up from your dreams. When you wake up, you'll see that bhajan is already going on.

What is this entire srishti (creation)? It is one bhajan. Srishti is happening by itself, bhajan is happening by itself. You say you are separate and the srishti is separate. You have an opinion and conclusive views on everything, including nature, as if you are separate from it. The bhajan is happening, srishti is happening. You just conjoin in it. You are also happening. You are not someone with a separate identity. Everything is just happening and you are comprised in it. You are nobody, you are nothing. You were never there and you can never be. Your separate being is a lie. "Wake up Mohana, the dawn has broken and it is weary and restless, waiting for you to awaken".

WHAT IS DHYANA? HOW IS IT DONE?

Sãdhaka: What is dhyana and how is it done?

Swamiji: What is dhyana and how is it done? What is 'done' is not meditation, it is a method...not a method OF meditation but a method FOR meditation. The method if applied and done properly, leads to the dhyana happening. Dhyana is Astitva's grace. It happens! No one can 'do' dhyana. What is done is the method, the kriya. Dhyana means 'happening', it is something that happens. What is in our hands is the methods and we adopt those. Certain methods involve steps. After adopting those steps there are chances of the grace of dhyana happening. There's no guarantee that it will happen though. The possibility of it happening once, after adopting and applying the methods several times, is there. For someone it could happen in the first go itself, for some it may happen after ten sittings, for some maybe after a hundred sittings and some may keep doing the kriyas their entire life and the grace of dhyana may not happen. This is a happening, a grace of the Supreme Consciousness. One must keep applying the methods for meditation, the kriyas... dhyana can happen anytime.

What does dhyana mean? 'Dhyana happens' means there is no mind there. It's a state beyond mind called 'Amani Dasha' where there's no mind, no thoughts, no duality or conflict, no good or bad, no right or wrong, no holy or unholy, nothing. When you do something, there's a movement, a divergence, a duality and conflict in it and where there's movement there's no dhyana. Dhyana is calm, dhyana is peace and to be relaxed, one has to get out of all kinds of mental mathematics. Getting out of calculations is called dhyana. If you are caught up in a calculative mindset, a multiplying and dividing mindset, then dhyana has not happened. If dhyana has not happened, it means you need to get out of the arithmetic mind.

WHAT IS THE CORRECT WAY TO SIT FOR SADHANA?

Sãdhaka: Guruji, how should one sit in one asana if one has to sit for a long duration? For example, there's exercise, there's yoga and then there's effort that is put in for going beyond the annamaya kosha, the physical body which help in the sitting to become natural and simple. Which way of sitting or asana do you recommend?

Swamiji: One asana is of the body and another is of the mind! Body is psychosomatic. So, one must bring the body to use, as an asana, and the best way is to make a resolution and sit. Don't make any silly resolve. Make a firm decision to sit without moving for ten minutes irrespective of whether your legs break with pain or whatever else happens. Tell yourself you're not going to move. Then increase it to twelve and then fifteen minutes. Alongside you must do other things too, like consuming haldi-neem (turmeric and margosa).

This has benefits like bringing flexibility to the body and improving the immune system. One big benefit is that it helps clean the intestines and stomach. The entire energy gets involved in digesting food in the stomach or handling issues if any in the intestines. Hence, consuming haldi-neem helps to clean up the mess and problems there. Eating light also helps the intestines since digestion becomes easier.

The best way, if I may say so, is not to make big resolutions because that's damaging. Make simple resolutions and that too for shorter durations. If you cannot commit for ten minutes, keep it for two minutes and sit. It's helpful to set an alarm and sit so that the sankalpa (resolve) doesn't break by mistake. It's fine to sit for more than two minutes but resolve to sit only for two minutes. See that you don't break the sankalpa at any cost, come what may. Hence do the sadhana involving sankalpa (resolve) very carefully.

People resolve not to smoke a cigarette and give it up but within a week they're back to it. That is not good because you lose faith in yourself. It's better to make a resolve of having five cigarettes per day for two days instead of ten per day that you're used to. Stick to a decision of five per day, don't make it zero. Once you do that, your trust increases and it's easier then, to make a decision to have four cigarettes per day for three days. It's better to increase the number of days you want to stick to for your resolution slowly, so that the sankalpa doesn't break. Do not let it break. Fulfill the sankalpa at every cost and then with that as the support, do the asana. It's not just the asana of the body but also the asana of the mind that the sankalpa helps with. These small sankalpas help in steadying both the mind and body. Asana means to become steady, stable where there's no movement, no agitation, no distractions. The lesser the agitations and distractions, more the asana. To achieve this state, you can use the power of sankalpa.

Sãdhaka: I want to talk about the diversity of asanas as well. There is sukhasana, vajrasana, siddhasana and padmasana out of which sukhasana is mostly recommended. Someone may be comfortable doing all of the above. Which one according to you will prove most beneficial out of the lot?

Swamiji: Look, siddhasana is a very good asana, although tough. If you can keep the legs positioned the way it's supposed to be done in this asana, only then you go ahead and do it. If legs are flexible enough to come into the position even slightly, then practice to perfect it. The advantage of siddhasana is that the body takes the shape of a proper pyramid wherein the spine becomes straight. The spine should be straight but one mistake that is often seen is that of stiffening the shoulders. Shoulders should be absolutely relaxed, spine should be straight and body should be stress free.

I see people when they sit. They shut their eyes with such force as if the eyes have made a mistake and you're punishing them. Shut your eyes softly with great love. In fact, they should shut by themselves softly. I say cover your eyes with your palms very softly and gently, just as a flower petal would gently brush against them. Why are you pressing them so hard? Who has asked you to press them so hard? I'm asking you to do it softly, gently and not hastily or harshly. When you do it with love, the Divine Darkness will reveal itself, and the mind will come to rest and relax, with minimum movement or restlessness. In fact, there should be no agitation or movement of the mind after a method for meditation has been used. At this stage when the Divine Darkness happens and reveals itself, a stage free from thoughts and defilements is reached. For a little while there are no thoughts and one gets a glimpse of the Ultimate Truth. I'm taking you directly to the glimpse of the Ultimate Truth which people don't get even after lifetimes of sadhana. Lots will be seen in that, but it should happen with a lot of love.

Whosoever is equipped enough for siddhasana, they must do it. It's a very good asana. There are many asanas but siddhasana and sukhasana are good enough. I recommend following your body's situation and requirement at the time. If required, even sofa-asana (sitting on a sofa) is also good, isn't it? I am in favour of that also, as long as you reach stability within. Stillness should come within. The progression has to be towards stillness.

DISCOMFORT IN BODY DURING A DHYANA SITTING

Sãdhaka: Pranam Swamiji! When sitting in sadhana, body should be calm and relaxed so that it can sit for a long duration. If there's pain in the knees or back or if there is discomfort due to any stress in the body or any other unforeseen reasons, what should one do?

Swamiji: You want to know how to deal with the body which is not rendering conducive support while doing the methods for meditation, right? Look, you're living at the level of the body and want to go beyond it, then body itself is the support that will help with this. If the problem which is troubling is related to the body, that means you are living at the level of the body. One way to go beyond the body is to accept all that is happening in the body. If there's pain, accept it and keep observing it, knowing it. Just accept whatever is happening, as it is. The moment you accept, all conflict and duality drop off. Duality is all about non-acceptance. It is born out of non-acceptance. If there's total acceptance of all that's happening, duality dissolves. Instead of accepting, you fight it, "This isn't right. Why is this happening with me? My body is not supporting me for sadhana", so on and so forth you go on, pointing out issues. You are creating duality by not accepting whatever is in the moment and in the process feeding the mind. Non-acceptance is the method for strengthening the mind and you do that with your mind. You yourself make it strong and propel it. Reaction is a result of non-acceptance. Why else do you react? It's because you don't accept things as they are. You want to change them as per your liking or suitability. Your reactions give birth to problems. Reactions give birth to a vicious circle (dushchakra). They give birth to the mind and it's activities and patterns. So, first of all accept whatever is happening. That is the solution to the problem. Acceptance and knowing becomes the base and support. Then the body will be seen and whatever is happening in the body will also be seen, whether it's pain or anything else. It will all be seen not through language, not through definitions or words but through a 'knowing'…this knowing will happen from afar. The body will be seen and known from afar and you won't remain a body then. So just accept whatever is, as it is. Acceptance opens the doorway to the next road worth treading on.

Chapter 2

Seven Bodies and Seven Chakras

S ãdhaka: Pranam Swamiji! My question is related to chakras. It is said that there are seven chakras in our body. What is the importance of these chakras and what happens when they get activated? What is the mystery of these chakras and the basic science behind them?

Swamiji: What is there in the seven chakras? One chakra is active in everyone and that is the mooladhar chakra, the root chakra. That is the reason for the universe functioning. It is because of the mooladhar that flowers blossom, the fruits are present, the butterflies and birds are there. It's when the mooladhar is active that you find people run helter-skelter upon seeing a bear approaching. That means the emotions of fear are there and when a fearful situation arises, that emotion gets activated and starts working...in this case fear. If there's little awareness at the time, you'll observe sensations in the Nabhi chakra (navel center). Similarly, when you're full of love and affection, you'll feel sensations in your heart center. Actually, what happens is that the lower two chakras remain more active, the mooladhar and swadhishthana and sometimes you'll feel sensations in the hridaya chakra (heart center). The rest of the chakras are almost asleep. When you progress in sadhana, then the rest of the chakras i.e. visshuddhi (throat), agya (third eye) and sahastrara (crown) start getting activated and sensations can be felt in them.

There are seven bodies and seven chakras. As far as the chakras are concerned, there are varied opinions on them. Some say there are twenty-one of them and some boil down their number to fourteen. Tomorrow somebody might wake up and say that there are twenty-one thousand chakras followed by someone else who might increase the count. When I say, "What is truth?", I'm referring to that which is infinite, endless, without boundaries, without qualities and is formless. This world is the Ultimate Truth's way of expressing itself. What this means is that srishti is not an act of creation. Srishti is a Self-Expression i.e. the Eternal Self is itself getting expressed as creation, "Srishta ne srishti nahi banayi. Srishta swayam srisht ho raha hai". It's important to note that this is a continuous process, and not something that has happened and is over with. The Eternal Self is itself getting expressed as 'Anahad Naad' (eternal sound or vibration) i.e. Anahad Naad is the manner in which The Eternal Self is happening. It is happening as the Triad Shaktis and is also happening as Adi Shakti. It is happening as the creation and as the seven layers too. Everything that is seen is the eternal, the beginningless, the endless, the infinite, the formless itself happening. The seven layers are a way of the Eternal itself happening, although appearing in the form of separation to our mind and intellect, due to a shape and form it has presented itself as. There is no separation at all but just accept the separation as leela, a divine play and keep moving. This table, chair etc. here are part of the leela. You can see one layer of this table but the other six layers behind it are not visible to the naked eye. If you go behind into the invisible layers, you'll know that this table also has an etheric body and a causal body just as a human body does. It's just that unlike the etheric and causal bodies of a human body, which are more fluid, the etheric and causal bodies of a table or chair are more solid and asleep. They also have a mental body but it is absolutely asleep. Essentially, everything that has a shape has a center which keeps it intact, holds it together. That center holding the shape together is the atma, the soul. The tables and chairs too have atma. That means they have a spiritual body as well as the brahma kaya and the shiv kaya (bodiless body). What I'm saying is that everything that has a shape and form is Paramatma's way of expression. He is present in this way as the seventh body. Ultimately, everything that can be seen as manifested, is the Eternal Self. The table, the tree, the ant, the human being, the earth, the sun, the universe, the multiverse are all a way of 'Paramatma' happening. The seven layers contain different shapes in them. It is Adi Shakti taking those different shapes. This is the leela but innately it is the ONE alone happening as the leela. It is a way in which the Eternal happens.

These seven bodies are the seven steps within that 'Self-Expression'. Of those seven steps, the one which is visible is one dimension, and similarly the other steps with little difference at each step, make up the other dimensions. Within those also there'll be seven steps and their way of happening will differ from each other. Those are also dimensions...dimensions which are not visible. In this way, there are sixty-four dimensions. This is the way 'The One' happens.

Now talking of the chakras, one body represents one chakra. The talk of twenty-one chakras or fourteen chakras is utter rubbish and madness. Maximum garbage that's available in the world is the spiritual garbage. There is so much nonsense being spread in the name of spirituality. This body, this visible body is the first body and is connected to the mooladhar chakra. In this manner if you go ahead, the second body being the etheric body i.e. the akasha sharir is connected to the swadhishthana chakra. The causal body, sukshma sharir is linked to the manipura chakra, the mental body is linked to the heart chakra, the atma sharir is connected to the vishuddhi chakra, the brahma kaya to the agya chakra and finally the shiv kaya, the bodiless body is connected to the sahastrara chakra i.e. the crown chakra.

To further explain, supposing I have seven sheets of paper of the same size, kept one on top of the other. A pin is kept on one spot on the topmost sheet of paper and inserted in a way that it creates a pin hole in all the seven sheets. It will create the holes at the same spot in all the sheets and not hither-thither. Similar is the case with the seven chakras present in the body which means that the seven kayas (bodies, layers) are present in this body. Every chakra gets a place to manifest in the body just like the example of the pinholes on the sheets of paper. The only difference is that unlike the seventh sheet of paper which also gets punctured at the same place like the other six sheets, here in the body, the seventh chakra is independent of the other six. The first six chakras in the body are connected through junctures one behind the other, seemingly in a line, barring the seventh chakra. The seventh chakra is without any imprints, which is why its effect is on the sahastrara, the crown chakra. It is in this body itself but at the top, known as the 'tenth gate' and is connected to the Akasha, the Omnipresent, the Endlessness. It is in this manner that the seven bodies and seven chakras are connected.

If one chakra in your body is active, that means the others will also become active and when they do, you'll come to know. One chakra which is active is the mooladhara. The second chakra, the swadhishthana, also makes its presence felt on and off. If an accident is about to take place, the effect will be transmitted through the navel center. If there's a danger posing itself, there's an immediate effect on the navel. Situations such as paragliding or standing very close to a deep ditch and looking down, bring about sensations in the nabhi, navel and immediately the swadhishthana also starts working. When you are loving and affectionate, you start feeling sensations in your heart. There are several methods for cleansing that have been provided, one of them being the seven-chakra alignment. With regular practice of these methods, the chakras do get activated...there's nothing that can stop them from getting activated.

Sādhaka: What role does the kundalini play in all this?

Swamiji: Kundalini Shakti is a possibility of the fourth body, the mental body. What is mind? Concentration! I repeatedly say, "Don't concentrate, don't focus during sadhana", reason being you have to go beyond the mind. Beyond the mind is called the 'amani dasha' (state of no mind) which arrives when dhyana happens. Concentration only leads to the mind getting stronger. You're strengthening the mind using concentration, but one has to go beyond the mind. It's contradictory. Dhyana is spoken of maximum in Bharat (India), but sadly maximum misunderstanding related to dhyana also exists in this country only. Many who have taken the responsibility of teaching dhyana are themselves not aware that dhyana cannot be taught; dhyana is not something to be done. Dhyana 'happens', you cannot 'do' it. People teaching dhyana are themselves 'doing' it and do not know the ABCD of dhyana. Concentration should not be used at all. What is the use of concentration in dhyana? It is not that there is no good use or utility of concentration. In the beginning, at some level it helps.

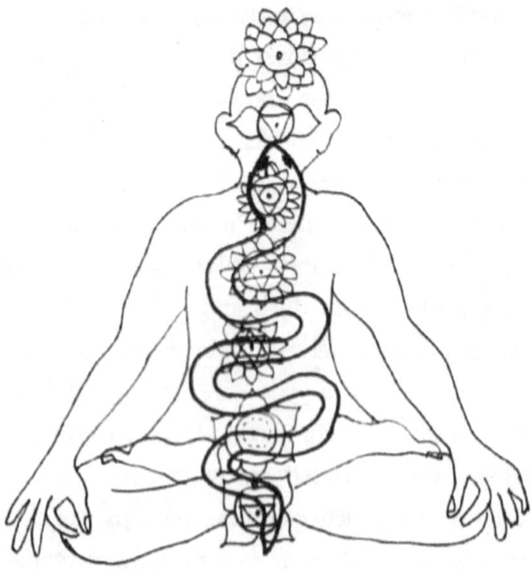

In sadhana, things come into alignment till the fourth chakra, and then the energy reaches a certain state wherein the sushumna nadi gets created. The energy gets accumulated in the fourth chakra and the sushumna nadi gets created. Once you reach the fourth body, with the sushumna nadi getting created and reaching the fourth chakra, then there's no obstruction to the rising kundalini energy. Once the alignment of energies takes place properly, all obstructions till the mental body are gone, and the kundalini has reached the fourth chakra, then nothing blocks the kundalini shakti flow. It then goes straight to the sahastrara chakra, unobstructed. Blockages are all in the lower chakras. If the energy reaches the fourth body, the fourth chakra and the barrier at the fourth chakra gets broken somehow, then there's nothing stopping this energy from rising up. There's no barrier in the atmik chakra, so in a few cases in which the energy flows through the atmik chakra, it doesn't stop there. Why I say few cases is because in most cases the energy flows directly to the brahmarandra. If this energy flows with great force to the brahmarandra, it creates a hole (randra) in the brahmakshetra. The bone here gets broken and this energy within gets merged with the energy without and becomes One, 'Aham Brahmasmayi'. This is the end of duality.

A lot of people wonder and worry about the bone in the brahmakshetra breaking. Let me tell you, you don't even come to know that it's broken. It's much later that you realise there's no pain or anything else related to that, and neither is it a matter of any medical emergency requiring a treatment. Nothing happens and nothing needs to be done for that. A hole is created by the rising kundalini shakti and you don't even come to know of this hole. Awakening of the kundalini shakti is a possibility of the fourth body.

Sādhaka: My questions are related to the chakras. First is, how do we come to know the level we are at? Secondly, you mentioned that when the chakras get activated and the activation goes beyond the heart chakra, one can see colours etc. I would like to know about this.

Swamiji: Look, I'd like to say one thing over here that many things happen. If you get into calculations related to these things, the result will be huge manuscripts and you'll start getting entangled with them. Talking about myself, I never got into any calculations of what, why, how. These chakras and other related aspects got clear much later when I heard and read about them a little. I did not have to read or hear much though, because everything unfolded with just a little bit of listening and reading. There was no need to go deep into it. With a little help, things got clear; clear in terms of the names given to experiences that had already happened unto me. I wasn't aware of the names as to what is what. I didn't know the name anahad naad. It had already happened with me. I got to know the name given to it later at some point in time, "Oh! so this is called anahad naad!" Similar it was with the chakras, when I got to know they were called chakras and that there were seven of them. All this information regarding names and labels came much after the experiences had happened. I didn't know chakras had mantras assigned to them. I never entered these zones of mantras related to chakras or for that matter any such zone, hence everything happened at a fast pace. If you get into a loop of these things or get yourselves involved in these things, you'll get confused, with your mind getting fickle. A lot of people are all out for the spiritual garbage being presented to them...this data and that data being provided by influence streams. What happens with this kind of a mindset is that it looks for data even in sadhana, thinking there should be data for sadhana too. Data related to what happens, how this happens, why this happens, what is its exact something something...and so it goes on, data, data, data. This data has eaten you up. You are so consumed by the data that it has ruined you. One shouldn't get involved in these data loops. You will further strengthen your mind with all this data, which will then lead to mental projections. The mind might show you some colours and you'll get embroiled in things like this chakra has got activated and that chakra has got activated. The mind is very strong and you'll get caught up in its web.

Ram Krishna Paramhansa would see Maa Kali appear the moment he would shut his eyes. She would speak as well as respond to him, a proper conversation at that. What a strong mind he must have prepared that it would project the exact Kali in front of him and she would say things that would be very different from what a regular mind could fathom. That mind had been prepared in such a strong manner that the data would not leak easily. It was in the end that Totapuri Maharaj freed him from all data and from Kali.

Mind is very strong. It can project anything. If you get attracted and stuck to any data in any manner, the data will become strong and then you can forget about liberation. There are all kinds of things being propagated like a specific mantra for a particular thing, certain colours being attributed to something specific or the talk of certain numbered experiences, for example, the notion of 'three things' happening which may include divine light being seen, anahad naad being heard and a fragrance being smelled or something else that the mind projects. Then they'll say, "Oh I heard a sound resembling teee, peee, cheee" thinking that it is anahad naad. No, that's not anahad naad! That is just teee, peee, cheee and nothing more than that. Teee means teee, peee means peee and cheee means cheee. This is no experience, nor does it hold any spiritual value.

Sãdhaka: There are many Sãdhakas who say they've never had any spiritual experiences. They feel their sadhana is not happening properly especially when they hear others speak of their spiritual experiences. Kindly throw some light on this.

Swamiji: I repeatedly say that it's not necessary that experiences will happen in sadhana. It's not so important. Bhagwan Buddha never had any experiences nor did his kundalini rise. Supreme Knowledge, Param Gyan, Liberation happened to him without any kundalini experience or other spiritual experiences coming along the way. It's not necessary that spiritual experiences will happen. Even Janak never experienced any such experiences. Supreme Wisdom happened to him through a dialogue, a conversation. Hence, it's not necessary that experiences have to happen with everyone on this path. This is like gathering data, "this will happen followed by this and then that." A big fat textbook can be written on this and read. What will happen? The mind will get prepared as you read and re-read, leading to projection. You may not understand anything written but since you want to project, you'll have to prepare for it.

That's the reason I say "Achanak" (suddenly) which means don't give the mind any opportunity to prepare anything. You land up with only as much understanding as the quality and quantum of material that you've read and consumed. With me, it happened very simply and suddenly...why? Reason being, we people of the forests live a simple life and it happens to us very easily. I never read any Vedas, Shastras or Upanishads, not a single one. I don't know any shloka other than one that came my way, "Sarve Bhavantu Sukhinah..." This one I do know.

Sãdhaka: At times we see some scenes or situations being played out in dhyana and years later the exact scenes and situations take place in the reality being lived. Is this an extra sensory power that has awakened or is it something else?

Swamiji: When extra-sensory powers awaken, then all extra-sensory potentials and abilities awaken. Various kinds of fragrances, visions etc. will come. One is able to see future events also which then take place later. When the event or scene happens later, you recognize it and then you know stepwise what's going to happen next. Extra-sensory powers start getting active. This is a leela and all kinds of things happen in a leela.

Sãdhaka: Someone who is unmarried and alone is relatively free to take decisions which a married man or a householder caught up in responsibilities of parents, kids and spouse is not able to. Please throw some light on this.

Swamiji: Whosoever is caught up in life for whatever reasons, should be extremely grateful to those reasons, whether they are familial responsibilities or any situations. It is because of those reasons that you experience being entangled and understand what separation is. You should be grateful that you're getting to experience what living a life of separation is like. What I'm saying is that there is a separation, that's why this restlessness is arising within you because you want to taste freedom. You'll be ready to pay any price if this restlessness is for freedom and liberation. There won't arise any fear, even if your ego dissolves while experiencing the process of internal freedom. Listen brother! We know what feeling stuck is but liberation is a big thing. Freedom from ego, freedom from atma, freedom from paramatma; everything must get dissolved because being stuck in anything is going to bring you back to where you started. After all you have to come out of all entanglements.

Why be stuck? There's an entanglement at every step - your job, relatives, any program, even dharma for that matter, isn't it? You're entangled, stuck even in your own body. If any entanglement becomes a reason for your awakening, it means it holds the key to show you all those areas where you're caught up. It can throw light on whether you're stuck in the body or mind or feelings or atma or paramatma, and can help in getting rid of all at the same time. Anyway all these entanglements have to go one day, so why hold on to them. Let them go. Hold on to the one entanglement with the family so that the rest become easier to let go. Let it happen this way.

Sãdhaka: Swamiji, when you look at someone or while speaking with them, do you come to know of their past lives or the sadhana they have done in past births?

Swamiji: Where it has to unfold, it happens. I don't unfold anything about anyone. I do not read anyone's mind because that is wrong. That's like invading someone's privacy and insulting them. Having said that, in some particular instances, when someone with wrong intentions comes and stands in front, suddenly the mind reading happens. Another instance could be when a Sadhaka needs support and his/her time has come to receive some support or help, then the unfolding happens and I inform them. I don't unfold anything on my own. If it happens, it's fine. Why should I unfold anything? If it happens, it happens and if it doesn't, it doesn't. It has nothing to do with me. Distance doesn't matter in this. When it has to happen, it happens from anywhere.

Chapter 3

Advantages & Disadvantages of a Blessing and Recognising the Divine Plan

Sādhaka: Swamiji, Pranaam! Can we ask for a blessing from a guru, sage or Paramatma if we want to obtain something, like for my daughter's upcoming job interview?

Swamiji: To show the right path is also a blessing, okay! Whatever the Supreme Consciousness wants for us, whatever Existence wants for us is the right blessing. This is what right blessing means. Now you are looking for a blessing for your child so that she gets selected for the job. What if Existence has decided something else for her but she gets this job now, and this job later becomes a reason for her adversity and misfortune? She may become an officer but her life may get upset after that. It could be that something else, some other field or line was meant for her where she could have done wonders. Maybe education wasn't meant for her and she was to become a spiritual personality, a world-renowned motivational speaker or an environmental activist with a caliber to change the entire world and her name etched in gold in historical records. Her life may get spoilt by becoming an officer, as you want her to, by expending all her precious years there. If she has come with a higher and a bigger purpose in life, then Existence won't let her be successful in these kinds of jobs. Such things also happen existentially. I'm not suggesting that what I've mentioned before as examples of a higher purpose, is what she's meant for, in case she doesn't get the job. I'm only trying to make you understand that whatever Existence has planned for her is not something you can know or understand, right? Since you could not understand the existential planning, you put in efforts towards something and you've learnt something from those efforts. She prepared for the exams. If she gets selected, it's good but even if she doesn't, she will end up so enriched from this experience, be it in terms of her level of understanding, common sense, information and her experiential understanding, leading to an all-round growth and development happening for her.

You cannot decide the direction her life has to take. Existence (Astitva) decides that. Now you tell me, are we interfering in Astitva's work or not? You say you want this to happen and Astitva says no, this is not her karma-prarabdha. We don't have a foresight good enough to envision how good the will of Existence ultimately turns out to be. We see the situation only from today's point of view and may find that it's not favouring us as we may have wanted it to. Circumstances may not be in our favour today but if they do turn conducive to our wishes, it might lead to our misfortune. That, we are unable to see.

Like I said, by the way, if a child gets selected to become an ordinary officer due to a blessing and earns a lakh or two per month or a crore or two in a year, that'll be his misfortune. It could be that he is meant to become a big industrialist owning a firm or an empire worth thousands of crores or he's meant to be a big politician or a social worker. Whatever Existence decides will happen. Our lack of faith makes us doubt and wonder as to what will happen and how, which is why the thought then arises that this job is fine, since it warranties safety and security. There is no progress or growth with safety and security. Insecurity helps in one's expansion and progress. The more one is insecure and surrounded with excess issues and problems, the more he's led to right listening and right learning which further helps in the right intelligence quotient getting developed in him. This will then create his personality. There is one programme these days, what is it called? Personality development programme! This programme cannot help in developing a personality, not as much as the troubles and difficulties of life that arise existentially can. The lessons taught by Astitva in the form of difficulties and troublesome situations is the real personality development course. The formal classes that have been introduced for this, do work. I don't say that they are of no use, but in the end, that learning and teaching is basic. Right learning takes an existential form and comes. The circumstances and situations bring along with them lessons of suffering, difficulties and irritation which teach us well, making it a real personality development course.

You must be aware of how Albert Einstein would get expelled from his school and his parents had to request school authorities with folded hands to take him back, but he wouldn't last long. They would change his school again but a similar thing would happen, forcing them to take admission in another one. It would take two to three years for Albert to get promoted from one class to the next. Somehow with great difficulty, he would pull through, securing a third division and yet he is considered the greatest scientist of all times- Albert Einstein!

The bookish knowledge and education is all about rote learning. This kind of education cannot decide the actual caliber of a person. You'll find the educational background of most of the great scientists and great artists to be weak. They clear the exams with difficulty.

They don't find this kind of education useful enough and would rather spend time studying something they are interested in. They don't study to get a first division nor get into the rote learning system. They are open to the essence of what they're learning, which does not happen with rote learning. A person who receives the essence of something cannot explain much about it, but when something finally comes out through him, it's not the essence that was absorbed, but a whole new innovation. This innovation or an absolutely unique creation comes from his own experience. Something keeps working and churning in his subconscious mind and slowly the right intelligence gets aligned with some ideas and with those ideas, new things, new discoveries, new innovations happen through him, leaving the whole world stunned. One important thing here is that such people don't work intentionally, nor do they concentrate. Astitva works in a different way with people who don't work intentionally, don't concentrate and don't do any rote learning. They are the chosen beings and Existence puts innovative ideas in them alone, making them great, renowned and famous personalities of their times in their respective fields. On the other hand, people who memorize a lot of data and believe in 'repeat and learn', remain average individuals with an average job and are not really remembered upon their retirement or even when they pass away.

Personality doesn't develop with concentration. A person is intelligent if he is not able to repeat something that he's heard, in the exact words they were said OR if he's not able to explain it in the way it was told. One who is able to repeat things the way they were spoken is a fool. Memorizing something and repeating it is not intelligence. An intelligent man gets the essence. He doesn't have to do anything for it. Since he is equanimous and keeps himself open to receiving, essence comes through to him. All his senses are open and functioning properly for the essence to get adopted automatically.

He is not concentrating to adopt the essence, rather the essence gets adopted. His growth happens in this way and when he's asked to explain something on a particular subject, he'll say something new and ten times better than the past orator. His speech will be the best, despite not being able to provide data well. That is because it will have quality along with an appeal factor to it, unlike the other orator who has data and information but lacks quality.

There are many professionals who complete their education and take up office jobs, giving presentations which are replete with data but aren't appealing enough and lack quality. They are soon forgotten. Then there'll come along a person who'll give a speech or a presentation without being prepared like the other professionals, and he'll present something full of newness, something original. Such a person is never forgotten. You'll forever remember him because of his unique, simple and natural way of representing himself. He's not representing knowledge or information gathered from here and there. What he's representing and offering is the naturalness of his personality. The fragrance of his personality is mixed in his presentations. Such a person will leave an indelible mark, an everlasting impression on your subconscious mind. Your subconscious mind will never forget him, keep this in mind.

Your constant suggestions that you offer the child is pressurizing for the child. I feel you care too much for your child. You're doing injustice with your child by repeatedly suggesting what should or shouldn't be done. That is not the way to behave with a child. Being on their back constantly, asking 'why' or 'what' related questions, or giving suggestions many times a day is not good. It's not good if you're doing this with your child but if you're not, then that's a good thing. Never pressurize a child for anything and don't make him ambitious. An ambitious person cannot be intelligent. He'll move forward in life in a robotic way but his personality won't radiate quality, he'll be incomplete. There are many people who're rich and some who are ambitious but their personalities are not good and lack quality. There is no fragrance to their personalities. Where will this fragrance and quality in a personality come from? It comes when a person lives innately with all his senses open and is not ambitious. When an unambitious person grows, he can reach great heights.

One man might be at a very high position but lakhs of people abuse him behind his back. Another man may not hold a high position but has a blooming and fragrant personality with thousands and thousands of people loving him. He's neither rich nor in any high position but he has many people loving him. What could be the reason? The reason is his blossomed personality. On the other hand, an ambitious person or for that matter a selfish human being, who is neither sensitive or empathic nor is he humane, is like a robot. Who will love a robot?

The difference between a person who is filled with selfishness or any such low vibrational characteristics and a person who lives naturally, simply and spontaneously, is that the latter is liberal, flexible and full of unconditional love. He loves sharing whatever he has or receives, for example food. He will spread love and live in peoples' hearts because of his blooming and blossoming personality. His spiritual growth also happens by itself. The purpose of human birth is spiritual growth and growth of personality. The reason we are here today is for right listening to happen, so that it leads to spiritual growth. Someone may become materially rich and wealthy while learning his lessons, but lets his personality traits fall down in the process. He remains of no use because all material riches are finally going to be left behind in the world. It's not like someone who is a millionaire or a billionaire will call for a hundred or two hundred rotis (Indian flat breads round in shape), saying that he'll eat as many because he's a tycoon, nor will he call for a five hundred feet long bed to sleep on saying, "Don't you know I'm a tycoon? Get a five hundred feet long bed for me. I want to sleep on it." Have you ever heard of anything like this? He'll also sleep on a six feet bed and eat four rotis like others. Therefore, it's not that being a rich and famous person holds more value. What matters and needs to be seen is whether his personality is quality enriched, as in, does he have a developed, sensitive, understanding, loving and dharma conscious personality? These should be the benchmarks of a personality. So, never push your child towards becoming ambitious. If your parents did this to you, then somewhere you must be living the defilements that are born out of it. You must work towards freeing yourself of them so that you don't transfer them to the next generation.

What is worth sharing wholeheartedly is love, generosity, kindness, dharma. Share these things without holding back, so that you have an expansive persona. Sharing helps in personality development and that is right living. So be careful and never ask for any such kind of blessings for your children where you want them to become officers or get selected for jobs, or likewise. These cannot be the blessings. Blessing is what Astitva has decided for them and the development that happens naturally for them. Astitva's blessing is on every human being. Wanting to shape someone's personality using a specific framework cannot be a blessing but a curse.

Blessing is when you help in creating opportunities along with being open and supportive, so that the child can go where Astitva wants him to, and accomplish what is destined for him i.e. whatever Astitva has decided for him. This blessing will be liberating for them and will move them towards growth. It will move them towards their inherent nature, their divinity. The growth has to happen towards 'beingness', towards the divine that they are, towards living naturally. This will help in their flowering and slowly this blossoming will lead them towards being Paramatma. We are here to be Paramatma.

Paramatma cannot be touched but you can be Paramatma. You can never meet Paramatma but you can be Paramatma. One can merge in Paramatma and the moment merging happens, one is Paramatma. We are on the wrong path with wrong concepts, and we must make sure not to transfer these wrong concepts anywhere else. Allow the child's development to happen naturally, without trying to fit them in a specified framework. Do not seek blessings of this kind for anybody.

People do ask for blessings from sages and in response they say, "Mangal ho" which means "may you be blessed". How will this mangal happen for you? If there are any obstructions coming in the way of your wellbeing, they'll get removed. This is the blessing that sages give, whether you understand it or not. They will bless with a 'mangal ho'. I have given a guideline for future, as to how your thought process should be towards children. If you ever want to ask for blessings for children or for yourself, ask for mangal to happen. That mangal is sans conditions, sans any guidelines. Once this blessing is given by a sage, the esoteric group and group of deities work towards fructifying it because the blessing is a sage's word, and the deities will never let a holy man's word go empty. The path of this blessing starts opening, provided there's no blockage from your end. What you will understand about this blessing and when is a different matter. It's possible you may never understand it but your mangal will happen. The meaning of mangal is that your right intelligence must grow, right understanding, intellect and wisdom must grow. You should be able to live a successful life with wisdom and equanimity. Successful means, living the worldly life and the spiritual truth properly. Don't hurt people, earn honestly, be philanthropic in your own way, spread love, understand sadhana, include it in your life and grow. Grow, develop and progress to be Paramatma. This is the only real development. This is the only sadhana for a sãdhaka, no other! Many people say, we do this, we do that, but those are all useless. There is only one sadhana and that is to be Paramatma. There cannot be any other sadhana. There is a lot of rubbish going on in the world in the name of sadhana. There is no limit to the spiritual garbage being served in the world. Trash is being offered in the name of spirituality.

Do you know what adhyatma is? Do you know what sadhana is? Practice such a sadhana that you become Paramatma. This is the one and only sadhana. A holy man's blessing of 'mangal ho' means he is removing all obstacles coming between you and the Paramatma you are to be. He dissolves all hindrances coming between the present you, and the Paramatma you are to be. He creates and releases an energy force and to activate that energy force, the esoteric group and group of deities get activated and start working on it. They remove the obstructions lying in the way of your liberation, they remove obstacles coming in the way of crossing the ocean of this worldly existence. It is therefore the vani (wise words) of the sage that removes the obstructions.

Sãdhaka: Swamiji, today's students say that they have to compete with their peers and keep high aspirations to move ahead. They feel that a competitive spirit is necessary to an extent, if they want to be successful.

Swamiji: Competition holds great value in the world that we have created. Human beings will become ambitious if we make them ambitious, putting seeds of competition saying things like, "race ahead, race ahead". We are the ones who tell the children, "Son, you don't have to be a human being; you have to become a robot, you have to become a computer." What it means is that there's a robot with a computer installed in it, hence a super-robot and that's what people are being asked to become. They are being asked to stop being human and become machines instead. Good competitive machines, who are told that their efficiency should be better than the other machines. They are asked to grow themselves, update themselves, bring a new version of themselves, upgrade themselves with new technologies. They are asked to be less of a human and more of a machine, if they want more opportunities in the world.

Corporate culture likes skilled people. Skilled people are those who are equivalent to great machines and can give maximum output. This is the language of technology…Who can give maximum output? Who is most skilled? Who is a good manager? This is all robotic stuff and people are being pushed towards becoming a combination of a super-robot and a super-computer, saying they'll succeed in the world. They will succeed in the world for sure, but be unsuccessful in their life because there won't be much life left in them. They are machines and not humans anymore. Little of their humanness will remain alive within them, which will make them feel that they're human and at times others will also remind them. They'll be highly stressed. Intoxicating themselves and doing other things to lessen the effect of becoming a machine so they can feel life to some degree, will be a norm.

Even when attending parties, they carry the attitude of their corporate designations to see where it can come of use, where they can extract more output from, which relationship can be cashed in on and how they should behave with certain people. There's no love present, because for them, people they're meeting are just clients. Their focus is on how to profit from them. They don't meet anyone from the viewpoint of love. It's pure business for them and love is not business. But sadly, the meaning of love in their dictionary is "receiving". People demand love. Love is not something you ask for. It is something to be shared and given freely, wholeheartedly, not just to any one individual but shared with all and sundry. Love is not selective. It is unbiased. Living with this unconditional love in your heart and pulling out from the rat-race of aspirations and ambitions, is when the person grows and his personality develops. This is when he'll be totally relaxed and in his natural state of simplicity. When one is not ambitious, one is simple and natural. When one is simple and natural, one loves unconditionally and that's when the love spreads and is shared with everyone. The more he is loving, the more human and less of a machine he is. Now, do you want your child to remain human or become a successful machine? If he's truly human, he'll be like a natural flower reaching a peak, with its captivating fragrance spreading in the world, attracting butterflies and photographers alike. His flowering happens beautifully. His name, fame and personality become immortal, just like the picture of a butterfly sitting on the flower; but the body, like the natural flower, is mortal and withers away. If the child is ambitious, he's like a paper flower which never flowers, blooms or blossoms. Now, what you want your child to become is in your hands. Do you want him to be a robot or Paramatma? Meanwhile check yourself also, as to how human and how robotic you are. We have taken a human form so that we can be Paramatma. That's the lesson we are here for. We keep taking births and die, only to return again and again, so as to complete this lesson. Today's technological era is turning humans into robots and super computers, converting them into super-robots who look like human beings but are no more human. They are skilled and trained robots. They seem to be humans but are actually not, with a twenty percent human to an eighty percent machine ratio. Considering this ratio, you have to decide what you want your child to be.

WHY DO DIFFICULTIES ARISE IN LIFE?

Sãdhaka: Difficulties keep coming in life. Why do so many difficulties arise in life and what should a person do when difficulties come?

Swamiji: Challenges and difficulties will keep coming in life to teach us. They are here to teach us lessons we need to learn. We awaken through these difficulties. If it were not for these challenges, no human being would be prepared to wake up. Man wants to sleep and stay unconscious with this thought that everything is settled and comfortable. He wants to live in his comfort zone, which means he is happy living unconsciously. If his choice is to live unconsciously, then both nature and Astitva will give him lessons...lessons to wake him up by breaking his comfort zone. This is 'the law', rule of nature, and it works in a manner which will wake us up because we haven't taken birth to sleep but to awaken.

The reason for a sãdhaka facing more difficulties is that he needs to be woken up, since he has the potential and the sensitivity required for it. He can feel the difficulties which is a very important aspect needed for waking up. The non-sãdhakas are not able to feel the difficulties arising, and therefore picking up lessons from these arising problems becomes challenging for them. People keep running here and there unconsciously. When we take lessons from the difficulties, then solutions also come on their own... Astitva provides solutions. Question is whether we have picked up our lessons or not. Difficulties don't stay, but if we haven't picked up our lesson from one, another difficulty in a different form will be presented. This will keep happening till we learn the lessons we need to. We move ahead once we learn the lesson and our consciousness elevates along with it, post which we get ready for the next lesson. Any such individual who is cocooned in his comfort zone and things are congenial for him all the time, cannot be a sãdhaka. He/she could be a drama king/queen in the name of a sãdhaka, with no sadhana or development happening. Being in comfort zone forever and ever does not happen in existence. Lord Buddha said "Life is suffering", and there are reasons for that. It is in the form of suffering that life happens, and suffering is the greatest teacher. It helps us understand the futility - futility not of the world, but of the separation that we are living. It is because of this separation that the world exists. If we are not there, then what samsara are we talking of? Then there is only Paramatma. Samsara gets created from where we announce our separation. Where our announcement of separation dissolves, there remains only Paramatma.

Chapter 4

The Five Senses and Their Diet: Establishing Balance of the Five Senses and Their Diet

Sãdhaka: Pranaam Swamiji! How does diet affect our body and our spiritual sadhana? What precautions should a Sãdhaka take as far as his diet is concerned?

Swamiji: It is very important for a Sãdhaka to understand 'diet' since we have limited our understanding of diet mainly to the food consumed from the mouth, whereas diet is taken in from all five senses. Whatever goes within from outside, is diet. To begin with, we understand things related to diet with the food that we eat. We eat a light, normal diet for a few days and then one day land up having a special party diet and start feeling heavy. What we need, is to understand how we feel after eating. People keep eating without being aware of how the food they are consuming is affecting them – it's effect and impact on their health. A conscious individual immediately feels the impact of the food he's eating. Throughout the day, he keeps his awareness maintained on what he's putting in his mouth and what impact that diet is leaving on his body.

The vaidyas (practitioners of ayurvedic medicine) have spoken so much about incompatible food combinations (viruddha ahaar). You trust their word on this and follow the guidelines they provide on this topic, but by yourself, you lack the right knowledge and understanding on the subject. You don't really pay attention when it comes to eating. You are totally unaware as to what food combinations are leaving what kind of an impact on your body and health. You are blindly following the knowledge the vaidyas share. What should be eaten with what, what combinations of food should not be consumed, which food is beneficial in the morning, what helps to take in the afternoon or in the evening...where has all this knowledge come from? It has come from the people who kept their awareness while eating, and were conscious of the impact it had on their body after consumption. If you keep watching the entire process of eating from start to end, you develop instant awareness with every move, which then remains steadfast. Then, if something doesn't feel right in the body after a meal and you cannot understand which food or ingredient might have caused it to happen, you can use a 'trial and error' method with different food combinations. This will help you in knowing their impact, before coming to a conclusion of what suits your body and what needs to be eliminated from your diet. In this way, one has to be aware towards diet on a regular basis. If one truly intends to regulate one's diet patterns and habits, an understanding of what, when, how and why one eats becomes important, so that a disciplined and mindful practice of eating is developed.

This was about regular awareness towards the food we consume, but if the awareness deepens, we will be conscious of what we are taking in through all the five senses. Secondly, speaking of eyes, they are one of the most important sense organs. Maximum energy is used up and exhausted through the eyes. We're continuously seeing with our eyes and whatever is being seen, is our diet. One must be discreet with what should be seen and what shouldn't. Even when it's not required, people are watching out of a forced habit. If nothing else, they're reading the hoardings that are put up everywhere. What is the need? And ever since this thing called the mobile phone has come, everyone is hooked on to it, watching various things available on it. Let alone the mobile, even the television has become a major source of compulsive watching. The screens have become a constant companion, providing food through the eyes which has a poison-like effect when consumed indiscreetly. Like the food we take in through our mouth has an impact on our physical body, the food we consume through our eyes impacts our mental body. Mental body is also one of the bodies, isn't it? Whatever goes inside the body leaves an impact on one of the bodies. When it comes to the ears, here also one has to be careful and mindful of what he's listening to and what he should avoid. Lending ears to some rubbish will create poison within.

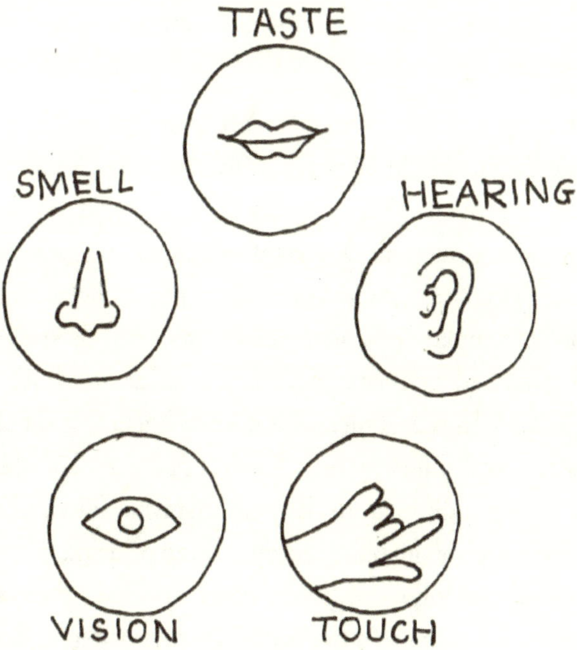

A Sãdhaka, a serious one at that, is willing to take risks. If he finds that the city he's staying in is getting polluted, noisy and the energy of the place is getting disturbed, he takes the chance of shifting base and moving elsewhere. He knows that even if the energy inside his house is fine, the thoughts etc. in the collective sub-conscious mind of the city are impacting him. That is a collective energy which one cannot really escape from, and he knows that. That propels him to leave the place for a quieter, remote place, maybe closer to the forests, where people are simpler and conditions favourable. He does this, only because he doesn't want to consume a harmful diet. Sãdhakas have to be careful that their diet remains healthy. For that, they may have to take chances of such kind to protect themselves from poison entering their system. That is why the talks of having an ashram or a community outside the village boundaries, closer to the forests and in a place which is demographically suitable for sadhana, keep coming up - a place where population is less and people are simple and good, so that we get to consume a good and healthy diet in all aspects.

Whatever is taken in from the five senses of touch, smell, taste, sound and sight should be proper and balanced. A balanced diet is extremely important. This also includes right contemplation (samyak chintan), which plays an important role in our progress on the path of liberation and protects us from falling prey to illusions. Hence, till the time contemplation is taking place, it should be samyak chintan i.e. balanced and right contemplation or reflection. If it's reflection, it should be right reflection and if it's intelligence, it should be right intelligence, and similarly, right intellect and right knowledge which take us on the path of truth. It is the Samyak Tattva (The 'Right' Principle) which is the balanced diet. If the principle of balance and rightness are not followed, things won't work out. Samyak tattva is the middle path, samyak tattva is liberation. Therefore, this principle should be lived and a sãdhaka should make sure he expands and 'lives awareness' throughout life.

Living in a mechanical way highlights the unconsciousness of that person. One's way of living and moving around depends on the kind of impetus present within him. If samyak tattva predominates, then the style of walking and working will be different. It will have a naturalness to it. Expansion of awareness and living consciously your whole life is a pre-requisite for sadhana to fructify, or else you won't experience success. Walk mindfully, eat mindfully, be mindful while talking or when doing any other work. Only then will your life be rightly balanced. This balanced and mindful day to day living is sadhana. After this stage is reached, the need for intense meditation starts weening off. All activities of your life now happen from this principle, the samyak tattva.

Don't bathe in a robotic manner. This is one more thing that can be very enlightening. Don't rush this activity. Do it joyfully and at the same time, being mindful of the divine water element touching your body and refreshing you to the core. Having a bath mindfully helps in saving water also which otherwise gets wasted a lot. You'll take water in a mug and slowly pour it over yourself, scrub your body, doing everything with ease and in a relaxed way. You may end up spending a little more time than you normally would, but you'll see the difference. You'll be more mindful, feel more refreshed and you may have an experiential understanding of the fact that you are not this body in a profound way.

I had my first realization of 'I am not this body' at a very young age while I was bathing. There was a sudden realization, "I'm not this body, this is somebody else. Bath is happening and it is being known. This is a body, water is flowing over the body, everything is a happening. This body is not the knower of all that is happening."

Living consciously, with full awareness, enlightens one that the 'I' is not the body. Witnessing the body walking, eating, bathing, brings about this right understanding of 'I am not this body'. With this becoming clear, the element of absolute truth, along with balance and equanimity, start growing within and lead to a balance in daily life, without which sadhana will not progress.

We need to understand hypnotism and come out of it. Talking of food hypnotism, you're eating time and again, without being mindful of what you're putting in your mouth. Where is the awareness? I am seeing that there's a variety of things you want to eat along with the tea you drink. First of all, tea itself is unhealthy and secondly you are eating things like fruit also with it. This confuses the whole body terribly. The body is confused, with various kinds of food being put in it over and over again. The entire energy goes into digesting that food. In such a case, how will right intelligence ever blossom? Energy being involved elsewhere, is not free to develop right intelligence and awareness. The first thing you want, upon waking in the morning, is tea. Even tea engages the energy, you know! Tea also has to go through the process of digestion. Then it's not just tea, since you want to eat something along with it. Two hours later, you're eating something again and another two three hours pass by and you're hungry once more. Your entire energy is expended in food and it's digestion. Where is the energy left or when is it free to help your intelligence grow? 'Right intelligence' doesn't grow if your intelligence doesn't grow. What happens is, you are then bereft of the right intelligence, which is a prerequisite for liberation. Your entire energy will remain stuck and entangled in the stomach and intestines. Later when the life force energy is asked, "what did you do?", it says, "I was busy with the stomach."

There are many who live to eat and their entire energy and intelligence is spent there. Eating this, eating that, eating here, eating there, this isn't getting digested, this food is giving me trouble so I'll visit the doctor etc. etc. After all this, they still wonder why they aren't feeling hungry and look for solutions. They're eating so many times a day, how will they feel hungry? In fact, they are victims of false hunger and they're caught in a viscious circle due to their biological clock which has gone corrupt. That is the reason the food hypnotism must break. Till the food hypnotism does not break, this wisdom that 'I am not the body' won't arise. Although criticized at times, the scientific wisdom of 'Sanatana' (eternal, everlasting, ageless) is profound. It has spoken of the concept of fasting once a week. Even if people follow this wise advice, they do it in such a way where they're eating the whole day. They will have food like a heavy sabudana khichdi, moraiya khichdi, boiled potatoes, a dense sweet made from water chestnut flour, fried potatoes etc. If this wasn't enough, to make things worse, you now have companies which send food home at the click of a button. What I'm saying is that people fast in a way where they eat more, and want more and more throughout the day. Not just food, there's beverages also that we haven't spoken of, with tea scoring a victory here. This is how people get caught up in the name of fasting, whereas the science behind fasting suggests having water once in twenty-four hours and nothing else. Try doing it for thirty-six hours, if possible, followed by a light meal. If you find this difficult, you can follow the naturopathy way of fasting, which calls for a sixteen hour fast. During the remaining eight-hour period starting in the morning, eat only twice.

People aren't aware that even tea is a diet in itself. That also goes through a process of digestion. If you have two meals in a day, drink tea three times a day and munch on something twice in between, it will be counted as seven meals. Milk and tea also take time to digest. Your body gets completely involved in the process. With fruits, it's slightly different. Fruits take around thirty minutes to get digested although it is said that they take twenty minutes, but that depends on how good your digestive fire/energy (Agni) is. If the digestive ability of the body is good, then the fruits get digested in twenty minutes. A well-balanced diet with healthy food items is very important, so that the right understanding of 'I am not this body' happens.

The first barrier in the way of sadhana is the misconception that you are the body. Till this barrier is crossed and the right understanding of 'I am not this body' happens, you cannot progress in sadhana. Till the time you consider this body to be you, all the hypnotisms related to the body will hold onto you, typically the 'my, my' syndrome. With the realization that you're not this body, this syndrome collapses, and the ego which is central to this syndrome, also collapses. Right now, this is in relation to something, be it my relatives, my house, my things etc. There is attachment and insecurity involved with it, since the bond with this body still continues. Once this relationship with the body is broken, and you're well established in this truth that you are not the body, then comes a state of being alone. This is the time when staying alone, staying in unfamiliar settings, living amidst new and unknown faces becomes important, to start off. Until and unless these steps are climbed, depth in sadhana won't be possible. 'Prem gali ati sankri, tame dui na samaye' which means the lane of love is very narrow, two cannot fit in it. Neither God can fit in, nor the Guru. You have to gather the courage of being alone. This is the fundamental courage without which climbing further is a little difficult. You have to gather this courage and take the first step. You will have to take this step at some point in time, so why not today for things to work out. There is a variety of sadhanas available. Many centres are available these days, where so many types of sadhanas are going on. There's so much happening and so much talk around these facilities and sadhanas. Many people have been associated with these facilities, but years have gone by and nothing profound has happened. Doing more sadhana leads to enlightenment is a myth.

I hear people say that they've been meditating for the past twenty-five years and some say they've been meditating for the last fifty years. I tell them yes, you've probably been doing it for the last fifty lifetimes and will continue for another fifty or maybe hundreds more. Don't worry, you'll continue doing sadhana as you have been doing till now. The thing is, what should have happened has not happened. Self-realization should happen. What needs to be understood is, there's nothing wrong with intense meditation and it should keep happening but it's vital to know that until sadhana becomes a moment to moment happening in your life, Truth won't reveal itself. Even in the midst of a celebration, dancing, conversations, jokes and laughter, the lamp of awareness should remain alight. If this lamp remains lit at every step, things fall into place and then there's no harm whatsoever. Once this stage is reached, Krishna's Leela will be understood. His full incarnation will be understood, wherein He does everything from Raas Leela to celebrations to taking care of His kingdom to giving sermons. Things work out well when sadhana happens while all activities are being carried out.

Intense meditation is not about all this. Intense meditation is for sãdhakas who are beginners. They are taught this meditation by giving instructions like 'A is for apple, E is for English, G is for goat', followed by 'A is fine but apple must be removed, E is fine but English must be removed, G is fine but goat must be removed. Be aware; be aware as to what you are holding onto and sitting over.' Intense meditation is fine in the beginning. You spending twenty-five years or fifty years of this golden era on a one-hour or a two-hour intense meditation sitting daily, doing all kinds of practices, should not be the case. For a few days in the beginning this is okay, but slowly you should come into the 'Samyak Sadhana', which should spread through your entire life. "I am doing sadhana for the last fifty years." What sense does this make? Sadhana must expand in your entire lifespan and The Ultimate Truth should get revealed. This 'Ultimate Truth' is the liberator. It is 'The Sadhana' itself, sadhana of ultimate reality. This is the middle path (madhyam marg), the middle system (madhyam nikaaya). The middle path, the middle system is the emancipator. There Kabir das Ji's vaani will hold significance, "Sadho sahaj samadhi bhali" (O seeker, natural/effortless union with the Ultimate Reality is best). This sahaj samadhi remains forever, unobstructed. Intense meditation is not going to help when leaving the body. The naturalness of sahaj samadhi keeps getting profound and even while leaving the body, it will remain intense. Everything at that point will be given up, the first body will be given up followed by the second and then third and in this manner all the six bodies will be given up. Then, entry into the seventh will take place, where the final merging will happen and this game will end.

IMPACT OF FOOD ON OUR BODY

Sãdhaka: Pranaam guruji! What impact can the food that we consume have on our mind, our desires?

Swamiji: It affects greatly because the body is psychosomatic. This physical body and the mental body are very closely linked and connected to each other, so the impact is instant. Even the craving, the food craving is first born in the mental body and then becomes apparent in the physical body. Whatever is then put in the physical body has an immediate effect on the mental body. That is why a lot of caution is required when it comes to food.

The mental body comes after the physical body, so the physical body should get shattered first and only then will the mental body break. There are many steps to it. First of all, if a person is a very sensitive human being, he should be a vegetarian and protect himself by avoiding any kind of animal diet. Secondly one should stay away from eating too many times in a day. These days there are various kinds of influences, related to science as well as the recently born therapeutic modalities, which are being fed incessantly to mankind. This new age medical science born barely three-four hundred years ago does not have the depth or profoundness to it. It has been prescribing things which make no sense at times, like asking people to eat little at regular intervals through the day. We don't have to get into this madness. Ayurveda has a research history of thousands of years and it says, "Ek baar yogi, do baar bhogi, teen baar rogi khana khata hai", which upon translation means: One who has a single meal in a day is a yogi, one who eats two meals a day is a bhogi (enjoyer who enjoys worldly life and pleasures) and one who eats three meals in a day is a rogi (unhealthy/diseased).

Looking at today's environment and giving oneself some concession, a person can have two meals a day at the most. As per naturopathy which has branched from ayurveda itself, a sixteen hour fast must be observed. This must be followed every day, with the two meals being consumed in the eight-hour window, and only water consumed when needed during the sixteen hours of fasting period. The two meals being spoken of can contain grains or cereals, but non vegetarian food should be refrained from. Out of the two meals, the evening one should be kept light if possible. A soup or a light khichdi or daliya would be beneficial. There is no hard and fast rule, but keeping one of the two meals lighter and at times even skipped would help. Skipping it means having only one meal a day and if possible, do a complete fast on some days which means not having any meal. This helps in purification of the body and also helps in clearing any blockages in the system. It is important that blockages in the body are cleared because when that happens, the blockages in the mind also get cleared. There are many common blockages since the knots of the body and mind are tied together. When we say 'Neti Neti, I am not this body', we need to understand that the body is made of food, so we need to work on the food and diet aspect. Without working on the food aspect, we cannot get over the body. Going beyond the body, one comes to the realization of 'I'm not this body'. Sadhana does not progress until then. The sadhana that will happen till this realization takes place will only be hypothetical, with all kinds of imaginary things involved in it. Hypothetical sadhana leads nowhere and is nothing but big talk, like a phrase in Hindi language goes, "Unchi dukaan, phika pakwaan" which literally means 'A high end shop but below average goods.' All the conversations and talks around hypothetical sadhana will be big and fanciful, but it won't take you anywhere and what you're working towards won't happen. That is the reason one should be careful with what one eats because the variety available when it comes to food is unlimited. What helps in going beyond the body has to be given preference, since body is made of food.

Diet is that which is taken inside from out. One is food, one is what we feed our mind and likewise whatever is fed to the other senses. All that is fed to the five senses is diet and this diet impacts us. What kind of thoughts should be taken in, what company one must keep since company matters a lot...all this plays an important role. Lord Buddha said one must not be in the company of a person with inferior energy/character. Although he said it's okay to keep company of people with mediocre energy, but discussing sadhana or any such deep topics with them should be avoided and the conversations should be limited to common topics. It is best to keep company of those with high energy; a virtuous and spiritual friend who wishes well. This is the friendship or connection which is most benevolent. The other kind of friendships are not beneficial.

The kind of company we keep plays a very important role because we imbibe thoughts from them. The quality of company shapes our thoughts and those thoughts create a framework of concepts and ideas within us. Spiritual and virtuous friends do not give ideas or concepts, rather they break the existing concepts and conditioning. Conditioning and concepts must break. On the other hand, one must behave and speak to mediocre friends with caution, avoiding any profound discussions with them. Company holds great significance. Everyone is friends with mobile phones and internet these days which is certainly not good company and caution needs to be maintained. This has both good and bad contents to offer, with the percentage of bad being at 99.9% which means that 99.9% of the content is rubbish, with a lot of it being spiritual garbage. There are so many influencers serving so much content in the name of spirituality, but sadly there's nothing spiritual about any of it. There's definitely some talk of spirituality in them, but that is not what spiritual is. Someone who hasn't attained spiritual wisdom in his life is speaking about it - nothing can be more dangerous than that. Dangerous because that individual has no experience of it. He is attracting and influencing people not through any personal experience, but just by repeating things that he's probably picked up from different sources. As an influencer, even if one sentence spoken by him goes wrong out of a hundred spoken ones, it will be detrimental and prove very harmful, because you will take that information to be true. You may not be able to recognize the fallaciousness of that one statement. Since ninety-nine percent of what he said was right, you may be led into trusting that one percent of the wrong as right too.

You see, you felt good listening to the ninety nine percent of the content the influencer shared, but it lacked life force, because he was speaking without any experiential understanding. Whereas whatever a Sadguru says, even if he speaks in a broken language, it has a naturally penetrating effect. Why does a Sadguru's word have a profound effect? It is so because he is speaking from experience and innate wisdom. His vital energy, the life force energy, is inherently present in it. That is why Kabir Das Ji's 'saddhukadi bhasha' works (blend of five dialects, a vernacular dialect from medieval North India also known as 'language of the saints'), whereas an influencer's long and over the top talks, drown. For such people, Kabir Das ji says that when one blind man (ignorant) guides or shows the way to another blind (ignorant) man, they both fall in the ditch and get destroyed. Great care has to be taken so as not to accept any information from inexperienced people. Although these people are good at learning things by heart, reciting shlokas wonderfully, saying verses from the holy texts fluently, giving great examples, but they have no personal experience at all. Kabir das Ji when asked, said that he had never held a paper or pen in his hand and that he was illiterate. He could not read or write, yet his words will continue to leave a profound impact on us, like they always have.

THE PATH FROM NIRVANA TO MAHAPARINIRVANA

Sãdhaka: Guruji, There's a path to Nirvana and one leading to Mahaparinirvana. Once the path of Mahaparinirvana opens for a sãdhaka, can he at any point derail from this path again, or can Astitva stop him from moving ahead on this path?

Swamiji: Nirvana happens, but if mahaparinirvana does not happen after nirvana, then the final liberation does not happen. Nirvana means that the person cannot be held up for long, and mahaparinirvana will definitely happen in his case. If it doesn't happen in this life, it will happen in the next one. He is a 'sakadagami', once returner, so he will take one more birth and not more. For mahaparinirvana to happen, there are existential arrangements made in some cases, wherein the available esoteric support systems hold back a few people through whom auspiciousness and well-being has to spread, and in due course they transform into sakadagamis. Some are transformed into sakadagamis without this divine arrangement also. In this case, if any limitation still remains to be worked out or if any new attractions happen to take over, which is possible and can happen even after nirvana, then these become the reasons for taking one more birth. It's not that they will take many births.

If one has attained 'srotapanna', he will take seven births at the most, with the number getting reduced to one or two births only, if nirvana happens. Post nirvana, there is also a possibility that he may enter the 'anagami loka'. If he enters the anagami loka, then he won't take birth on this earth but will be born in a higher realm and will get liberated from there. This happens often in cases where nirvana has happened. In the anagami loka, their journey is very long because the awareness of time is very less, so they have to stay there for a very long time, but the 'final liberation' is guaranteed from this realm. The number of sakadagamis who come back once to spread auspiciousness and well-being is more, since they did not attain mahaparinirvana after attaining nirvana. They are the ones who take birth in the human form, who play a special role over here, role of an auspicious and virtuous friend. They are chosen to play this role and they take one more birth after nirvana for this reason. Whosoever then comes in contact with these 'kalyan mitras', virtuous friends, will be benefited and transformed. To what extent one is benefited in the company of these virtuous and high energy beings, depends on how open and receptive one is; open to letting go of one's ego and receptive towards the wisdom being shared. Gurus and Sadgurus are kalyan mitras.

RIGHT REFLECTION (SAMYAK MIMANSA)

Sãdhaka: When does 'Right Reflection' happen? Does it happen after the 'I' is dropped? Does it become the reason for shedding and destruction of karmic impurities?

Swamiji: 'Samyak Mimansa', right reflection- everyone reflects upon things but the question is of 'right reflection'. Right reflection is a state where the person is very intelligent, with a very high IQ level. The intelligence quotient is very high, but only if the sadhanas from past births have been good and the accumulated old merits emerge and come forth, can the intelligence transform into right reflection. The conditions for this are good sadhanas from past births, and accumulated merits from those sadhanas coming forth. Emergence of accumulated merits plays an important role for right reflection to happen. The emergence of old merits means fading of the ego, ego losing its strength and becoming feeble. Right reflection is possible when ego loses its strength. As the merits from past births start showing up, ego starts to emaciate and right reflection happens. This quality of right reflection then destroys the ego completely. Once the ego is destroyed, there is no need left for right reflection. What is the need for samyak mimansa after ego has fallen apart? Samyak mimansa in itself is one of the paths or systems, out of the six systems of Hindu Philosophy called 'Shad Darshana'. Being one of the paths of shad darshana, mimansa contributes to the feebling and fading of the ego, but it is because of the emergence of merits from past births that the ego is destroyed. Since his IQ levels are already high, the individual without wasting any time on worldly things and on any hypotheses or research of any kind, will only work towards dissolution of the ego.

The path of pure knowledge or wisdom has to be 'samyak mimansa'. There are two things in this and we can take two examples. Taking King Janaka's example- when King Janaka met Ashtavakra, right reflection was already integrated in Janaka's life, which is why he was interested in the knowledge of all the wise men he came to know of. If he found them to be good, he would invite these scholars and wise men to his royal court and welcome them wholeheartedly, showing immense respect to them. He would shower riches, valuables and a lot of respect on them, asking them to share their knowledge and wisdom with him. He would go on listening to them and then bid them farewell. Having given them a sendoff once, he would never call them back again because he felt they had delivered what best they could, but what he was looking for had not really worked out. He knew something would work out for him only if it was worthy of 'right reflection'. If that wasn't delivered, he would respectfully see them off. Different scholars would keep coming for the scholarly discussions, debates and discourses on scriptures, which the king would organize time and again. He would announce big awards for these events, thinking that someday, out of the hundreds who came, one such scholar, Guru or Sadguru might appear, whose deshana would help him attain samyak mimansa completely. Wishing that someone would arrive one day to satisfy his thirst of right understanding on this path of reflection that he had chosen, King Janaka organized another such event. It was in this event that Ashtavakra's father came to participate. To call his father back, at the behest of his mother, twelve-year old Ashtavakra with eight deformities in his body happened to arrive at King Janaka's court.

Ashtavakra entered the royal court of King Janaka to call his father back. The court was full of scholars, priests and courtiers. When they saw young Ashtavakra walking into the court, they laughed at him, at his deformed body and the weird way in which he walked. The way he moved was so crooked and weird that they all burst out laughing. When everyone laughed at him hysterically, Ashtavakra stopped, looked at everyone present there, and burst into a laughter louder than theirs. He laughed so loud that there was pin-drop silence in the court. They all went silent because they couldn't understand why Ashtavakra had laughed at them. They thought they had a reason to laugh at him, but the reason for his laughter was unfathomable for them. When nobody could understand or come to any conclusion as to why Ashtavakra had burst into laughter,

King Janaka asked him, "Son, I understand why these people are laughing. They have a reason to laugh. What could possibly be the reason for you to laugh? Why did you laugh?" The twelve-year old boy said, "Rajan (king), there is a scholarly discussion going on here in order to find the highest form of truth. You think these chamaars (derived from the Hindi word chamdaa which means skin; referring here to people operating from the level of body consciousness)

sitting here will reflect upon the Ultimate Truth? You think these chamaars whose outlook is limited only to the body, will examine and evaluate the truth? These people whose vision operates from the level of the body will give discourses on what Supreme Reality is? Your Highness, you should be fully aware that scholarly debates and discussions on scriptures to find the truth happens with learned and wise people, not with chamaars. Does one invite chamaars for the scholarly discussions (shastrarth)?" The king was left astounded, with all his invitees screaming as to how dare the boy call them chamaars. Ashtavakra continued, "Rajan, these people saw my body alone, this flesh and the crookedness of this body. They did not see the real me. They did not recognize who I am. They did not see the light within me nor did they recognize the consciousness within me. They couldn't see the light of my consciousness. They are seeing the body, the flesh and its shape and size. Rajan, those who see the skin and its shape, size and form have to be chamaars. You think chamaars will determine what the Ultimate Truth is?"

Ashtavakra had given a definition with which all challenges, problems and issues of the world can end. All distinctions based on caste and lineage can fall off. He proved in the court that just because someone is a scholar, priest, researcher or learned, doesn't mean he is a brahmin. This does not determine the caste nor does birth determine the caste. He said that a poor man's child could belong to any caste, even a lower one, but if that child is on the path of sadhana, he will be a brahmin. No caste is determined by birth, be it brahmin or any other. With this major happening, King Janaka was enlightened and the gathering was fruitful and productive. The reality of people operating from body consciousness had come to light, and a rare opportunity to be in the energy field of an Enlightened and Liberated Master had happened. That day King Janaka did not dare to go behind Ashtavakra, but the next morning he got ready and left in search of the young boy. He had gathered information about his whereabouts and knew which road he was wandering on. He asked his charioteer to stop the chariot, got off and did 'sashtang dandavat pranaam' to Ashtavakra. Sashtang dandavat pranaam is a gesture of complete surrender and respect shown, where one prostrates in a way that the eight limbs - the forehead, chest, both hands, both knees, both feet touch the ground. This is performed with arms stretched forward. After this prostration, Janaka said, "Bhagwan (Lord), please grace me with your benevolence. Kindly accompany me to the palace and accept me as your disciple. Please bless me with your supreme knowledge." He then took Ashtavakra to his palace and made him sit on his throne. King Janaka sat on the floor in front of Ashtavakra and again did sashtang pranaam, washed his feet and requested him to provide the teachings.

A young boy, twelve years of age, but who had the eyes to recognize him!? No one but Janaka had those eyes. He himself was the path of reflection, and recognized Ashtavakra's truth. Everyone cannot be the path of reflection or profound contemplation. He used to listen to all kinds of scholars and learned men and knew how to discern milk from water. Great scholars who were well respected and had earned a name in the world would come to his court. He would give them a whole lot of respect and riches before seeing them off with a 'Ram-Ram'. 'Ram-Ram' meant take all this material wealth and never come back again. Your knowledge was heard, it was rubbish, please leave. What this conveys is that Janaka would not get influenced by wrong knowledge. He had the eyes to see, the right vision. He himself was the path of right contemplation.

The scholars would recite big holy texts and shlokas seamlessly in a flow and cite quotations and statements from all over fabulously, but King Janaka would donate worldly riches and send them away with a "Ram-Ram", which meant please don't come back and kindly take your rubbish with you. Janaka never got influenced and that's the reason he progressed. He kept moving ahead and never got entangled in any spiritual garbage. The path of right reflection and contemplation cannot get entwined with spiritual garbage.

These days a lot of people are seen giving fantastic talks and statements on the vedas, shastras and upanishads but that's all rubbish. Why rubbish? Rubbish because the orator is not speaking from experience. All of what he's sharing is not his own experiential knowledge. It is borrowed. He is giving borrowed information which won't help at all. However profound the knowledge may be, it is still borrowed and not his own, so it's of no value. The speaker's life force should be integrated in his speech, like Kabir's saddhukadi language, which consisted of strange words and yet they were pure gems because they were coming from the great mystic poet and saint Kabirdas Ji's mouth. Reflection happens when the speaker's vital life force energy has merged with his words. It then has the quality of bringing transformation.

The second example after King Janaka's is that of Lord Mahavir. Lord Mahavir said that between the 'shravak' (listener) and 'sadhu' (the holy man/ascetic), the listener is supreme. Sadhu is ranked second since he has to do sadhana and he progresses one step at a time as he does not travel on the path of reflection or contemplation. The ones travelling on the path of mimansa (reflection) are the best but they are rare. Therefore, the shravaks are supreme in comparison to sadhus. The thing is that definitions change over time, and for that reason, all those who come to listen now, those huge crowds that gather are also called shravaks. Shravaks are of higher order and level. You think those huge crowds of people gathering up to listen are shravaks? Shravak is a very high stage. King Janaka was a shravak when he met the Sadguru of those times, Ashtavakra. Ashtavakra was the Sadguru of mimansa, the philosophical discipline of reflection and investigation. It was upon meeting the Sadguru that the disciple was born. A great disciple was born and a great guru was born. Both happened simultaneously, the birth of the disciple and the birth of the guru. The world then received the great holy text, 'Ashtavakra Samhita'.

Listen brother, about mimansa – if it's not your path, then it's surely not. Ask yourself whether you are a shravak. If you are, then it's for you. If not then it's only going to delude you. You have to know whether you are on the path of mimansa or not. Mimansa is the path of repeated cutting, neti-neti (not this, not this). It will keep cutting - cutting all the lies and throwing them, cutting all the illusions, the entire illusionary being and throwing them all. Mimansa is all about 'not this, not this, not this'. That is the reason King Janaka was saved. All the great and big-time influencers came and he heard them, but he was clear that wasn't it. He gave them what they were looking for - money, gold. "Take all this with you, along with the knowledge you have shared" – this was his take when he would see them off. He was clear and knew, "this is not it, don't want this". Apart from this he would also check the 'I' within, like 'who am I, what is mine' and realized 'not this, not this'...hence it was mimansa in the perfect state. A state of perfection takes birth with mimansa.

King Janaka was enlightened and everything dropped from him. He did not try to leave anything, everything got dropped. He stayed in the palace, but there was no palace he was holding onto. It had got dropped. Where was the need to then leave the palace? The palace had already got dropped, so what was the problem staying in it? You can keep using the palace as it has anyway dropped. You also don't have to leave the palace or the money. The money gets dropped and there's no more holding onto it. 'I am not this body' will also come in neti-neti. Once the body is understood as an illusion and gets dropped, videh (bodiless) happens. Dropping the body means you are bodiless i.e. you have gone beyond body-consciousness. 'I am not this body' is the way the body has got dropped. When this clarity comes and the right understanding happens, videh happens. What this means is that despite being in this body, you are bodiless. There will be times when there'll be no awareness of the body because we are not this body but the body is used. This is what happens in samadhi.

If it can happen with Janaka, it can happen with everyone. When samadhi happens, videh happens, we go beyond the body. Whether it was Janaka or anybody else who experiences samadhi even today, isn't he videh? If he is not videh, how can samadhi happen? Hence the state of bodiless will happen to him as well. Samadhi means the right understanding has dawned that 'I am not the body nor am I the mind'. Just as videh is no-body state, amani dasha is no-mind state. Amani state is higher than videh. Videh means 'I am not this physical body' and amani means 'I am not the mind - I am not the fourth body'.

I say, talk of something beyond this also, as in, 'I am not the atma, nor am I paramatma', neti-neti. Ultimately what is all this? Which liberation, what kind of liberation, whose liberation, what emptiness, what nirvana, what mahaparinirvana...not this! not this! Ultimately everything has to go. The 'Mahamukti', the Final Liberation one talks of, there everything must go, nothing can stay. Nothing should remain there.

Chapter 5

Supreme Science of Breath
Mystery of the Subconscious Mind

'SUDDEN EXHALATION' METHOD FOR MEDITATION: THE MOST NATURAL, SIMPLE METHOD FOR CLEANSING

Sãdhaka: Pranaam Swamiji! Kindly explain in detail about the 'sudden exhalation' method for meditation that you've given for cleansing. How must this method be applied? How does this method prove effective in breaking the patterns of the subconscious mind? Why is it the greatest of all methods? Can it be applied anywhere, anytime and any number of times?

Swamiji: This great and most supreme method that I have shared needs to be understood properly. This method truly is the greatest because it is most natural and simple to apply and doesn't need any arrangements before doing it. One doesn't need to make any schedules for it or remove any time for it because time and space come under the mind-game category. Barring this method, rest of the intense methods for meditation require a negative part to be applied wherein time and space is involved.

There are two parts to meditation. One is the negative part and the other positive. Why does one have to use the negative part? Reason for this being the involvement of time and space required to practice these methods. There's a preparation involved before the sitting takes place, like a venue is decided upon and a time is scheduled for the same. One decides which method is to be practiced in that particular session, so on and so forth. Now, what do you think all this is? This is all a part of the mental knowhow. Mental manipulation is involved in it. If the mind is involved, that means all this is happening within a mental framework. The involvement of the mind, somewhere or the other, becomes an obstruction for the intention of the method to fructify. Look, what are these methods for meditation? They are techniques and methods to go beyond the mind, right? But who is involved in the planning of these methods? The mind itself is involved - sit at this time, this place, do this method, do this, do that, repeat this method etc. That is why this is called the negative part and it has a role to play. When we talk of doing bhastrika, omkar naad, catharsis, gibberish etc. etc. what do you think all this is? It is the negative part, and we say negative part because all this falls under mental planning. For that matter, nothing happens without mental planning. Mind is involved in everything you do. There is one part of the mind that inspires us for sadhana. There is another part of the mind that says, do everything but don't get liberated. The mind agrees for sadhana also only if it falls in its own framework.

If the sadhana is happening as per the mind's planning, then it is ready for it because then it's a game that the mind itself is playing. The mind may get a little organized with it but then going beyond the mind doesn't happen. A lot of people have challenges in their practical life where they cannot remove time for meditation. How should they remove time and from where? It gets them wondering whether they can anyhow manage to steal some time in the morning or evening. They also wonder what will happen if they face any disturbance in the afternoons. What if a mental pattern hacks them in the afternoon - if stress takes over or maybe anger, greed, fear or anything else, how will they manage to get out of it? This is their concern. Something needed to be given for handling any such issue if it arose, hence this method has been given...this method involving the breath.

It's very important to understand this method. Every sãdhaka must understand this method properly. This is the greatest method. There is no planning involved in it. Whenever the thought arises, you instantly exhale without wasting even an iota of a moment. Even before your thought reaches completion, the exhalation should happen. The moment a trigger, a memory, a disturbance or anything of the sort arises, that very instant exhalation must happen - sudden exhalation. The arising of the thought and sudden exhalation, happen simultaneously. This exhalation must happen without any preparation or planning. The first exhalation that will happen will be different and a unique one. How will this exhalation be? It will be one hundred percent wrong and it won't help in dhyana at all. Now understand well. It hacks the patterns of the subconscious mind. What does it hack? It hacks the breath first. In every situation, be it a situation where one is afflicted by lust, anger, greed or be it an environment of love or peace, the breathing pattern is different in every situation. Without a particular pattern of breath, the emotion associated with it cannot arise. When in anger, the breath is fast, in love it's different, in fear it's different and similar is the case with all other emotions or defilements. Whenever a defilement or pattern hacks you, it means it is hacking your conscious mind and for that to happen, the breath is hacked first.

Your conscious mind is very small and the subconscious mind is quite big and more powerful. When the conscious mind gets hacked, it is left with little power, but with this little power we have to clean the subconscious mind. This small conscious mind has to clean all the patterns, defilements, memories which are stored in the subconscious mind from many lifetimes. What is needed for this is the power of discernment and technique. If a person is asked to dig a mountain, it won't happen even with lifetimes of effort. But there is a technique that has been made available now and this job is not impossible anymore, thanks to the JCB, a mechanical excavator. Now if you tell the person to dig a mountain, he may agree to do it within a stipulated timeframe. This is what a technique can do. The technique is now given to you all to clean the entire subconscious mind with your small conscious mind. That technique is the sudden exhalation method.

Something we really need to understand is that new patterns are also getting created. New patterns are getting created and the old ones are getting updated and becoming powerful. What is the solution? Sadhana of awareness is the solution. Increasing our awareness will not allow new patterns to get created, they won't stand a chance. With awareness, old patterns will get cleansed. They won't get updated or become powerful and new patterns won't get created. That is the reason this sudden exhalation technique is needed. I have given you this technique so that you can make it a part of your daily routine. Whenever a thought arises, exhale immediately and how should this exhalation happen? It should happen without any planning or preparation. What this means is, from wherever the thought arises, the exhalation must happen from there itself. If at that thought-arising moment, your breath is on its way in and only twenty percent of inhalation has happened, you will exhale from that point itself. You will not inhale completely and then do the sudden exhalation. The twenty percent of breath will be exhaled, not a hundred percent of the breath. This is because you are not going to complete the inhalation process since the thought had come when only twenty percent inhalation of the breath had happened. Whatever amount of breath was inhaled will be exhaled. If it's little that was inhaled, that much will be exhaled. If it was twenty five percent inhaled or fifty percent inhaled, twenty five percent or fifty percent will be exhaled. There is no measuring or calculation involved in it. Wherever the breath has reached while inhaling, it will be exhaled from there. The moment the thought of exhalation arises, exhalation should have happened then and there. This way the mind doesn't get time to plan. The mind thus, neither gets a chance to get involved nor manipulate, resulting in an event beyond the mind. A happening beyond the mind takes place because mind is nothing but time, and it needs time to get activated. Without time, mind cannot get activated and we are not going to give it any time for exhalation. The more time the mind gets, the stronger it becomes so we won't give it time at all or we will give it very less time, so less that it doesn't get time to execute a plan. We will give it such less time that no plan can be made nor executed. Exhalation once done is followed by inhalation which will happen naturally, slowly and with ease, on its own. There is effort involved in exhalation. There'll be no effort put in when inhalation happens. Inhalation will happen naturally, taking its own time. In the next exhalation, a complete hundred percent of breath will get released since a hundred percent of natural inhalation had happened before. With this next exhalation, all the defilements will get released. You have to couple it with a feeling that all the defilements related to the six chakras are leaving this body. The seventh chakra, the uppermost chakra has to be left out. Exhalation will be coupled with the feeling that all defilements like lust, anger, greed, attachments, pride, ego, pragmatism, jealousy, aversion, hostility, hatred, fear, procrastination and the like, related to all the six chakras are getting released.

This exhalation is one part of the method. It is the negative part because there is 'doing' involved in it. Since it is the negative part of the method, we can add other things to this already existing negative aspect for cleansing. How do we do it? You think we are going to get calculative, taking the name of each defilement separately for it to be removed? Will we take names like lust, anger, greed, attachment etc. separately when exhaling? No, this is just for the sake of understanding. When we just understand that defilements have to go, it gets integrated in the exhalation. We won't say ego, pride, jealousy, aversion, hatred etc. We will just say, "All the defilements are getting released with this exhalation. All the defilements related to the six chakras, whether we are aware of them or not, are getting released with this exhalation. All the patterns are getting dissolved and released with this exhalation. Inner purity is getting revived." This needs to be a part of our understanding and it will happen automatically when exhaling; it will remain inbuilt in it. That is the reason I repeat these things often and if you too keep repeating and reminding yourself of this, then it will happen with every exhalation that takes place. This was the negative part of the method. What will be the positive part?

The positive part of the technique is the 'happening', which involves our natural breathing. The coming in of the breath is a happening i.e. the inhalation happens on its own, at its own pace, without any effort being put. Whatever is coming in is Paramatma's gift and it is auspicious. The breath that we are taking in is actually paramatma's exhalation...paramatma is releasing that breath. Paramatma is releasing the breath into us. What do you think paramatma will release? Will he give out anger, greed? Will he release lust, pride? It is love, compassion, peace, silence, loving-kindness et al, that paramatma is releasing, and these supreme states are entering us. This happens naturally. All the defilements and patterns get released with exhalation, so the more we do it, the better. Maintain an unbroken awareness towards this practice, along with other jobs at hand. It doesn't matter if you forget about it in between. Be in gratitude that you remembered to do it as and when you did, and that it has brought about some changes. When the thought comes back again, exhale and then allow the inhalation to happen naturally, followed by the exhalation and a natural inhalation again. This process continues and the cleansing will keep happening. You don't need to sit for this nor do you have to stand still for it. It can be done anytime, anywhere... while working, while walking, while cooking, while talking, when bathing, when eating. It will happen suddenly.

At any given point if you feel disturbed, anxious, unaligned, stressed, restless or anything else, sudden exhalation is the answer. If we've been hacked by a pattern, if we still talk to people the way we're used to, if we try to manipulate people, if we try making them understand things, that means the mind has pushed us into doing that. Many people are in a habit of giving unsolicited knowledge to others. Any such behavior means the mind has hacked us. Mind is getting powerful, leading to the personality getting stronger. At such times sudden exhalation will help and we'll realize that we were in the grip of a pattern which was operating us. The patterns of the subconscious mind operate us and those patterns must get destroyed.

What is the meaning of destroying patterns? Is someone present as a doer to destroy them? It will happen, naturally and simply. We won't do it, it will happen. It will come in our memory by itself and happen naturally through us. The 'I-ness' will keep reducing which means 'I have to do it or I will do it' will keep fading. The 'I' as a doer should keep reducing and then it'll happen...the sudden exhalation will happen. When it's sudden, then it's an event that has happened beyond the realm of the mind. It's a happening outside the mental realm and hence the mind fails to understand it. The mind did not plan or organize this, so no patterns of the subconscious mind can get activated. There is no environment for any defilements, any thoughts or patterns to get activated and where there is nothing happening, there the 'thoughtless state' happens, the 'amani dasha' as it's called. When the mind doesn't understand what's happening, it gets de-activated. When the mind is not active, then it is in a thoughtless state, the amani dasha. Thoughtless state or no-mind state is sadhana's primary intention and purpose.

There's no question of remembering anything in all of this. Like I said, you just have to understand. I keep repeating those words and you hear them and you understand what is being said. There is no need for you to remember those words and absolutely no need to repeat them. Whether you understand what defilements are or not, it doesn't matter. All the vikaaras, defilements, those we're aware of and those that we're not aware of, all those whose definitions we know and those that we don't know of, all these can be together termed as 'samast vikaara'. We just have to put an intention that all the defilements (samast vikaaras) are getting released from the body. This statement is also going in your subconscious mind. An antivirus needs to be put in the mind as there's too much in there. If you are excavating a mountain even with a JCB, it has to be drilled inside the mountain. The part of this heavy equipment called the drill, has to be put into the mountain to excavate it. In the instance of a virus having affected a software, an antivirus has to be put to clean the software. The mind is also like a software and an anti-virus has to be used to clean it of all that is stored in the subconscious mind. This sudden exhalation technique works as an anti-virus for cleaning the subconscious mind of all its contents. To save the software from a virus, like in the case of a computer, an anti-virus is used to save it. In the case of the mind, it needs to be cleansed completely. There's no question of whether you can keep some good stuff behind. Whether good or bad, all that lies in the subconscious mind has to be released, and the mind has to be completely cleansed because all that lies in the subconscious mind is nothing but rubbish.

There's one thing that has to be made clear about this technique since a lot of people have doubts about it and that is the breathwork involved in this. If not understood and done correctly, it won't benefit the sãdhaka, rather it may prove disadvantageous. Many people, even after doing it for a month are making mistakes. At the time of the first 'sudden exhalation', if the practitioner by any chance inhales before exhaling, it will go completely wrong and will not benefit at all. It will only lead to the mind getting stronger.

Chapter 6

A Principle to Be Free from Maya-Krishna's Guidance for Today's Times and Environment

Sãdhaka: Guruji, Sri Krishna had a multidimensional personality and something or the other from his teaching serves useful for everyone in every era. Keeping Lord Krishna's teaching in mind, what is its importance in the present era?

Swamiji: Tomorrow is Krishna Janamashtami, celebrated for Lord Krishna's incarnation on this earthly plane in a human form. It is in His memory that this day is celebrated. You're asking how useful is Lord Krishna for this era? Lord Krishna is known as 'Purna Avatar', complete incarnation of the Divine. The most special thing about Him is that He is a purna avatar and not a partial incarnation or 'anshavatar'. To be a purna avatar is the demand of this era, leaving no possibility for an anshavatar. Lord Krishna's teaching is extremely useful for this era. You are surrounded by too many influences of various kinds. There are multidimensional influences ready to take you astray in every dimension. Are you able to see your life? The influence of material wealth and riches attracts you so much. It has such an impact on you that it shakes you up, pushes you and takes you away. Similarly, the political influence, societal influence, religious influence and who knows how many more influences impress you.

Observe carefully how much the education system of children is influencing you. Look around you, in your neighbourhood, within your family, and you'll realize that the number of people influencing you has increased. A huge variety of new concepts is being served to catch your attention and influence you. Then there's all kinds of fear being served on your plate. The influence of medicine and treatment is taking over you, leaving an impression on you in such a big way. People were living life, falling sick and recovering even in the olden times, but they were not influenced to the extent people are today. People are being influenced into buying health insurance policies and maintaining them. 'Take this medicine for this issue, take that medicine for that issue, this 'pathy', that 'pathy', all these kinds of advices are being given. Some of the prevalent modalities or so called 'pathies' are without any logic and make no sense at all. They are inducing such chemicals in your body which are a threat to the survival of your natural life. Influences are of many kinds. There's chemical in your food which is affecting your body and mind as your body is psychosomatic. All the intoxicants that people consume are also chemicals which affect the mind. They make the mind spin, creating instability. Some chemicals influence by generating excitement. With the presence of so many influences, the simplicity, spontaneity and naturalness of life is missing.

Certain influences were there in times of Krishna too. They were more political and societal. To deal with them Krishna had to further develop and exhibit his multi-dimensional personality. That was an era where authenticity was not working. For example, when a person tells you that he is trustworthy but ends up cheating and backstabbing you, authenticity is lost in this case. Hence, in

His times fulfilling responsibilities while remaining authentic was not possible. Living a natural life was impossible because nobody's word could be relied upon. That is why His teachings speak of living artistically, performing as an actor or artist in life. Influence streams will continue, but you perform actions like an actor. Act as if everything is normal but stay unaffected from within and use diplomacy also wherever needed. What does influence mean? Isn't it diplomacy? These influence streams are nothing but diplomacy, where false is being presented as the truth and an impression is created such that you accept and adopt it exactly the way it is being presented. False will be served in the guise of truth. That is what influence is!

People ask what are influence streams. Influence means lies that are fed to you. A lot many 'so called' scientific, technological and technical facts are gilded nicely with many ingredients and painted with some spiritual mention here and there along with a few references included from the veda shastras. This lie will then be presented in such a manner that it appears true to you. I have named this as 'Spiritual Garbage'! This era has a lot of spiritual garbage, in fact more than required. Looking around, you'll find spiritual garbage being presented in a manner that seems very spiritual, with the presentation appearing as a spiritual event. What all do they propagate!? Twin flames, soulmates, wingmakers, 5-D. What is all this? Spirituality? Rubbish is being adorned and offered to you in a way that it seems true. The principle of Goebbels suggests that if a lie is repeated innumerable times, it starts appearing true. This is how you are being presented with lies and being influenced. If you sit amidst such people and oppose any of this, you'll be eaten alive, snubbed and oppressed in a way beyond imagination. Since human beings are social animals, you have to stay amidst such people and maintain relations. You can't survive without society and relatives, so you have to maintain the relations, irrespective of what extent you maintain them to. In this case the question arises as to, how can one do this or how will this even work? You will have to live as a performer, an actor, an artist. You will have to live like this so that the influencers don't feel that you are in their opposition. If the influencers or their followers get a hint that you are not on their side, they will make your life miserable. They'll project you as a fool and simply outdated, but since you have to stay amongst them, you must act and say things that make them feel you are in tandem with them and that you're on their side. After that you simply leave from there. Don't get too involved or entangled with them. How will this be possible? It will be possible with Krishna's teaching of living a performance-based life. Make use of diplomacy as well. It is in this way that you can keep yourself protected from these extra smart individuals who have all kinds of material to influence you. Be an artist, use diplomacy to protect yourself and do your sadhana in secrecy, without revealing. Krishna's teaching will work in this way. If you manage to protect yourself from the influences and the garbage being served, it will be considered your biggest achievement. To be able to protect yourself in this era is a big job because living authentically has become a big problem. Suppose you are angry with someone and you remove your anger at the person in an authentic way, exactly the way you're feeling towards them, it might lead to unpleasant consequences. It could be that you felt like hitting the person and if you did so, you may land up visiting the courts for years on end or may even end up serving a sentence. All this may further lead to some unforeseen repercussions as well. Your hitting the person in a fit of rage is an offence, and you'll have to face the boomerang effect it will have. Living authentically in today's era is not possible.

Using diplomacy and acting to sail through today's times is a demand of this era, but this must be done with complete awareness so that no impressions are formed within. Perform with the 'knowing' that performing is important. Perform and live, keeping minimum contact, just as much is required. Maintain minimalistic need-based contacts and spend the rest of your time doing sadhana. Whether you are a part of a small sangha or not, go into a sadhana which can liberate you. Many illusions pertaining to sadhana will take birth. Many people claim to be doing sadhana but that is not the sadhana that will liberate. Either it is not a sadhana at all, or even if it is, it's the kind which will make you wander. Sadhanas which take you off track or make you wander will be termed as the liberating sadhanas in these times. Whereas people who practice the liberating sadhana will be called foolish.

Krishna is very useful in today's era. There's an absolute need of His diplomacy and performance-oriented life. He is called a trickster (chaliya), isn't it? The influence streams want to trick you, deceive you. Krishna used to deceive the influence streams. We too need to become chaliyas like krishna if we want to do sadhana in this era. We will be able to do sadhana only if we become diplomatic and protect ourselves from the ill-effects of influence streams. Tomorrow is that chaliya's birthday, Krishna Janamashtami and we have to learn from Him. This chaliya is going to protect us in this era, this golden era. His deshana, teaching is of 'Oneness', "I Am this, I Am this, this also I Am, that also I Am, I Am everything, there is no second, there is no other!" How can there be a second or another? There is no other, and there cannot be another, ever, and this is what I repeatedly explain that there is no creator who has created this universe. Paramatma is himself getting expressed as creation. It's a continuous process...one of never being separated.

We have to come out of this madness that there is somebody known as Paramatma who has created the universe, and after creating it, has opened an office from where He runs the universe. This utter madness has really taken over and resides as a dominant thought in many people. They think there is a God sitting somewhere and running the show. What systems would he have made use of to run the show then? If He has made the world, then He surely must have bought the chisel and hammer from somewhere. If He had bought parts and accessories to make the world, then certainly there must have been factories that already existed. That means people already existed, otherwise where and from whom would he have bought the raw material from. Since He has maintained an office, He must have bought it with the help of a broker, right? He must have kept some staff also to help with the office maintenance, isn't it? There must be computers installed as well, smart computers and that's why the world is operational. Everything on this earth has to be managed, and so many mad people have to be managed and maintained by Him! Yes, this earth is like a mad-house, full of mad people. How must He be managing them? This idea that people are living with regarding Paramatma, has to be dropped. They have to come out of this conceived notion, this concept they are holding onto.

Srishti is not the creator's work. He has not made the Srishti, the universe. Universe is not an act of creation. Srishti is a happening, a SELF-EXPRESSION i.e. the Eternal Self getting expressed as creation itself. There is no mountain, the mountain is happening; there is no river, the river is happening; everything is happening and everything is the SELF, unbroken, undivided Self, which never got separated. If it breaks, it cannot come back together as before. Anything that breaks can never become one again. When nothing has broken, the question of joining or becoming one again doesn't arise. It is all an illusion, maya, a divine play (leela). The word leela is associated with chaliya, isn't it? What does a chaliya do? Leela! Leela means they make use of diplomacy and live tactfully while enacting every scene, knowing well that it is all a play, an illusion, and in this way no impressions get formed within. Impressions getting formed inside is the problem.

Lord Krishna says whatever action one performs should be performed without getting attached to it, so that no impressions of the action are left within. Actions should be performed with awareness, mindfully, in a detached way. If any impressions are left within, they will give birth to a series of cause and effects. This will result in the individual taking birth again and carrying the school bag once more, learning the unfinished lessons of 'A for apple, B for boy'. Thus, it is important that the whole life is lived consciously, with awareness. One's whole life should be a sadhana. There cannot be anything like a part-time sadhana if one has to stay detached. If one lives unconsciously, attachments will be formed and one will get associated with some pattern. That pattern will then get activated, such that, it will either get updated or a new pattern will be formed. Hence, living consciously is very important so as not to get attached.

We have to clean our subconscious mind. Sadhana to dissolve all the patterns means, all the patterns that exist in the subconscious mind must dissolve completely and new patterns must not be created. This will only happen when we live with equanimity, with complete awareness, so that no attachments have any opportunity to remain stuck or get stuck. If there are traits like insistence and obstinacy in us, then we are not balanced, we're not at peace or equanimous. If we are not equanimous, it means we are attached. What does detachment mean? Detachment means we are free from traits like insistence and obstinacy. It means we are conscious. If we have traits of insistence and obstinacy within us, they will come to the surface.

They will come up from the subconscious mind to the conscious mind, looking for a release. If we are conscious and equanimous at the time they surface up, they will not be able to hack us. They will not be able to hack us: the 'us' here is the small conscious mind, the awake and aware part of us. This awake and aware part of us cannot be hacked because we are equanimous. This will lead to the dissolution of those traits and patterns. They will play their games but will not have the energy to take over us because we are now conscious. Only if we are unconscious will they get the energy to hack us. We don't feed them when we are conscious. We will not give them our energy. Our being is a form of energy and the patterns are also smaller forms of energy. This being so, if we don't feed them, the patterns get discharged, dissolved and the game ends. In this fashion other patterns will keep coming up and their dissolution will keep happening, and dissolve they must. The dissolution must happen for liberation to happen. When patterns come to the surface, we will know them with equanimity. We will not react, not analyze, not categorize nor will we define them. We will not do anything.

People who tend to 'do', spoil everything. Without 'doing', everything becomes alright. If you do anything, if you try to understand the pattern and react towards it, analyze it, categorize it, define it or if you get associated with it in any way and become unconscious, it will hack you. It will hack your breath and change your breathing pattern. Whatever the pattern is like, whether related to fear or greed or desire or whichever other emotion or defilement, it will lead to hacking the breath and changing the breathing pattern, as per the surfacing defilement. It will change the breathing pattern according to the samskara that is surfacing, and operate you accordingly, which then goes to say that your conscious mind has now vanished, it has got hacked. With the hacking of the conscious mind, the patterns will get updated and get stronger than before.

They will get stronger than before and get restored again. Then the next pattern will surface. This is what goes on when we remain unconscious.

What do you think is going on? It is the thoughts that are going on, what else! That is what thoughts mean. The related patterns come on the surface and hack. Hacking has happened, now what is the sadhana? Being conscious is the sadhana. When you're conscious, the pattern that tries to hack you, fails in its attempt to do so because you are not co-operating with it… you're not reacting, analyzing, categorizing, defining or doing anything else. Nothing can go wrong now, since you're not doing anything. Things get spoilt when we try to do something and become fine when we stop doing. Everything will become fine when you don't do anything.

When we speak of right and wrong, what is 'right'? 'Right' is the complete erasure of the patterns that hack us and enslave us. When those patterns cease to exist by our 'not doing' anything, that is termed 'right', since everything becomes alright when we don't associate with them in any manner. The pattern that keeps us enslaved has dissolved. One pattern being dissolved, next one comes up and we remain equanimous. To remain equanimous, one needs to be conscious. Without being conscious, equanimity doesn't happen. Till the time all the patterns of the subconscious mind don't get cleansed, liberation is impossible. This sadhana technique is one which can liberate. There are various methods of cleansing that have been given because cleansing is a necessity. Only then the sadhana techniques can be helpful in one's liberation. The illusory nature of maya is gripping and in excess.

The sadhanas which don't lead one towards liberation are the entangling kinds of sadhanas. They keep one hooked on and can be termed as maya. There are many such sadhanas prevalent these days. They are claimed to be sadhanas which can help in one's liberation, but it is all spiritual garbage. This is nothing but wrong influence. If you buy into these influences or get caught up in the loop of the influencers selling them to you, your school bag is ensured. It's a guarantee that you will come back to do 'A for apple, B for boy' in your next birth. Sadhana cannot be just any sadhana; that doesn't help. It has to be samyak sadhana, the 'right sadhana'. Liberation happens with right sadhana, not with the wrong one. You have to understand which sadhana will liberate and which will entangle you. It's a must that you understand this very well because the influence of the entangling kinds of sadhanas is more these days. The sadhana which can liberate is not being understood. Very few people are understanding it. There are many people who attend the retreats, and few are heard saying that they liked it a lot and everything was good, but they listen to other speakers as well thinking where's the harm in listening to others also. They feel there's no harm in listening to the influencers. They are not yet clear as to which sadhana is liberating and which is an influence, and for this reason, their chances of landing up carrying the school bag again in the next birth is very high. There's no guarantee of how many times they'll have to come back. What I'm saying is, there are so many good sãdhakas who have been doing good sadhana for years or maybe lifetimes and will continue to do so for lifetimes to come. They'll keep doing sadhana in every lifetime but where will they reach? Why were they doing sadhana? What is sadhana for?

Sadhana is for liberation. What is the need for a sadhana which continues for lifetimes, hundreds and thousands of lifetimes and has to be further continued for lifetimes after lifetimes? Sadhana should be a liberating one and for a sadhana which liberates, where's the need for lifetimes!? The liberating sadhana will be 'here and now'. It will liberate you here and now. Why will it free you in the future?

Freedom is possible here and now. It's important to wake up to this truth and live consciously. Sadhana cannot happen part-time. It has to be a full-time sadhana and you'll have to protect yourselves from the influence streams. In order to keep yourselves protected, you'll have to be a chaliya like Krishna. Be conscious, be a chaliya and celebrate Krishna Janamashtami tomorrow. Right sadhana will be possible only if you can protect yourselves from wrong influences.

Sãdhaka: Pranaam Swamiji! Osho, in his discourses has said that one doesn't have to be a bhogi (enjoyer of worldly pleasures), nor does one have to be a tyagi (renouncer). My question is, when does this wisdom awaken in a sãdhaka?

Swamiji: Neither does one have to be an enjoyer nor a renouncer. To be any one of these two, you need to be in favour of one – either enjoyer or renouncer. To become either one of them, you have to categorize them; what is bhogi? What is tyagi? Categorization means to be broken from the whole, which represents duality. Whether an enjoyer or a renouncer, they both are living a duality. The bhogi is also living a duality and the tyagi is also living a duality. What is liberation? Balance, right balance is freedom. There is freedom in balance, in equanimity. We should be both enjoyers as well as renouncers. The subconscious mind has a different language, a pictorial language! It's not the language that is spoken. It is the language of the animal world. The language of the subconscious mind is that of the animal world. In this world, if it is said that enjoying is bad, then enjoying will become bad.

Now consider a man who is absolutely fresh after a bath and is standing outside in the open. The weather is good and he is basking in the sunlight. While he's enjoying the weather, a lovely breeze is felt and he says, "Wow! This is wonderful". His hands go up, his eyes shut and he gets totally immersed in that. He has become a mahabhogi (enjoyer beyond limits, extreme enjoyer) since he is now enjoying not just some small things, but has now started enjoying the entire Astitva. He has started enjoying the sun, the breeze, the sky, and the subconscious mind will say, "this is a sin, this is a sin. Enjoying is a sin, enjoying is a sin. A sin is taking place." The subconscious mind may say this and you won't even realize because its language is different. The subconscious mind does not make use of the language that we use. A person who is in right balance will say, "Wow, this is wonderful! This is the supreme essence, this is Paramatma. Expansion has happened, mightiness has happened, Paramatma has happened, Paramatma has happened." Enjoying or bhog led to Paramatma.

Now, consider a renouncer, what will he say? He will talk of tastelessness. He'll look for food that is tasteless. He will not go for tasty food. One who has right understanding will say, "Paramatma is so delicious, chew well and eat, enjoy it. Paramatma is really tasty." Food will become the path to attain Brahm. Brahm will happen through food as the medium. There are five senses and one can go beyond these five senses with a balanced and right enjoyment of pleasures. With this right understanding of enjoyment, when you're going beyond any of the senses, who do you think will manifest? What lies beyond the senses? The truth lies beyond. If we go beyond senses through all the five senses separately, we don't reach a different truth. The truth remains the same. It is one, while the paths being five. Whether it is going beyond taste, going beyond touch, going beyond hearing, going beyond smell, going beyond seeing, only 'One' is revealed. The 'One' that is beyond, that is formless, that is beyond merits and virtues but that which is the 'all-knowing', reveals itself. Everything is happening and it is being known. Effortless knowing is happening. If you try to know it through effort, you'll break it, divide it. Effort will break it.

The doers spoil everything and when there's no 'doing' involved, everything becomes fine. Everything is being known without doing, 'knowing' being our nature. Knowing does not mean that we concentrate on one thing and come to know of it, that's not what it means. It means everything is being known simultaneously, simply and naturally. Naturally means everything is being known simultaneously with an innateness which is existential. We don't have to put any effort into that because that's our inherent nature, our way of being. Everything is known simultaneously. If an incident has taken place with someone and later asked as to what happened at the time, he will give you the details of what had transpired. When he's describing the incident, write everything down and maintain a record. After this is done, take the same individual, hypnotize him, take him back to the time of the incident, and ask him to tell you what exactly happened. Write down the details and maintain that record too. Then check both the maintained records and you'll find a lot of difference in them. You'll find that the details provided by him in his conscious state were far less than what he gave in the hypnotized state. This is what happens. In the hypnotized state a person will give you details of things which he is not even aware had transpired at that time, but they were all being recorded within him, for example, the sounds all around, an ant biting his leg and more such minute details. He will tell you everything. In a conscious state, he will give you an approximate or rough details of what happened, leaving the rest out. Everything was being known within him, and when hypnotized and taken there, everything was already there without anything being left out. But how is he living in the present? He is living with concentration and operating selectively. Whatever he chose at the time, only those details were provided by him. All else that was left out in the details, had not been registered in his conscious mind. He did not have that record with him but when hypnotized and taken there, every detail was there, even the smallest ones which he had not made a choice towards. Nothing was left out...everything had been recorded. When you choose, you pick up some and leave the rest. Paramatma is whole, Astitva is whole, it is not some broken pieces or divided. We spoil everything by making choices. Making a choice means we are 'doing' something. Doers spoil everything while everything becomes simple and natural when 'doing' is given up. Without 'doing', everything is undoubtedly and unquestionably fine. Why are there so many problems and issues in the world? It is because social reformers have taken birth. They have spoilt everything. A world without social reformers would have been heaven. They have ruined everything. No reformers, no problems. That would be the 'right balance'.

Osho has spoken of this in a different manner. Buddha called this equanimity (samata). Osho spoke of it in a language understood in today's times. He said the enjoyer and the renouncer are both incomplete. According to him, there should be a harmony, a balance between the two. Balance liberates. Leaning towards one side is either insistence, stubbornness or obstinacy (aagrah-duragrah). Right balance means you are beyond any rules. No rules can bind you. You don't have to commit or make promises. Krishna would commit to something one day and break it the next day. That is why He was called Chaliya. A promise was made at the time that it was made. Next day whatever was necessary would be done. He was acting as per the necessity of the moment. There is no need to walk as per set rules and regulations. Rules, self-made rules will turn you into a slave. Even rules decided by others turn you into a slave. All rules take you on the path of enslavement. Whatever the rule, slavery is certain. It is only going to kill your freedom, isn't it? What is the rule of 'here and now'? It will arise from this moment. How can you plan for it beforehand? That is liberation, freedom from rules. Rules are the influence. They influence, and along with those influences come more new rules and new concepts. One has to get liberated from concepts completely. Neither does one have to pile on new concepts, nor do the old concepts have to be replaced by new ones. Fitting a new concept in place of the old one by removing the old one is not to be done. You have to be free from concepts. Freedom from concepts is liberation. Freedom is not in replacing concepts, and what are the influence streams spreading? They are propagating removal of old concepts and bringing in new concepts in their place. 'Use this instead of that, this is the truth and this is false' is their verdict. I say, chuck both truth and false into the dustbin. Both are concepts, some of the truth and some of the lies, but both are concepts. Liberation means trashing everything in the rubbish bin. All knowledge (gyan) is rubbish, whatever knowledge it may be. Knowledge is forever rubbish, which knowledge are you speaking of? Be it of concepts, be it of explanations and interpretations, knowledge is all rubbish. The word 'gyan' itself has gone corrupt. What was gyan referred to as in the olden times? It was referred to as a state where thoughtlessness happens, where defilements dissolve, where there are no words and language left, where there are no concepts, where there is nothing. A natural state, free from defilements and thoughts was termed as 'gyan'.

Today, what is the meaning of gyan (knowledge)? Data! What is data? Data is information. Information is being considered as knowledge these days. Please understand, we are talking of gyan as in, knowledge. Information is being collected from books and other sources here and there. What is paramatma? What is atma? It is just information, it is a concept, it is a hypothesis. What else is it? Put it all in the dustbin and get liberation. Put it all where it belongs! Rubbish needs to be trash-canned. What is atma, paramatma, god? Garbage, so throw it in the garbage bin. Be free. Listen, there is no name for 'That'. Neither is its name paramatma, nor atma and not even god, it cannot be. This is your language, words that you have given. How can there be a name for Him!?

You say, "this is an aam tree" and others also call it an aam tree. Aam is known as mango in english, so "it's a mango tree". Does this really define a mango tree? Just understand that it is not a mango tree. These are words you have given. The word 'mango' is not the fruit. The fruit doesn't have a name. In fact, even the word fruit...what is it? What is mango...a tree? These are your words, a temporary arrangement. Neither is it a mango nor a fruit nor a tree. You say, "No, it is a tree...a mango tree. This is called mango in english and belongs to the fruit species. This is the king of fruits...", etc. etc. You are so caught up in this hypnotism. Listen brother, language has a utilitarian purpose attached to it, so use it. Why do you get hypnotized by it? Take its utilitarian benefits for what they are. Why get hypnotized? Have you got hypnotized or not? Ask yourself. People will die fighting over this also.

It's not like you're lying. It is a mango and it is a tree. It is called a tree. It is mentioned in so many books and shastras and it will become a lie if spoken otherwise. You are right. It has a utilitarian purpose attached to it, temporary usage. Use it, but having the right understanding is important. It is neither a fruit, nor a mango nor a tree. If you make a tree out of it or a mango, how will you ever have the grace-bestowing vision of Paramatma? How will you behold that supreme essence? You are living a duality. You will live the concept of duality!! That is 'tattvamasi' which translates to 'that thou art or you are that'. How can there be another? For utility purpose, we have given names and we call them by those names such as a tree, a mango or something else. But there is no other, no second. 'That' alone is, and 'That' alone happens in the form of a tree, a mango, a stone etc. All of nature is a way in which 'That' happens. Language was made for using. Use it, but know that it's not a tree nor a mango nor a fruit. These are just the way that ONE is happening. Whose way of happening? There is no name for 'That'. I say, how can there be a name for 'That'?

Imagine if you are the only one in the world, what will your name be? How can there be a name for that 'ONE' which is happening in the form of the whole existence? 'That' alone is, there is no other. How can there be a name for it? When there are too many people, we have to give them names and call them by names. That's how we recognize them and that's very helpful. For 'ONE', how can a name be there? For a name, two have to be there...one's name being this and the other's name being that or one's name being one, and the other's name being two, or whatever. Being 'ONE' alone, how can it have a name? Its name is Paramatma, its name is Khuda, its name is Ishwar; how is it possible? One alone is! How can it have a name? How can it have attributes? For attributes, there have to be two. Attributes are relative and are present in relation to something.

They are not absolute. If 'absolute' is all there is, which relativity are we talking of? We need two for relativity, isn't it? How can 'absolute' have attributes, virtues, merits. Now the thing is, we are entangled in forms. For the purpose of understanding, we say that all forms are His. But all forms are not His. Forms are the way in which 'He' or 'That' happens. Forms are 'His' way of happening. He has not made anything, nothing. Everything is happening.

People say things like, "Oh creator of the world, why did you create this world? What came into your mind?" There is no mind of that 'ONE". He has not made the world. He is happening and He is everlasting, timeless and eternal. Never did the world begin, it has eternally been there. It's not like it began one lakh years ago or some four billion years ago. In fact, four billion years ago, an infant was born which we call as the Brahmaand, the Universe. Our universe, this small little child was born four billion years ago. What does four billion years even mean? What does 'year' mean? Draw a huge map of this small child, the universe, which we're saying was born four billion years ago. A huge map on a paper big enough to cover Kashmir to Kanyakumari. A small line will be visible, barely visible which is called the milky way. It'll be visible as a needle pin on this huge paper. Take another huge paper, the size of Kashmir to Kanyakumari again and draw a map of this milky way on it. There will probably be visible something very small, as small as the size of a grain. That is called the solar system. Now if you draw a map of the solar system on a huge paper again, there you'll find a needle pin sized something known as the earth which makes two different types of movements, it rotates as well as revolves.

There is a small star, a very small star, I think it probably is the smallest star in the milky way and we call it the Sun. It's a small star, a small star emitting minor light because of which there is sunlight and shade, and a play of sun shade goes on. A calculation is then made, and who does this calculation? Set up a huge telescope on this map of the solar system and what is visible is these insects with two legs moving here and there, very small insects. These insects did some calculations and came to conclusions about this sun shade. The movement of the sun shade led them to making certain calculations and then calling them hours, minutes, day, night, week, month, year. Now, the four billion years refers to this concept of year that was born out of the calculation based on the sun shade. Four billion years ago the big bang happened. Every second, there are not just one lakh, ten lakhs or more, but endless such big bangs happening. Endless big bangs happen every second like the one that is spoken of. Not just one crore, ten crores or twenty crores but endless big bangs happen. Infinite happens within the infinite. Everything is infinite, no calculations involved, and so endless of these happen. Four billion years ago, what year was it by the way? When such a huge happening had taken place, was the world even there? This world is eternal, everlasting. It never begun in the first place, and this truth the small head can't grasp. These two-legged insects or creatures seen from the big telescope, sit in their small cocoon and say, "We know everything, we understand everything." This small little head says it understands everything, it is very wise, it is this, it is that. Can that head really understand?

They discuss the infinite; who? The school going kids. They keep repeating the information they have been fed on infinity. Infinity is like this and it is like that. If infinity is understood properly, the brain will go numb. People repeat gathered information without understanding it. Have they lived infinity? Have they known it? They've only gathered concepts from here and there. The world is full of foolish people giving definitions of Paramatma. Is it possible to define Paramatma? They try to give away a lot of information in the name of knowledge, saying Paramatma is like this and like that.

The two-legged creatures and insects seen through the telescope give big lectures on Paramatma. Where are you stuck? It is only in equanimity that the mystery unfolds, where nothing is done. Beyond enjoyment and renouncement, where there is equanimity, that is it; then it's done, it's happened. The definition is not possible, but knowing oneself surely is.

You surely can dive within yourself. The moment you know yourself after going within, you come to know that there is no duality whatsoever. I alone am, and all this is my way of happening...the entire mystery unfolds. Trying to solve this mystery with your head is futile because the head is very petty and small. The one holding the head on his shoulders is also small and negligible, and so is the earth on which the man with the head lives. The solar system as well as the milky way, the universe and the multiverse are all very small, very negligible. When compared to infinity, a sand particle and this multiverse are equally small. It is not that one is small and one is big. In relation to infinity, their value is zero. They both are equal to zero, whether it's the multiverse or it's the sand particle. The head will not agree to this. But how much is the power of the head? How much can it contain? Talking of the head, how much can this small head understand? These are the entanglements. When all the concepts have withdrawn, then what remains IS. That is ONE. Duality has dissolved. Where there is ONE, how can duality remain!? I alone AM, I Am; there's no known language for this I AM, I alone AM, Aham Brahmasmi, this, that. These are used just so the message can be put across. This is a flow that happens... a flow of 'that' which has to get revealed externally. But ultimately, this is an internal happening. There is ONE and that nature reveals itself... it's a natural revelation.

This separation, this pettiness and trivialness that is being lived is manufactured through efforts. Trivialness is manufactured, and the material used for its produce is efforts. Trivialness, pettiness has to be made, created. Vastness is timeless, eternal and does not have to be made. The Eternal divinity or God doesn't have to be obtained. He is not something you can touch...never. He is something you can BE. You can never meet Him. "I have bought a deck of cards in the hope that when I meet Him, we'll play a few games of cards. But He doesn't meet. I've been looking for Him, trying to find out where His office is. I've tried to find a way of messaging Him, to invite Him over lunch, thinking we can talk over lunch and play cards. But there's no information regarding Him or His office as to where it is!" Brother, this is a big lie! If there was an office belonging to Him, it would have been located since when! We would have made Him understand and charmed Him enough so that He would come over. Great effort is put in, "Please do this work for me and I'll offer you one and quarter kilos of sweets. Please do this, please do that." But He never came, not even with the bribe offer of one and quarter kilos of sweets!

Sãdhaka: Swamiji, people go to temples. Some believe in Lord Rama, some in Lord Krishna while there are others who believe in Devi or Lord Hanuman. The day they don't visit the temple of the deities they worship, they feel their work might get disrupted due to them not paying homage to the deity that particular day. The question is, why is there so much fear in the subconscious mind?

Swamiji: That is what I have been saying that the language of the subconscious mind is different. It is a pictorial language, an animated language that goes on in the subconscious. There is fear lying deep within, and the influence streams enhance it further with different kinds of things. Now they are saying that there will be some special planes coming from the higher dimensions and will take some chosen ones who are special. The rest of humanity will face a downfall with things going haywire for them and will die as per these influencers. Someone shared this with me about special planes coming from higher dimensions for special people, so should you work around getting a ticket for yourself? There must be some authority somewhere to make the pass for this trip, some designated broker or agent sitting with an office, since these are special planes that are arriving! One may have to make friends with these authority figures and follow some assigned rules and regulations they have made for this trip, don't you think so? Only then will you get the pass and only then will you go!! Whosoever doesn't get in touch with them or follow their rules will be denied the pass. Yes, the so-called VIP 5-D pass!

Just observe yourself as to how influenced you are by these shop sellers. If someone is speaking of those shops as well as criticizing them, it means he is confused and puzzled. What is the need for getting confused or confusing someone else by talking about things like, "It's like this in gurudwaras and like this in temples and like this in masjids, this is like this and that is like that". Why is anyone confused? One needs to look within oneself. If you understand correctly, come out of it. Either you will take someone's side or you won't. Being in favour of someone or opposing someone means you are affiliated to them somehow. Without feeling the connection or affiliation to what anyone says, you won't side them or oppose them. In both cases, there has to be some kind of a connect. Why are you talking about them? Where is the time for all this? Why is there time for all this? Discussing someone else and criticizing!

People ask me to tell them something about twin flames and what not. I say I'm not aware of all this. Then someone asks, "Have you heard of this?" and I say, "Yes, people like you mention it and I listen to them." Anyone talks about concepts like twin flames etc. I stop them from speaking of such concepts here. I don't accept garbage. I don't want to understand all this nor get into a loop of such conversations. Why does one have to? Why does anyone have to get into this spiral of whether temples and masjids are right or wrong?

I am a chaliya. You visit a temple and you'll find me bowed down. You'll find me going there and also bowing down, but I don't come under the influence of any temple. I know the science. One must bow down. I know the science that they are old temples and have been made in a certain way because of which the energy works there. Wherever there's positive energy, it becomes known from afar. 'Yes, the place with positive energy has come!' It becomes known and I reach there. I reach there, bow down, sit and experience the bliss and leave without getting involved in any influence streams present there. Neither do I side it nor do I oppose it. My work is to see what's inside the bowl, not the bowl or the spoon. If whatever is inside the bowl is good, I eat quietly, leave the bowl and move out. There's nothing else to give or take from there. Whatever sweet is offered in the bowl should be good, be it kheer or halwa. If it's fresh and of good quality, I eat quietly and leave. I am very selfish. I don't know anything else.

We are all out to know the meaning of the Self, but what is the meaning? Why should we be interested in anything else that's going around other than what we're looking for? What do we have to do with all else that's going around? We took birth to know the Self, the meaning of the Self. You've been offered something, eat quietly and leave. Why get into calculations of what, how, why; how the bowl was, how the sweet was, this is right, this is wrong etc. Peeping into the bowl, if you find that what's inside is not of good quality, just throw the bowl. I don't touch it if the quality served isn't good, not even the bowl and spoon. If it's good, pounce on it, eat, drink and leave. It's not that one must know the science behind it. During the making of these temples, mosques and gurudwaras, the science applied must have been fantastic for them to have such positive energy. Meditators need places to sit, isn't it? These positive and high energy places were made so that meditators could make use of these places for their quietude and sadhana. That science is lost now. There were no shops there in those times. Someone must have grabbed the land and opened a shop and this trend began. Pilgrimages were made on mountains so that the climbing would make the body light, and it was a natural breathing exercise too. Body relaxes after climbing such heights. With this, the negative part of the meditation takes place where the 'doing' is involved. Putting in the effort to prepare for it and then climb, get tired and finally sit. Once one sits and closes his eyes, he feels relaxed and his mind becomes peaceful. When one climbs the mountain in close proximity with nature, with no roads and a very difficult path, a whole lot of awareness comes into being. If one slips, he's done for good, and for that reason he has to be fully conscious. He cannot climb unconsciously. Consciousness is needed. Having arrived consciously and sitting with closed eyes, his mind relaxes completely and a dip into the thoughtless state (amani dasha) takes place. He then gets a glimpse - of whom? Of Oneness! He gets a glimpse of the Oneness. The use of the supreme science was made in these places so that supreme energy could be present at all times. The flow of people who have reached this no-mind state, has been constant there. The energy is working there. With many having attained the amani dasha there, there's possibility that someone may have attained enlightenment as well. The energy of those who attain Buddhattva or enlightenment in these places remains there. It is forever there and supports those who go to that place later. This is all a play of energies. There are the esoteric support systems that play a major role there. Temples in the mountains have been dedicated to certain Devatas (Deities) and their energy is literally present there and working. If not one, then it's a group of deities working together over there. You feel that energy when you sit there. Whether that energy is supportive of you or not, just see that. If it is supporting you, just sit with your eyes closed. One of your chakras will get purified and cleansed there. Sit and observe. One of your chakras must be getting cleansed. Cleansing will happen but knowing the science helps. If science is not known, everything will be entangling.

Chapter 7

Stage Prior to Attainment of Liberation

Sadhaka: Swamiji, when does the last glimpse happen and what is its experience like? What I mean is, what is the state of a sadhaka before enlightenment happens?

Swamiji: When does the last glimpse happen!? If it was possible to predetermine when the last glimpse will happen, it would be possible to measure everything else too. We would then be able to measure paramatma as well – how paramatma is, what paramatma is, what truth is. A detailed map of paramatma could have been removed. How will the last glimpse happen! This will forever remain a mystery. For Lao Tse, the last glimpse happened while seeing a dry leaf falling. For Ramakrishna Paramhansa, the experience was something else – he was embracing a method given by Totapuri Maharaj to dissolve duality and that proved to be the last glimpse in his case. For Buddha, watching a star of dawn happened to be the last glimpse. Every person goes through different experiences. For a zen sadhika, it happened when she was carrying two mud pots full of water in a kaanwar (a bamboo stick with two baskets hanging on both ends and placed straight on the shoulders from behind). It was a moonlit night when she was walking, while gazing at the reflection of the moon in the water. Her foot hit something, the pot fell down smashing into pieces and the reflection of the moon disintegrated. With the breaking of the pot and the disintegration of the moon's reflection, she arrived! That was the last glimpse for her.

For every individual, it is different. Nothing can be said about the last glimpse, nothing at all. There is no yardstick for deciding how the last glimpse happens. Yes, there are certain parameters which can be spoken of, like lessening of thoughts, thoughts and feelings becoming known beforehand. These are signs of progression and expansion. But even with these signs being present, nothing can be said about the time it may take for the last glimpse to happen. Whether it's going to take six months, six years or six births, nothing can be said. There are no predetermined maps or rules in spirituality and that is its beauty. 'Nothing is predetermined' is the beauty and not a challenge or a problem. If there's anything at all that you need to observe or understand, it is how much are you holding onto things. Recognize wherever you're stuck and which areas of your life are you still holding onto. The more you hold onto life and all that it offers, the further away liberation gets. Letting go of your hold or loosening your hold will bring your 'arrival' closer. The whole issue is of holding on. Holding is maya.

There is an old saying, 'Tumne kambal ko pakda hai ya kambal ne tumhen pakda hai!' which translates to, 'are you holding onto the blanket or is the blanket holding onto you!' It may seem difficult to decide, but on close observation you will see that it is you who is holding the blanket. The issue is from your end. Paramatma has not created any issues. Existentially, there are no problems. Your separation is a divine play, a leela, but that leela has come to its last stage. You have the free will unlike other beings. Only a human being has free will. When and how he uses it depends on whether he is a mumukshu having a sincere desire for liberation or not. His longing and yearning for liberation will decide the length of the remaining journey. If it's only excitement, the destination remains far-fetched. If there's curiosity, information will come through regarding the journey to the destination; and if there's a yearning and sincere desire, the destination isn't far. Despite all the yearning and sincere desire, which glimpse will prove to be the last glimpse cannot be decided. Who knows what may happen. When the destination is just two kilometers away, you may decide to settle somewhere nearby and keep sitting there for lifetimes to come. If this happens, the destination will remain where it is – two kilometers away. If your free will says, "this is it! Let me settle down here", you may stay there for many lifetimes, with the destination that you were yearning for at the start of the journey still being two kilometers away.

You've almost completed the journey and have sat down very close to the destination; eating, getting into all kinds of worldly affairs and still going on asking people as to how far the destination that you want to reach is. How will you reach the destination? You left for the place and got off on the outskirts of the city and settled there. It's just two more kilometers of travelling and you'll be there. Yet you go on asking the whole world how to reach there, and the problems you may encounter on the way. After all this, you still wonder if you've made mistakes and why god is angry with you!! etc. etc. These are nothing but justifications. You have travelled this far. Can't you travel a little more? Did someone else make you travel so far? Was it someone else who obstructed your journey? When you've travelled this far and are sitting on the outskirts of the city, what is stopping you? You just need to enter the city using your free will, but you say you don't have a free will. You say you have been entangled and manipulated, that you're being deprived of grace and you're being made a victim of discrimination. This is a tough situation you are in. After having travelled thousands and lakhs of kilometers, there are ifs and buts that are now stopping you from making the remaining two kilometers journey.

Look within yourself, the deception lies within. Within lies the fear of this journey coming to an end. Fear, that once you reach your destination, there is no way of returning or coming out. An ending, a completion will happen with no one remaining. This thought whether 'you' will remain or not after perfection is reached, predominates, "Will I survive or not? If I don't survive, what is the point of this journey!?" Whereas, what is coming off clearly from the beginning is that 'you' are the problem when you say, 'I won't survive'. You clearly need to know that it is 'you' who has to go, 'you' who doesn't have to survive. You are the issue. No other problem needs to be removed. There is only one issue and that is 'you'. There is no other problem. You are the problem, and who are you? You are a matrix that resists, and due to this process of resistance 'you' are born, otherwise you were simply existing. You resist, "this should be like this, this should be like that." You just want to change the situations and circumstances.

Sadhaka: Swamiji, then what role does the Sadguru play in this situation? When one is in the last leg of the journey or if one gets stuck for some reason, what should one do?

Swamiji: 'Acharyo mrityuh', Sadguru is he, whose presence and proximity pushes you towards 'mahamrityu', the ultimate death, the great liberation… and what is the ultimate death? Not remaining on the outskirts of the destination but entering it. You all strive to build palaces on the outskirts, live there and keep doing seminars on what paramatma is, what atma is, how far your destination is etc. You sit there and keep doing seminars, keep reading books, keep talking and lecturing. Sadguru's job is to push you to the destination. You are afraid of dying, and for that reason you settle on the outskirts. Till the time you remain on the outskirts of paramatma, unwilling to die, there's no chance of you ever being Paramatma.

You are the obstacle that is stopping Paramatma from happening! Your separation prohibits Paramatma. Your announcement of separation denies Paramatma. If you as a separate self are there, then you cannot accept paramatma. All the nonsense you talk is your version of paramatma. That is hypothetical paramatma. You don't have any problems with your own version of paramatma, the one you have created because your own created Paramatma does not disturb your separation. Your created paramatma accepts your separation because he is of your caste; he is a part of your mind itself. That paramatma is a part of your mind and a living Sadguru doesn't let your tricks and clever maneuvers work. He eradicates your false paramatma along with you. That is the ultimate death and that is the role of the Sadguru. Sadguru convinces you to die. He tells you that there is only one matrix and that is 'you', there is only one lie and that is 'you', there is only one problem and that is 'you'. Till the time 'you' remain, problem remains. You are a separation. The moment 'you' withdraw, Paramatma eternally exists – the ocean is there, it's just a matter of the wave bidding farewell.

Paramatma is forever ready to embrace you. He gives you a message every day, "Come, merge in me, dissolve! Leave this childishness of separation, of being a separate entity. You are not separate. You've played enough games. Now come back." Paramatma gives you messages every day, in fact a thousand times in a day and those messages reach you. You define them in wrong ways. You're being given lessons every day, many times in a day and you disagree, saying it's not like this but like this. That is why it's a problem. You keep saying, "It'll become alright. It'll become alright if I do like this. It's not like this, it's like this." Listen! Nothing becomes alright. Nothing of separation becomes alright. When there's no separation, everything is anyways alright. If you see simply, everything is perfectly fine, nothing is wrong. But when you think in terms of your separation, what are the thoughts like? What does the separation think? Separation thinks there is something like a permanent happiness. It thinks, "I am permanent, this body is permanent and if not, then I have to struggle to make it permanent. To make this body immortal, I have to put in efforts." For whom? For this body! Separation is being lived, with the body being taken as the truth, and who is this body!? I am this body, this is my name and form, this is my way of being! This is who I am. Separation wants to make this body immortal, this mind immortal! Mind is a conglomeration of concepts and separation wants to make this immortal. Separation wants to make the body and mind immortal and you believe it. Look deep within yourself and see whether this thought ever occurs that you will die. Take a good look within. You'll hear yourself saying, "No, I'm not going to die." Nobody accepts their own death, "Others die, I won't", and all the effort is about making oneself immortal.

One is running behind money and other material riches. Why does he want to earn so much material wealth? He earns as much is adequate for him, and then he earns more than that and yet isn't satisfied. He then goes on to make more. Why? Does he think that he's going to live forever? This is what happens when one has a lot of money; he gets deluded that nothing can happen to him since he has so much wealth. With this thought that nothing can ever happen to him, he takes his false identity to be true. What is truth? Truth is that which doesn't get destroyed. What is forever, remains as it is! That is truth. It's qualities and nature never change. What are its qualities and nature? It is devoid of qualities, is without attributes and is formless. What does it look like? It doesn't have any looks. It is endless, infinite and has no boundaries. Truth is that which is still and unmoving. We, on the contrary consider separation to be the truth. Separation, which is a process, which is forever in movement, which is restless and which is a sum of distractions, seems to be permanent and hence the truth. We want to put it on a prestigious platform in place of the ultimate truth. What is the entire maya? That which is moving, that which has a name and form, is maya and we want to put it in place of the formless and eternal. Can you see the madness? What kind of madness is this!?

We are trying to make the impossible possible, and that is maya. What is the meaning of maya? Trying to make the impossible possible. We announce our identity as the truth, against that of Paramatma's, and think that it will remain so permanently. What that conveys is, we are separate and paramatma is separate, making us two. Two is the problem. The path of love is very narrow and two cannot fit in it. Two cannot fit in it but we want to meet such a paramatma where I'm also there and paramatma is also there. 'I must remain here and I must survive anyhow! What sense does it make if I'm not there?' We want to save ourselves. We want that both paramatma and I should remain and then play a game of cards together! This is impossible because you can't sit with paramatma, as there is no time factor playing out there. There is no binding of time in the infinite, endless, formless, the one without attributes. Even if there was a paramatma with whom you could spend time, what would you do? You'll keep seeing each other? Even if that were to happen, for how long? In the infinite, and endless, will you keep looking at each other endlessly? How much will you speak to each other? What will you discuss? How much material do you have for discussion? Once the talking material is over, then what will you do? What is left ultimately; a deck of cards to play a game of rummy! Look at your madness, your mental neurosis. Just look at how far you can go with your justifications to protect your separation!

COMING OUT OF SEPARATION; DISSOLUTION OF THE 'I'

Sadhaka: Swamiji, when you explain separation to us, it seems simple to get over it. But when living our practical life, the separation somewhat remains. How does one move ahead from this?

Swamiji: 'I' will do it, 'I' will do it, 'I' will withdraw the separation. How can the 'I' withdraw separation? What the 'I' will withdraw will be some hypothesis, with the 'I' standing outside of it. The main issue, the main problem, which is the 'I', will keep standing outside and some imaginary separation will be withdrawn by an imaginary process. The difficulty lies here, but if this subtle truth is understood and understood fully, then the 'I' gets immersed. We want to immerse the maya but not ourselves. We want to get out of maya, and that is the biggest issue. We ourselves are the problem, we don't have to come out of maya. The 'I' has to immerse, 'I' has to die. With the 'I' taking leave, maya will also leave. We want to come out of maya but without anything happening to us, and that we, as a separate entity must continue to be. Understand, wherever we are, there maya is. Maya is our way of happening. We want to solve the problem, but how can we? We are the problem! We want to remove the separation, but we are the separation. How can we remove the separation? This is the biggest problem. Ego must not remain and what is ego? You yourself are the ego. You say, ego should not remain, so 'I' will remove the ego. But we are the ego! How can we remove the ego from ourselves? When the 'I' as a separate entity dies, ego gets erased. If the 'I' lives, ego will remain for sure.

Our presence is the presence of the ego. 'I am' means, I'm announcing the presence of my identity against that of Paramatma, and this is the ego. How can I erase the ego? My presence is ego itself. My presence is the separation and my presence itself is the problem. I am the matrix. When this is properly understood, then the jump will happen. The 'I' does so many exercises to get rid of maya but 'I' can never get rid of maya because 'I' is maya. 'There is some maya which is troubling me and has kept me entangled. Like everyone else, it has entangled me too'. Listen, everyone's maya is different. There is no common maya. Maya is my way of happening, my separation. It's not that there is some gigantic maya which has trapped crores of people, including you. The announcement of 'my separation' and all efforts to maintain it, is maya. Maya takes birth in such a way that the 'I' does all kinds of exercises to protect it. Exercise is maya, and wisdom is deciding not to do any more exercises from now on. When no exercises are done, the 'I' won't survive. The exercises give birth to the sense of 'I'. It gives birth to separation. Separation is not a permanent thing. If it was, no power could have erased it, not even Paramatma. If separation is the truth, no power in the world can eradicate it, no sadhana can dissolve it. If separation's existence holds true, then no methods, no sadhana, no meditation can dissolve it. The only truth of separation is that it is an illusion, and the meaning of illusion here is that it is an effort, and a continuous one at that. To protect an illusion, a continuous effort has to be put in. The moment the effort is given up, the illusion vanishes. The illusion needs continuous repetition to survive. 'This is the truth, this is the truth, this is the truth' needs to be fed to the illusion. The illusion has to give birth to the hypnotism of 'This is the truth' to stay alive. It has to follow this process. Hypnotism means a continuous process.

One has to give auto-suggestions to oneself for the illusion to stay alive. Hypnotism is a continuous process. Once the process stops, hypnotism goes, maya goes, the 'I' goes. Maya is born out of this process, so it is a child of hypnotism. It is an illusion. From this illusion, another illusion is born i.e. the 'I'. From maya, the 'I' is born and from the 'I', maya is born. In fact, they are one and the same thing. 'I' is maya. Using that process if someone says, "I am a lie, I am like this, I don't exist" etc. that is nonsense. One needs to understand how that process is continuously going on, and withdraw the energy of the efforts from the process. This will happen with the understanding that I myself am the process. It is not that the process is taking place through me, rather I am the process of maya. I myself am the process, not that someone is creating maya. I am the process and due to this process, maya exists. The name of the process is maya and from this process, an illusion called 'I' is taking birth. Once the process stops, maya leaves and so does the 'I'. Only Ram remains!

SHRAADH AND SPIRITUALITY; JOURNEY OF THE 'I' AND IT'S IMMERSION

Sadhaka: Pranam Swamiji! During the 'fortnight of the ancestors' (shraadh paksh), people make an offering of rice and barley balls (pind daan) for departed ancestors so that their souls find peace and liberation. Is this just a ritual or does it hold any spiritual significance?

Swamiji: Look, spiritual significance is an absolutely different event. Spirituality only speaks of how maya can be immersed i.e. how can 'I' get immersed. Nothing else is included in spirituality. Lots of things take place but they aren't spiritual. Spirituality is all about one thing, which is, how will the ultimate death take place and liberation happen. But the mind loves to create and it gives birth to a thousand things in the name of spirituality, so that it remains busy somewhere or the other. The thousand things he is giving birth to are all maya, but they are given the name of dharma. Yes, there are certain things, some sciences being applied but all these sciences are the science of maya. The word science is not heard of in fields of creativity, art and expression, nor is science seen through the lens of creativity. All kinds of words are made use of in it. One way that science is applied is for removing the obstacles on this path; obstacles which are counted as defilements. Many such applicable sciences are promoted on the path. What are these sciences actually? They are detractors, they are maya. Do they work? Maybe, but they are not spirituality. It is some science but it is not spirituality. Why do you connect it to spirituality?

Spirituality means complete annihilation. Any other process including science does not involve annihilation. It involves little safeguarding, little ornamenting, little improvising and so on. Some kind of give and take...receiving blessings, receiving energy etc. Someone will take care of us and we will take care of someone, but it has nothing to do with annihilation. Agreed, it is some kind of science but why is everything termed as spirituality? These days the internet is full of spiritual garbage. What do you think all that is? Spirituality? Spirituality doesn't come that cheap.

Spirituality is that which is simple and straight forward. It doesn't mean a thousand things. "Dying" is spirituality, and who will die? Everything that can get annihilated has to die and what is that? Illusion; illusion will get annihilated because it can. In fact, it doesn't exist, it seems to be and hence it can get eradicated. What is eternal cannot be annihilated. Annihilation is spirituality. Once illusion goes, Truth that forever is, remains. It's not like you have to bring truth from somewhere, as though the truth had vanished and to bring it back you need an aircraft! You'll obviously need an aircraft to bring something special like truth back, isn't it? It can't be brought back in a bullock cart! What insanity is this? Illusion has to be annihilated. Truth doesn't come and go, it forever is, it's been there since eternity. It cannot be destroyed, nor does it increase or decrease. It is insufficient as in, it is never enough. If at all there is anything outside of the truth, where will it come from and where will it go? Saying things like 'truth has to be brought or wanting to get the truth' is absurd. It means truth is somewhere far and it is difficult to catch, hence, "once you come in my clutches, I'll hold you in a way so you can never leave." Which truth are you talking of? Looking for truth as if truth is hidden somewhere! Take a strong noose with you wherever you go. If you come across truth, throw the noose and catch it and speak to it, "You really troubled me.

Where did I not look for you!? Now that you're caught, I'm not going to leave you." Tie its hands and feet otherwise it may run away again!

Truth is that which is infinite and eternal. Nothing exists outside of it. Truth cannot be brought nor can you have an access to it. Who is the illusion? 'I' is the illusion; my presence and the announcement of my separation. 'I' means, an announcement that I am something and I am standing against Truth. If I am, then I am against Truth and is it possible for me to be against Truth? No, it's not possible because nothing can exist outside Truth. I cannot be against Truth, but it seems so. This is a futile process which is understood later through sadhana. In the depths of sadhana one understands that he is involved in a futile process which can never succeed. One reaches this understanding, "how much ever I may raise this illusion, take care of it for thousands of years or for that matter even crores of lifetimes, it will still remain an illusion. It will never become the Truth." You can bring up the illusion for lifetimes, thinking it must hold some value, or some truth must have seeped into it by now, "I have brought up this illusion and separation for thousands of years. Some truth must have got absorbed into it for sure!" Will this happen? Will it? Will Truth enter the illusion? You can take care of the illusion for millions of years if you want, it will still remain an illusion. Ultimately, illusion will get dissolved, separation will get dissolved. Take as much time as you want; the time that you use belongs to your free will. Free will means living the time.

We create the illusion called time. Our existence, our declaration of being separate gives birth to illusion, otherwise there is nothing like 'time'. Time is a great lie and so is death. There is nothing like time or death. We want to stretch this play that is going on and that is maya. This play of our separation will end at some point and the divine play, the leela will continue. The leela is never going to stop, but we can withdraw our separation with the right understanding that 'I' am the problem. If you think that you have to correct the problem to attain atmagyan, then you can forget it. 'I' as a separate entity can never attain atmagyan or buddhatva. Where there is no 'I', there buddhatva already is!

When the illusion of 'I', the illusion of me as a presence, my existence, my separation gets dissolved, the realization happens. In other words, with the ending of our involvement in this process, the realization of buddhatva already being present, happens. In the great divine play which goes on forever, this other play takes place where the illusion of separation is born. The wave keeps travelling, and having travelled far it feels it is something, and that it has a separate identity otherwise how could it have travelled! With this feeling that it has journeyed for so long in the ocean, it starts considering itself separate from the ocean. But ultimately it is Paramatma himself happening in this way.

Agreed that you began living your separation in the form of a stone. From there you moved to becoming sand, soil and continued further as algae, fungi and then taking the forms of aquatic beings, leading to taking forms on land and then air and as amphibians and so on. You have travelled long. Your journey has been a long one, but that doesn't decide that you are separate. The wave says since it has travelled so far, there is some truth to it. But when it hits the shore, it's separation ends. The end is inevitable. Every wave has to disintegrate but does it get destroyed after it's disintegration? Understand, the wave was the ocean in the first place and will remain the ocean forever. It was never a wave but the ocean itself as the wave. Wave is just a way the ocean happens to be. Ocean forever is and will be. This is just an example being given of the ocean and the wave. The ocean won't remain forever, but from this example what I am pointing towards is the Ultimate Truth; the truth which is infinite, endless, eternal, without a beginning or end. That great divine play has forever been and forever will be. That is its way of expression. We feel that we have covered a long journey from being a stone to where we are now and so we have an identity of our own. This illusion of a separate identity makes us believe that 'we' are making this journey. The wave could be on a very long journey, but the truth is that it is not a wave but the ocean itself.

PURIFICATION OF THE ANTAHKARAN (THE MIND, INTELLECT, MEMORY AND THE SENSE OF 'I') IN THE PHYSICAL LIFE

Sadhaka: Swamiji, it is said that one can experience paramatma after the purification of the physical body and the inner body, the antahkaran. But in today's times, in order to balance the transactional and relative reality, the antahkaran, the conscience, becomes impure. Kindly give some guidance on this.

Swamiji: If we are living the relative truth and trying to manage it, the antahkaran is bound to get impure. It does get impure and talking of today's era where the relative truth is lived with such cunningness, the conscience has to become impure. Now what is it that we can do here? See with a lot of depth and you'll notice this is the reason that Lord krishna is called 'Purnavatar'. He was seen fully entangled in the relative truth, but He Himself opened this mystery that it was done as a performance. What is this 'performance' in reality? Performance is a great art, a great skill, not just an ordinary skill. This has nothing to do with performing in movies. The performance being spoken of here is one which happens with this knowledge that there is no duality, that two does not exist. Despite this 'knowing' that there is no other, the play is still going on, so enjoy the play. There is no need to take it seriously.

In the worldly life, day to day life, the more serious we are, the more problems we create. Becoming serious means that the relative truth is no more relative, but is actual or ultimate. Why are you serious? Acting is never about seriousness. Can acting be serious? Acting, performing is a play. One doesn't become serious in acting. What is the reason behind calling acting a relative truth? It is just a play, just an act being performed so it is called the relative truth. There is no need to take it seriously and no need to get upset, in case you are. If it's being taken too seriously, it means it is no longer a relative truth. Now that you are getting so upset, it means you are taking it pretty seriously. Look within yourself. If there is depth coming in the sadhana, you need not take the relative truth so seriously. When you don't take the relative truth so seriously, then enacting of the scenes happens.

Enacting means we're performing without the thought of winning or losing pressurizing us. Everything is just happening, whatever the times maybe like, whether it is times like 'this' or times like 'that'; whatever happens, happens. There's no calculation of winning or losing involved. I don't get into the loop of profit and loss. Acting is also a kind of obstinacy. It involves somewhat of a refractoriness. Whatever has to happen, will happen! Take it all simply, whatever happens – profit or loss. There's nothing like opposing or taking sides in this, and nothing like duality or conflict. Whatever is happening is fine. It's just a play where duality is being known but not being lived. I repeat, duality is being known but not lived. If duality is lived, it will instantly become the truth, but if it is being known it will be a play. In just being known, it'll be a play and upon being lived, it'll become the truth.

You being serious in the drama means the act is being lived... duality and conflict is being lived. If it remains as a game being played, it means it is being simply known. If the performance is being known in a simple and natural way, then even duality and conflict will be like a game, and when that game ends, there won't be any attraction left. With no persistence left there, the game ends completely when it finally ends. But if you play seriously, the game won't end. The persistence will survive in this case with you constantly muttering, "what has happened is wrong, it shouldn't have happened, this should have happened." This kind of insistence will survive and you will have to carry the school bag again. You will have to continue your journey with the urges again; the urge and persistence like, 'this should happen, this shouldn't have happened, I will make it right.' But if you're not serious, then it's simple - whatever happened has happened. You're playing and so if you lose, you laugh out loud and if you win, you still laugh out loud. You win and embrace the one who has lost and you embrace the winner if you lose. When things remain the same in all circumstances, the game ends or else the school bag is ready. Insistence is what becomes the school bag i.e. when there's no acceptance of the way things happen. Not accepting and being serious means relative truth is being lived and not being known. Witnessing is knowing, and living means separation. Witness consciousness doesn't discriminate. The moment you discriminate, you start living and the 'knowing' ends. When you don't discriminate, things are just being known as a witness; detached and impersonal. Everything is happening and is being known. Everything is fine the way it is. Everything is just perfect, the way it should be.

Chapter 8

Conversation with Sadhakas from U. S. and Europe; Database Is Ego – 1

SADHANA FOR CLEANSING AND PURIFICATION OF CHAKRAS

Sadhaka: Swamiji, during meditation, there's some pressure on my chakras, especially on my heart chakra and after a while it subsides. These days it's happening on the upper chakras also including the sahastrara, but subsides after some time. What is all this and why is it happening?

Swamiji: All this is the development of sensations and wherever the development happens, the energy gets diverted that way. The chakras get activated and what happens is that the sensations lying dormant in those areas become natural as they should be. Till the time they reach the normal and natural state as they should be in, some kind of pressure, different sensations, a pull can happen. This will continue till the state of right alignment is reached. Something weird and unnatural is felt because the right alignment has not happened yet. But this is a sign that the work of alignment has begun. Even the sensations and pressure being felt in the upper chakras as you say, is a sign that the work of alignment is happening. The work is happening with speed in the upper chakras but you need to be careful with regards to your lower chakras. Keep paying attention to the cleansing of your lower chakras. Keep doing the method for meditation called 'sapt chakra sandhaan' or the 'seven chakra alignment' that I have provided. This will help in balancing the lower chakras in case they are imbalanced and will help in cleansing them also. This will help in cleansing and purifying all the chakras and bring them into alignment. The work on the upper chakras happens because of the sadhana done in past lives. The activation felt and seen happening in them is because of sadhanas from past lives but the lower chakras become the reason for a rebirth. Why are you born again? Rebirth has happened because the lower chakras were not cleansed properly. Why have we taken birth again? Why have we carried the school bag again? Why did we have to do 'A for apple and B for boy' again? It's not just this; even in this life, ever since birth there have been influences. There have been many influences, many circumstances we have been through, and more so we weren't fully conscious while dealing with them. Lack of awareness has led to new sanskaras, new patterns and new garbage being collected. All of that needs to be cleaned too, hence the cleansing of the lower chakras must be done regularly. The cleansing of the lower chakras is very important. The work on the upper chakras is going on and that's very good, my good wishes are with you. This is a good sign but cleansing must go on simultaneously. Cleansing is in our hands.

We don't have to obtain paramatma nor do we have to bring him from somewhere. We don't have to get 'enlightenment', we cannot get it. We cannot obtain or get atmagyan, buddhattva, enlightenment, liberation. We can only do the cleansing part. What do we have in our hands? It's the cleansing that lies in our hands. If the cleansing keeps happening properly, a state of innocence, a state of absolute purity is reached. That state of innocence and absolute purity is called Paramatma. There is no separate paramatma other than this. That purity and innocence is called Paramatma, so we need to go on with the cleansing of the chakras regularly. All the six chakras out of seven need cleansing because impurities come in them, barring the seventh chakra which is absolutely pure and has no impurities. We will have to cleanse the six chakras from mooladhara to agya regularly. As these six chakras get cleansed, the energy blocks get cleared completely. Energy is anyways ready to climb up. It is always in motion and is not something that remains still. Energy means that which is always in motion. Its movement happens upwards, starting from mooladhara (the root or base) which is where this energy is stored in the little reservoir called kund. That is the center of this energy. The storage of energy happens here, and it is from here that all the chakras receive this energy, including the mooladhara.

What happens is that when the alignment of the chakras is not right due to certain negative experiences, then certain negative attractions related to those chakras lead to the vikaras or defilements getting formed there. Some of these distortions then usurp this energy, due to which it is not able to rise up properly because of its flow getting disturbed. It is not able to rise up in the natural and straight forward way in which it should i.e. going straight up to the sahastrara. It gets sucked on its way up. What we call patterns are actually forms of energy, and every pattern is related to different chakras, for example, a pattern of fear is related to the swadhishthana chakra. Different experiences are connected to different chakras, and so the kind of experience a person has gets related to the chakra to which that pattern belongs. The rising energy is usurped by these patterns on its way up. Patterns are forms of energy and their food is energy, so they'll keep sucking the energy. Since they need continuous energy to survive, they keep drinking this energy. This is the reason that the flow of energy which must rise up to the brahmakshetra in a natural way, gets slowed down. If that flow simply rises upwards with speed, only then it is considered as the natural flow of the energy going upwards and that is called the sushumna naadi. Sushumna naadi means that the energy is flowing naturally upwards, beginning from down below. If there are defilements that it encounters on its way up, then this naadi breaks and scatters because these defilements suck this energy. If this sushumna naadi is complete and unbroken, then the flow is natural and it is like a silver cord. When this energetic silver cord remains active, then this energy rises from the kund and goes straight to the sahastrara kshetra. If it is in its full form without anything disrupting its flow upwards, it will create a hole in the brahma kshetra, leading to the opening of the brahmarandra. The hole that is made is called the 'randra' and that is why the term brahmarandra. This is all an energetic work taking place. The defilements and the patterns that obstruct this energy have to be dissolved. Sadhana is the sadhana of cleansing and not of obtaining paramatma.

What is the path to be Paramatma? Cleansing, right cleansing. Paramatma is already present i.e. if proper cleansing happens. We are already there because we are Paramatma. We are Paramatma; it is because of the impurities that this illusory identity took birth and that is the vikara, the defilement. It seems as if this illusory identity holds value. It gives a sense of someone with a separate form, name and looks, giving birth to an illusion. It is because of this illusion that it seems we have a separate identity. This identity with the separation at its core is the obstruction. This separate identity, this illusory being, is the obstruction and this needs to be immersed. Immersing this means that all the different patterns in all the six chakras will have to be dissolved. This illusory being is not sitting somewhere that you can go and catch hold of it or get rid of it. The coming together of lakhs and lakhs of different kinds of patterns is called the 'illusary being'. These patterns are spread out in the six chakras and that is why when a pattern gets activated, it first hacks your breath and your breathing pattern changes. The flow of the breath changes and its style shifts, for example when in anger, the breathing pattern changes from how it was before anger arose. When greed arises, the pattern of breath changes and likewise it is when lust or any other pattern takes over. With different defilements and patterns, the breathing pattern differs but when the breath is in its natural flow, that breathing is very different. The natural breath flows till the hara center, two inches below the navel. It is soft and slow. The natural breath always flows softly and slowly, during inhalation as well as exhalation. If the breath is flowing from the hara center, it means all the chakras are cleansed. It is then that the stomach rises and falls naturally like that of a child. What do we have to do? Cleansing and lots of cleansing. Cleansing is the sadhana and we need to understand this well. It is because of the sadhanas done in past lives and all the achievements from these sadhanas, that many of our chakras get activated easily in this birth. But the cleansing has to be done 'here and now'. We will have to do the cleansing otherwise we won't achieve anything. The day cleansing is complete, that is the day we happen to be Paramatma. We are Paramatma, it is the veil of illusion that just drops and the false identity dissolves. That is why I say that the false identity must dissolve and when that happens, fear arises. The fear of death arises and it seems that we are going to die. We ourselves are the problem because we are the false self. There is no problem within us; we are the problem. The moment the 'I' dies, the illusory self dissolves. That is why Guru Gorakhnath Ji says, "Maro hey jogi maro, maro maran hai meetha. Tis marni maro, jis marni Gorakh mari deetha!" (Die O yogi die, death is sweet. Die that death which Gorakh ji died and merged completely). Similarly, praising death, Kabirdas Ji also sang, "Jis marne se jag dare, mero man anand. Kab marihon kab bhentihon, puran Paramananda!" (The death that the world fears, I revel in it. I wait for the moment when death arrives and bliss is attained). These two dohas that I keep repeating are like an anti-virus. I want to make a pattern out of this anti-virus and put it in you, so that when it enters your system, it slowly dissolves all the other patterns that exist inside you.

THE MEANING OF GOING WITHIN

Sadhaka: Gurudev, sometimes you ask us to go within and sometimes to go deep within. You ask us to know ourselves and recognise ourselves. What is this that you say? Please speak on this.

Swamiji: Go within, go within, by saying go within, can anyone go within? It is true that just by saying go within, no one is able to go within. It is not even that by closing your eyes you reach inside yourself. You do reach one or two steps inside by closing your eyes, not more than that. As you go within, you find soldiers at every step ready to fight. They're standing there with swords asking you to fight with them first. Who are these soldiers? They belong to the opposing forces – they are the patterns, the sanskaras which will keep attacking you. As these patterns keep getting discharged, you keep going within, depending on how much they are getting dissolved. As you keep entering the depths of your inner self, you'll find this entire army at every entry point. You alone have to fight this army and defeat it. Fighting here means, 'not fighting'. We have only one weapon and which is that? You not doing anything, will defeat them. You can never defeat them by fighting. If you do something, they get strengthened. Even if you want to fight, who is it that you're going to fight? It is like fighting with King Bali, Sugriv's brother. If you fight with Bali, half your power goes to him instantly. Never fight with these patterns. There is only one way to win from them, and that is 'not doing anything'. You don't have to do anything. Let the patterns dance with the swords in their hands while you go on watching them till they dissolve. Why should the shadow be empowered!? We will lose a fight with the shadow, isn't it? If it were real, we could have done something, tripped it over and hit it. But it is not real and is impossible to catch. You will get exhausted fighting it. That is just a shadow, how will you trip it? In the process of trying to make the shadow fall, you will fall.

Never fight the shadow. We always lose when we're fighting shadows. We just have to see the shadow with equanimity, as it is. We don't have to improve it, manipulate it nor manage it. Neither do we have to defeat it nor understand it – we don't have to do anything. When we don't do anything, they dissolve and when that happens, the path will open. With the opening of the path, a movement forward happens. You don't have to 'do' the moving forward, the inner journey happens on its own. As the journey inwards happens even slightly, the next soldier comes and stands in front but seeing them with equanimity, our power keeps increasing. The more we come into a balance, into equanimity, the more our power increases. Then whatever our sight falls on, gets dissolved. You have heard of the third eye opening; in this state whatever is seen turns to ashes. Whatever pattern arises, when seen with equanimity gets dissolved. Seen with an equanimous eye, they dissolve.

There are stories which are used to put across a point and when they unfold, they prove the point to be true. We go to different places to listen to these mythical stories and keep listening to them. What we have to do is to unfold them. This opening of the third eye, the Shiv Netra leads to the dissolution of whatever comes in front of it. What is going to come in front of it? The patterns which are the shadow will keep coming and keep getting dissolved. Their drama won't continue for long. In fact, as they come in your vision and you start seeing them, they get dissolved instantly. This is how our inner journey will continue to happen. What this means is, the inner vacuum will keep growing as the Shiv Tattva increases. As the ongoing drama in the vacuum becomes clearly visible, and is seen just as it is, its dissolution then is a simultaneous happening. The dramas will keep dissolving and the veils will also keep dissolving. Our entry into the vacuum will keep happening with the veils going further behind and the open space increasing. With the increasing of the open space, there will come a stage when all the attention seekers will be gone. With the attention seeking patterns gone, the drama also ends. What will be left in its place? Infinite vacuum (nirvaatiya anantata) or the Shiv Tattva! That which is beyond attributes, infinite, endless, never born, beyond time and space, eternal, then gets revealed. When that starts revealing itself, we start dissolving just like a pattern dissolving, and then our separation reduces resulting in the increase of the Shiv Tattva. That is the reason one feels very light when a pattern dissolves. How much the separation reduces depends on the quantity of patterns dissolving. The lighter one gets, the more spacious it gets and the Shiv Tattva keeps increasing. With the increasing infinite vacuum all the patterns get dissolved, resulting in complete dissolution of separation. You are but a conglomeration of patterns! These patterns collectively are called separation. As the patterns dissolve, Shiv Tattva will keep increasing and the Paramatma that we are will start shining through, and will keep getting profound with every dissolution that happens. The day all the patterns dissolve, only Paramatma remains as us.

The death of the patterns feels as if we are dying because of our association with them, just like when a child dies, the parents feel that a part of themselves has died because of their association with the child. The attachment to their child makes them feel as if they are dying. Between a husband and wife, if one dies the other also feels as if he/she is dying. Why do they feel half dead? It is so because of too much association with their better half.

Chapter 9

Conversation with Sadhakas from U. S. and Europe; Database Is Ego – 2

BALANCING THE PHYSICAL AND SPIRITUAL LIFE; WHAT IS PARAMATMA AND HOW IS LIBERATION POSSIBLE

Sadhaka: When the feeling is intense then dhyana happens very nicely but when engaged in a lot of other tasks through the day, it doesn't happen properly. How should one maintain a balance between the physical journey and the spiritual journey so that one can be equally devoted towards both?

Swamiji: This is a common question belonging to everyone; how to attain balance which is lost when we're too engaged and entangled in our daily activities. Losing balance means we are not completely present with the activity or task at hand. We need to learn the art of being fully present, of being one with whatever work we do. That is the summarized meaning of balance. You just 'be the action', being totally involved or rather, being one with the work in hand. Other than that, don't do anything. You just 'be the act, the work' yourself. Stop living this duality which projects 'this is the work and I am the one doing it.' When you are one with the work i.e. when work and you are not separate, then the completion happens.

Normally what happens is that we are working on something but we're simultaneously worrying about the other tasks that need to be done. But you can do only one work at a time. Whatever is being done now is the only work that can be done. By thinking of four other tasks that need to be done, you yourself are disrupting the one which you're working on in this moment. It is common sense that only one job can be done at a time. On this, someone may comment that they work on the laptop and do the cooking also. But if you look with awareness, you'll see that when you're working on the laptop, you're only with the laptop. These days what happens is, people work online from home and they are also cooking side by side. They feel they're doing two things at a time but that's not the case. They're doing one thing at a time...either they're working on the laptop or they're working in the kitchen. They have to leave the laptop to go and work in the kitchen. Two minutes here and two minutes there may have been the case, but those two minutes you were present with only one thing, i.e. either the laptop or the cooking. They're not doing two things simultaneously, at the same time. Only one work is being done, I'm saying something very deep. These are not two jobs, only one job is happening at a time.

We have to accept today's physical reality as it is. If one has to follow this kind of a routine, so be it. There's only one task happening, not two. Looking from a vantage point, from a higher perspective at that, you'll notice only one work is happening, not two. You're sitting in one place and working on your laptop and mobile and you're cooking. This is not two but one. But in today's era, whatever the physical reality is, has to be accepted as it is. However the physical reality is presenting itself, it has to be carried out in that way. It has to be performed, but with the understanding that it is one in the moment, not two. Hence, if you are divided in two places, it's a problem.

While eating food, if you be the food i.e. you are the food yourself, then there's no problem. The food will get transformed into prasad and there won't be any difference between the two. The food will be eaten peacefully and there won't be any duality. There won't be any opportunity for duality to arise and no opportunity for the balance to get disturbed. Balance only gets disrupted when you add some hypothesis. Example of hypothesis is, when you're sitting at home and working but also thinking about the function that is going on in your relative's house, then you're living a hypothesis. You may be sitting at home and working but worrying about the office. You can worry about the office work when you go to the office, or else if you need to finish some office work 'here and now', then you do it. If need be, call up the office; phone call happens in the 'here and now'. Now sitting at home and worrying about an office file which is not in your hands at the moment, you're playing with a hypothesis. The problem is that you are trying to be in two places at the same time. Sitting in one space, you're trying to accomplish four tasks although you're doing only one work at a time and not four. There is only one job being done at one time and if you yourself get transformed into the 'action', then there won't be any problem. It's an issue when somebody is living a hypothesis because the balance gets disturbed. Everyone must understand this thing very well – if you're living a hypothesis while doing other work, the balance gets disturbed. Hypothesis and speculation create imbalance. If someone is on the path of sadhana with a desire to attain paramatma, he will fall into a ditch because paramatma is a hypothesis. Will his sadhana ever succeed? Sadhana means to sit quietly, not do anything; getting firmly established in equanimity which will then sustain. Whatever is happening will be known. If one is sitting for sadhana and is living a hypothesis, how does he expect his balance to be maintained? This is trying to attain a hypothesis which doesn't exist.

What is paramatma for you? Do you know paramatma? Have you ever met him, had lunch or dinner with him? Have you played a game of cards, rummy with him? You're talking of that paramatma which is a hypothesis. Whoever your paramatma, he will be a hypothesis. If four people are sitting, you'll find each of their paramatma to be different. All the four will have a different hypothesis and as many paramatmas. You're looking for a paramatma who is unknown! When you don't know someone, all that you have is a concept about him. Every person will have a different concept. No two people can have an identical paramatma because their hypothesis will be different, since none has met paramatma. How will you know paramatma? You've never spoken to him on the phone, have you? But you'll say, "never mind if I haven't spoken to him on the phone, but I do know something about him". Which paramatma are you talking about? This hypothetical paramatma is very dangerous, very dangerous. First of all, he is not there and secondly, he destroys your entire sadhana. Imagine how dangerous he must be; not being there and yet spoiling your sadhana. Beware of such a paramatma! Save yourself, stay away. I have asked so many people to call paramatma over for lunch and dinner so we can chit chat with him and spend some good and quality time with him. It will be fun playing a game of cards with him. We'll entertain him well with good food and drinks. But nobody calls him. What kind of concepts are you living with, if I may ask? You're living the lies and expecting the truth!? You're living a hypothesis called paramatma and that too when you're sitting for sadhana! Do 'Ram-Ram' during sadhana if at all, instead of this! Just leave all this!

What is the need of paramatma in sadhana? When sitting for sadhana, you don't have to do anything. "Karne wale sab bigaad dete hain, bina kiye sab theek ho jaata hai", which means the 'doers' spoil everything and without 'doing' everything becomes alright. When you don't do anything, sanskaras will keep arising and keep getting destroyed. Once complete eradication of sanskaras or patterns happens, only Paramatma remains, as you; Paramatma who you existentially are. Paramatma cannot be touched but it is possible to 'be' Paramatma. It is true. No one can touch paramatma. There is no possibility of touching paramatma, shaking hands with him or sitting with him. Just see the kind desires people have! They want to do sadhana and enter paramatma's royal court! They desire to be seated next to the throne! Where do they want to sit? Next to paramatma.

You talk of paramatma as if paramatma has a royal court which must have been made by a contractor and you want his address. For what? For getting one made for yourself! Paramatma must have got the building material from somewhere, you think and ask "Can I know where the material has come from? I also want to get one made." Then you think of how well He is running the world and for that He must be having a good staff. You continue thinking, 'Oh! But all this must have existed before Paramatma, that's why he has been able to keep the staff. Even the shops and the contractor must have been there before Him. The person who made the throne must be the owner of a factory", and so you go on. Do you even think what kind of madness you are living? Thinking that Paramatma must be a perfect being running the world, and you wish to meet him. How insane can one be to live this madness!? God did this and God did that, God listens to me etc. etc. Come on! What insanity are you living? Correct yourself with awareness. Sadhana is about being conscious. Shake yourself up. Paramatma cannot be touched, but you can be Paramatma. Two never happened. Paramatma never broke and he can never break. Paramatma did not create the universe, rather He himself is happening as the universe. The world is His way of happening, His way of expression. Do not get into this madness that He separated himself after creating this world and has opened an office to manage it.

The One himself is happening as the world; that's His way of happening. He himself is the stone. It's not that He is present in the stone...no, there is no such thing. He Himself is the stone, He is happening as the stone. Stone is His way of getting expressed. There is no stone as such, rather the stone is happening. There is no mountain – the mountain is happening. There is no human being – human being is happening. There is no earth – the earth is happening. Similarly, the world is happening, the universe is happening, the multiverse is happening, brahm is happening... everything is happening. He is not making anything. He is happening as everything. Two never happened. It's an illusion which must be immersed. Paramatma alone is, there is no other.

All our self-created practices need to be withdrawn. Patterns are also a way of our happening – a different way of our happening. They are our attractions, the wrong ones at that. Patterns are our wrong attractions and a wrong way of our happening. It's not like some pattern got made on its own or someone put it in us – there are no patterns separately formed. Patterns are 'us' happening in a wrong way, they are our wrong attractions. Where will the pattern go after dissolving? It is energy, it becomes free. Where will it merge? It will merge with us. It is our energy which is playing in a different form. When it withdraws, we receive it back and patterns dissolve.

We convert our conscious mind into the subconscious mind, which means we form patterns and fix them in it. If someone is influencing us with their garbage, who is accepting it? We are the ones accepting it and not just that, we design that pattern and take it in.

It's not like the influencer has put it inside us. The influencer said something, we imagined it, we built a pattern with our imagination, we formed it and kept it in our storage. Somebody influenced us means we broke ourselves because of the influence. We break ourselves and then make a form out of it. We have broken ourselves into pieces. Every time you get influenced, you break yourself into a new piece. We keep breaking ourselves apart into pieces. When you take some spiritual garbage from an influencer, you break a piece of yourself and make it according to the garbage taken in. According to that you'll make a new pattern and reserve it. You broke a piece of yourself, your innate self and became a different self which is distorted. You created a separate distorted self and now you'll feed it. That distorted self is also 'you' happening; the distortion being a way of 'you' getting expressed. You decided to create the distortion. It is your own creation - a problem you have given birth to by breaking yourself up. That is why I say it is your child. When the pattern plays out and gets dissolved with right understanding and equanimity, its energy gets freed. Once it gets free, the energy comes back in you. Your energy which dissipated upon breaking comes back in you slowly and you are then whole.

How will your energy become? It will become as it should be. It will become like shivling. Whenever any energy becomes complete, how will its shape be? It will be oval like shivling. You've seen it right!? The earth moves in the solar system in an oval manner. All the planets move in an oval manner, all the movements being oval shaped. The motion of electron is also egg-shaped, oval. Shivling is also egg-shaped. Shivling means the energy is established in its innate nature. How is your energy now? You have converted your innate self into a distorted one. You yourself designed the patterns, broke yourself up into pieces and converted that innate oval shape into distorted forms. What kind of forms did you give it? Distorted forms. You are responsible for these forms and now you are yourself getting troubled by them. These patterns are troubling you but they are alive because you gave birth to them. They are your children, your attraction, your attachment to worldly illusions which you want to keep alive. You don't let them die. These attractions and attachments can end right now and they can withdraw instantly, but you are feeding and nurturing these problems. They are all pieces of you which you yourself are responsible for creating.

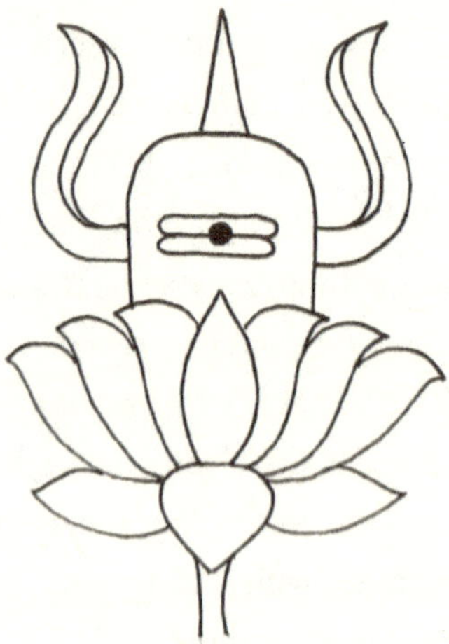

When you understand this, you'll understand the meaning of cleansing. Cleansing doesn't mean removing and throwing out. People think removing and throwing is cleansing. You don't have to throw anything out, you only have to know whatever is going on, as it is, with equanimity. When we know them as it is, the distorted form will dissolve and the energy which the distorted form of the pattern had taken up, will come back in us. Our wealth comes back in us, our investment comes back in us. Don't think that we have invested in our distorted self. We have not, rather we have invested ourselves in the distortion. We have invested ourselves in the distortions, in the sanskaras, in the patterns. The investment is a piece of ourselves that has been put there, which will later come back in its original, innate nature.

Swaroop, the innate nature means Shiv Tattva where the energy reaches its highest state. That is when liberation happens. Coming back to its original nature is liberation. Innate nature is knowing whatever is, as it is. In this, everything gets dissolved i.e. our duality gets dissolved. Our attraction to the physical body gets dissolved, our attraction to the causal body, mental body and subtle body also gets dissolved. Going further ahead, our attraction towards the spiritual body and the supreme body will also dissolve. That is why I say that the body must go, this body measuring six feet must go. The mind and the feelings must go, including the atma and paramatma. Everything must go. When you look deeply, you'll notice that hypothesis is a pattern. Every hypothesis in the end is a pattern. Mukti i.e. freedom must also go...release of the freedom! Paramatma must also be freed. Everything must be freed. You've played enough with Paramatma, now go and get free yourself. It is all a hypothesis. When everything gets freed, then there's Supreme Essence, Absolute Truth which doesn't have a name or form, which cannot be described despite using all kinds of words to talk about it and which cannot be spoken of despite using as many signs and signals. It can only be known when 'you be it'. Being it is knowing it! It doesn't have a name. It doesn't come under any name, be it Purna Shiva, be it Param Brahm or any other name. It cannot get contained in the vedas, upanishads nor can it get contained in any speech or any signs and gestures. It cannot be contained anywhere. It doesn't come in any hypothesis. Anyway, the hypothesis in the name of paramatma, has got highly corrupted. Recently it had to be called 'One' and 'Existence'. Something new needs to be done now since things have gone corrupt. Osho says 'Astitva', 'Existence'. The corrupt words have to be used to a little extent in this way.

But then they are removed slowly. He says, make use of the new word which is less corrupt. Although even that is corrupt, but in comparison it is less corrupt.

THE PROCESS OF THE SOUL CHOOSING A WOMB

THE ROLE OF ATTRACTIONS, DESIRES AND KARMAS

Sadhaka: Gurudev Pranaam! You had once said that after a human being dies, he is given an option of choosing which womb he wants to enter. My question is related to this – if the soul is given an option to make a choice, why would he want to choose a lower, sinful womb? How does a soul choose a womb?

Swamiji: There is a separation here. Separation is a conglomeration of a lot many attractions. When the body leaves, the attractions remain and this conglomeration of attractions survives and travels. 'Attractions' means that they want to live fully. Whatever the attraction is towards, the soul wants to play it out and complete it. How will the attraction get fulfilled completely? It has to be played out for its completion to happen. To fulfill any attraction, some play needs to be done. It wants to play out something in its own way which will turn out favourable for this completion. Everything should be conducive and favourable for the attraction to be completed. This separation which is a conjoining of many attractions is now the soul (Atma) and no longer a body. There are various kinds of attractions in the soul.

There are three bodies of attractions – the etheric body, the causal body and the mental body. The reason behind these three bodies being taken care of and held together is an equanimous state called atma, the soul. Atma keeps them clubbed together and then takes them along. It takes them and then what happens? Birth happens. Like I've said before, when death happens, an entire reel of all the leftover attractions revolves and gets condensed. They then become an Akashic Record, a pin pointed blue print. This blue print is very thin and a very small floppy is made of it, which acts like a link between the physical and the metaphysical. Now the soul has a lot of attractions in a condensed form, too many dangerous attractions of various kinds which it has to live. To live means it has to play them out. The soul has to play them out and to play them out means to live them. Till the time it doesn't live them properly, attractions won't get dissolved and till they don't get dissolved, the soul's journey will continue. If you see deeply and intensely, you'll find that the soul is neither born nor does it die. It doesn't come and go. It is a conglomeration of attractions which are on a journey. Now to play them out, it needs a body. This depends on the kind of attractions – if the attractions are the ordinary kind, then it finds a womb fast. Wherever it finds a womb, it enters there. Once it enters the womb, the program spreads inside. The attractions will then use this body and will want to play themselves out through this body. They will play and if they play right, the soul can be free from all attractions. It will be absolutely content and satisfied but if not played right, the attractions will get updated and get restored again. In the meantime, there are chances of more attractions getting added, leading to an increase in the number of attractions and thus the journey will go on and on, endlessly. Can it ever get over with new attractions being made?

All desires are hard to satisfy. Buddha says "vasna dushpoor hai" which means, desires can never be satisfied. Someone may desire for riches and wealth thinking if he gets a certain amount, he'll be satisfied. But when he gets it, does his desire end? No, he says he wants more. It could be lust or even sweets in place of wealth. You ask them if they want more of it. Their answer is in the affirmative. You ask the person with a sweet tooth to eat as much a sweet of his liking as he wants to. Later when you ask whether he's satisfied, he says no. He'll again ask for the same sweet two-three days later. Desire at all levels is hard to satisfy. They can never be satisfied entirely. The group of attractions has gone and taken birth in this way. Many souls don't get to take birth so easily because their attraction types are different. Their attractions are either very good or very bad. Both these types don't get birth easily. Attractions that are the aggressive kind, the peaceful kind or the positive kind, are not born easily. They roam around in the higher dimensions.

Now, what will this group of attractions do? They will use some other bodies also for example, when in anger, a person says he wants to slap an X person. He goes and not only slaps him but breaks him up in places. When asked later as to why he hit the person so much, his response is, "What do I say! I intended to give him only one slap but I don't know what got into me, what power took over me. I have no idea. I'm feeling bad that I broke his bones. I didn't want to do this." When you go into any kind of lust and desire, it seems as if some power has taken over and you've been hacked. Someone goes to earn money but then just doesn't stop out of greed. He only wants to 'earn more, earn more, earn more' after that. Why can't he stop? Why doesn't the brake get applied? The group of attractions hacks him and spreads temporarily inside him. When this group sees a greedy individual passing, it enters his body and then it's "earn more, earn more". Similarly, the attraction of lust will enter someone with lust in this manner, attraction of anger and fight will enter somebody who's an angry kind and increase the desire of hitting, instigating, to the extent of breaking bones. The attractions enter an individual like this. How will they play out otherwise if not through a body!? For playing out, it enters a body and takes birth and when it's not finding a womb to take birth, it temporarily enters an already activated body and tries to live the lust and desire it craves through that body. In this manner, the attractions keep entering bodies and try to play themselves out.

Now, why will a soul choose an inferior quality womb or one with lower tendencies? If that's how its attractions are, it will choose that kind of a womb. If it wants to choose hell, it will only choose hell! Its attractions are like that. There are such lousy and shoddy attractions that people have. If you roam around the world, you'll find people with such attractions, so much so that you'll get washed over with revulsion. Their attractions are such that you'll start loathing those individuals. It's surprising to see that such repulsive attractions exist in people. These are the kinds of attractions people have! People talk of living peacefully and with love in the world, then what is it that makes them do such aversive things? That's because their attractions are such. Bodies with similar attractions and bodies relating to these attractions are also used. They're like their counterparts. This is a deep mystery. If you go on unfolding it, it'll keep opening.

Sadhaka: Swamiji, in my opinion, the same logic applies to the cows, buffaloes and other animals as well. Am I right?

Swamiji: The state of attractions exists here also but human beings have a choice. Animals don't have a choice, as in, they have very limited choice. In their case, the level of choice and the capacity to choose is very less. Human beings are at the top of the ladder, hold the highest level in terms of the capacity to choose. Hence the soul of a human being can choose more. Their choices are stronger and have potential. It can stop if it wants to, but the soul of an animal cannot stop itself and takes birth very fast. The soul of an animal takes a new birth very fast whereas the soul of a human being doesn't take birth easily. Even an ordinary soul takes three days to take birth. Some take birth within twelve-thirteen days and there are many who are born after years. Not just that, it may take hundreds of years for some while some may take thousands of years before they're born again. When it comes to either very dangerous souls like Hitler and Ravana, or very good and evolved souls like the deities of higher realms – in both these cases, the souls don't take birth easily. They have a choice, a special choice for which they wait... they have to wait. When Astitva arranges and organizes circumstances conducive for them to play themselves out, they come. When a playground is made ready for them as per their requirements, they come. The playground has to meet their needs. Only then will they come!

An ordinary player will pick up the bat and play cricket in any lane or bylane. He will draw two separate lines showcasing as boundaries in case a 'four' or a 'six' being hit. Anything works for an ordinary player but for a special player, adjustments don't work. A special player will have specific requirements. He'll need a stadium of a definite kind, having a special standard...nothing short of an international standard, or else he won't come to play. According to them, the era is then created and when that happens, they get a womb and are born. Till then they have to wait. Their attractions are of a very special and unique kind. In this present era, there is a need for not just Hitler but much bigger Hitlers and they will come. The father Hitlers and grandfather Hitlers will be born, as well as father Ravanas and grandfather Ravanas and for that reason Rama like situations and circumstances will take birth. Beings of much higher stature than Rama will take birth because balance has to happen. This happens in every era. Those souls who have to come in this era, wherever they may be, would be getting ready to come and it is quite possible they have already taken birth. The fathers and forefathers of Ravana and beings of higher stature than Rama have already taken birth. They are getting ready for the play and we will get to see a lot many plays.

Sadhaka: Swamiji, this is the Golden Era. All this will happen even in this era?

Swamiji: Absolutely! Golden Era doesn't happen without Ravana. Rama will happen only when Ravana will happen. Krishna will happen only when Kans will happen. For Krishna's happening, Kans will be needed, Duryodhana as well as the army of Kauravas will be needed. There is a need for everyone. A huge play is going to happen here. This is the Golden Era and a very big play is going to happen in this Golden Era. A big play means a complete drama is going to take place. All the souls who've been waiting since very long will get a chance and will now take birth. Some would have already taken birth, some would be taking birth now and some must be getting ready to take birth. It's going to be a long haul.

GOLDEN ERA, ESOTERIC GROUP AND THE DIVINE COSMIC ENERGY SUPPORT SYSTEM

Sadhaka: What is the esoteric group and the divine cosmic energy support system? How does it provide support and protection to the sadhakas?

Swamiji: The divine cosmic energy support systems are always present. It's not like they're happening for the first time. They're always there. But this time, it's a special one, a mega one, a very big one…the biggest in history so far. Who has created it? Osho and Mahavatar Babaji have created it. The Golden Era began with Osho. He had started building this era and around the year 1986, he tried giving a complete form to this era. Since that time, Osho started working on this and then Mahavatar Babaji got involved, after which this era got created. Every Sadguru creates his own divine energy support system. A Sadguru has to do it. It is an inherent part of his process. He has to build it in the cosmos and that energy support system then gives a push to the sadhakas related to that Sadguru or those who enter his lineage later. They keep receiving this energy push-up. This time it was a big one and do you know what is special about it? The old energy support systems in the cosmos which were active but had gone weak, were recharged again. They were recharged and all were then interlinked. They were all joined together because of which it has become a mega support system and the biggest that history has seen so far. It has been the greatest experiment.

People say that Osho was unsuccessful and that the American government destroyed the Oregon Ashram, this and that. They say if he were alive, this would have happened, that would have happened. Let me tell you, Osho was not unsuccessful. He did his work. Not being in the body did not deter him from doing the work. He has done his work. You think Osho doesn't have a role in this program or retreat that you are attending and listening to? You think the divine cosmic energy support system has no role in this? Is there no role of Mahavatar Babaji and his support system here? What I'm try to explain is that, this retreat being organized by me is just a way of saying it, it's a way of speaking in the physical reality. In actuality, I haven't organized this retreat, rather it has been organized by them and I just have to play a role on their behalf. Everything has been organized by them; I don't have a role in organizing these retreats. Things are going on here and you all are receiving the support, aren't you? You're being supported, are you listening? You are receiving the support of this Golden Era. In these discussions going on now, it's not just hammers but guns that are being used. A big fat hammer is doing the work here, isn't it? This is what support is. What else is support? Support doesn't mean that you'll be taken care of. It means you'll be broken. Slightly fat hammers of upanishads help somewhat but not fully. In this era of technology, bulldozers work. This is a support. All your patterns have to be broken and shattered. Till when will you protect yourself? You've saved yourself for so many lives. Till when will you carry the school bag and repeat 'A for apple and B for boy'?

This support system is available to you and destruction of a strong kind is happening. All the disorderly and nonsensical things you'll witness in the world now will bring about a sense of disinterest and detachment. Whatever happens will awaken you to a sense of detachment. Then you'll come to know that even after attaining everything, one doesn't attain anything and despite losing everything, nothing is really lost. How much ever you attain and gain, it has no meaning. You losing anything also has no meaning. There's no sense or meaning in enjoying the world and fulfilling our attractions and desires with a separation. You keep looking at your attractions. Why don't you live those attractions? Even after its seeming completion, does an attraction get over? This wisdom will then arise that despite acquiring things of interest, the race to get more of it hasn't ended. The attraction has not ended even after its acquisition. That means even after obtaining, nothing is really obtained because the attraction is still alive as it was or maybe has increased further. You lose something but it doesn't end at that because you now try to get something new. Other thing is that even after losing something, you remain where you were. Nothing increases for you after obtaining something and nothing decreases for you after something is lost.

This is a very mysterious thing. This has to do with 'separation', where nothing is obtained even after obtaining and nothing is lost even after losing. The attraction of obtaining remains the same even after getting everything and in fact, keeps growing and after losing something, the attraction to get the same thing again comes back. This was about separation and what is the mysterious thing about it? The metaphysical thing!? Nothing is going to increase or grow how much ever you obtain. You are already whole and complete and even if you remove wholeness from wholeness, what remains is wholeness. If you add wholeness to wholeness, what you get is wholeness. What is whole will forever remain whole, it cannot be increased or decreased, so the support is there in that sense.

Now, what is the esoteric support system? Many people want to do something good for others, for their well-being and welfare. People with such feelings become deities of higher dimensions and what is their work? Their work is to provide support and this trait is inherent in them as a habit. Some people find contentment in creating obstacles for others. Till they don't spoil something for someone, their food remains undigested. They will criticize someone, pull someone's legs and so on and then their food digests. The other well-wishing kind of people wait till they find someone to share their food with before eating. If such a person has four rotis, he looks to find someone to share them with, or else he himself won't eat. Sharing is his nature. He thinks if he found even one person, they would each have two rotis and if four would come along, they'd each have one, but sharing makes him happy and content because it's in his nature - a habit to do something good for others. Till the time he doesn't do something for others, he's not at peace. What will such people become? They will become Deities/Gods of the higher realms after which some of their powers increase. Once they leave the body, their powers increase and then they look for a person who does sadhana or likewise.

There are many temple-deities whom people pray to, asking the deities for making things better for them and certain things come true also for them. These deities are like those helping and well-wishing kind of people who can't eat a meal without sharing. These deities help as much as they can but they are bound by certain restrictions, for instance they cannot make many changes in the destiny of an individual. They can make little alterations and modify things to some extent, like improving the health to a certain degree though not fully, and helping in acquiring a little wealth but then this is something related to maya. There are some deities of the higher dimensions who help those in sadhana. They help because they themselves could not make the jump which could have liberated them, when they were in sadhana. They did take a leap but got stuck in the higher realms, so their attraction also got stuck after reaching there.

One such discussion going on was about remaining established in equanimity when the body is dropping. A whole lot of things are seen; different realms are seen, but if you remain established in equanimity, they will dissolve, merge with the infinite. You'll see higher dimensions but remain established in equanimity. Don't get attracted, don't analyze it, don't categorize it, don't define it, don't do anything. Remember, this is the great mantra which will come of use everywhere. The dhyana/meditation I guide you through and what I repeatedly say during the application of the methods for dhyana, will come of use everywhere. Here also, when you see the next realm, don't concentrate, don't try to understand, don't react, don't attract, don't analyze, don't define, don't categorize. Just keep knowing everything as it is, you don't have to do anything. We don't have to understand anything, good or bad. Something may be very attractive but we're not reacting; what happens then? It dissolves. Then we will see another higher realm, a more beautiful and an attractive one with many attributes and qualities. There our own attributes and equanimity should be very well established.

The attributes of that higher realm are more but our state of equanimity should be much more established than that. There also we must not react, concentrate, analyze, categorize, define or try to understand anything. We must not do anything and it will dissolve. Then you'll see another higher realm and you'll keep going deeper and further; this continues till your equanimity is well established. Your equanimity reducing in any realm will become the cause for you to enter the next higher realm and get stuck there, since then the next higher realm will seem very attractive, beautiful and magnificent due to the equanimity losing its strength. You will enter and become a deity of that higher realm. Depending on how well the equanimity is established and till where, the soul travels up till there without getting attracted to the realms. Those realms don't attract them but the next ones keep getting better, more attractive and beautiful, with their attributes becoming more brighter and vivid. There the time zone keeps reducing and with the awareness of time becoming less, suffering isn't felt since it thins and lessens. On one hand the suffering lessens, and on the other, the joy turns into greater joy with no hunger, no thirst, no hot, no cold, nothing. It will be very attractive. If you get attracted, you'll enter that realm, which means that equanimity was well established till a point before this realm that you got drawn towards was seen; till just before you reached that realm. But not having been able to establish the equanimity further, you get entangled there and will have to take another birth. Now you'll ask when will the next birth happen…maybe after a waiting period of thousands of years, since the deities of the higher dimensions cannot take birth very easily. Another Golden Era will come after thousands of years and then you'll take birth. Deities/ gods of the higher dimensions cannot take birth in the ordinary era. You've been great sadhakas so how can you take birth in the ordinary era? You'll wait for the next Golden Era when you will take birth, do sadhana again, and get firmly established in equanimity. If you stay stuck in maya, then the equanimity won't be firmly established. If you get entangled in the web of maya, then the already established equanimity will also weaken. If equanimity keeps getting strong and firm, you'll come into a state wherein all the sixty-four dimensions will keep passing by, with each one getting more attractive, more beautiful, more magnificent, but we being the equanimous ones don't get attracted because we do not have any attractions left within us. We are in a state of total equanimity and our complete equanimity doesn't get caught up in any attractions.

However magnificent the realm maybe, however high it maybe, we don't get attracted, we don't react, we don't try to understand anything, we don't concentrate, we don't analyze...we don't get ourselves entangled in any such loops. Our equanimity is completely established; whether you now show us a movie, hollywood, bollywood, or anything else. Our equanimity is firm now. We are formless and free from defilements, absolutely smokeless. There is no smoke of any attractions. When nothing can attract us, then the sixty-four dimensions will leave. When we remain fully equanimous i.e. formless and without attributes, the sixty-four dimensions leave and what remains in the end...infinite, endless, limitless, Shiv Tattva, Shivoham, Shivoham!

The deities who are caught up in the higher dimensions have to do some bustling since they are still living the separation, irrespective of how high the dimension they're living in is. What kind of bustling will they engage in? That will depend on their habits. They will do activities based on their habits, based on what attraction they are living. If a sadhaka living in this world says that he is stuck somewhere in sadhana, this deity will tell him in different ways, "child! do sadhana, bring firmness in equanimity and make it stronger." If the sadhaka is going haywire, he'll hit him and ask him to walk properly. This is the esoteric group. What does this group do? It will start shaking and waking up the sadhaka at three or four in the morning, "wake up child, wake up, wake up, it's time for sadhana" and the sadhaka gets out of bed and stands up.

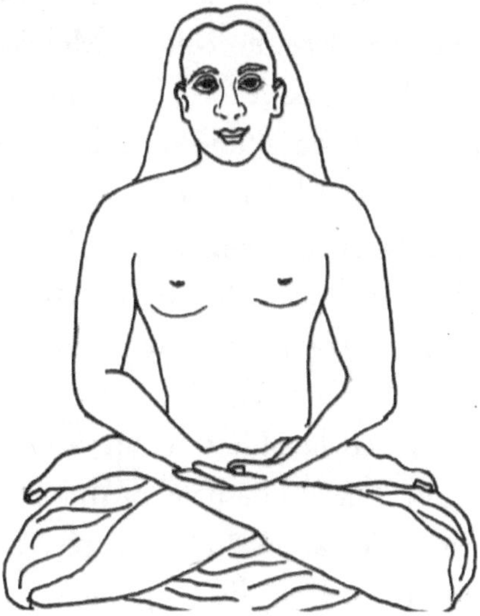

The support system says, "sleep for now, sleep, sleep, you need to stay awake at night". They support like this, making the sadhaka sleep in the morning so that he can stay awake at night because if he doesn't stay awake at night, he won't get the nectar. The support systems work like this. They give support based on the sadhakas needs, so the esoteric support system is in full form. Mahavatar Babaji leads this esoteric support system. The deities of the higher realms are fully active and the ones who had to take birth have already taken birth. These deities before taking birth tell their companions i.e. those who aren't going to take birth, that, "you are not going to take birth but my birth is decided. I'm entering the world so just take care of me while I'm there. Come and punch me and hit me if I go wrong somewhere. Keep an eye on me. I might get entangled in maya, so keep the stick/staff ready."

Maya is very active now. It has appeared in very dangerous forms – it has become the mobile, it has become the internet, it has become google. Maya has become the great deceiver. Kabir Das Ji had called maya 'maha thagini', the great deceiver. He didn't know then, but maya has become the great deceiver now. It wasn't this great a deceiver before. Mobiles have reached everywhere, be it villages, be it the Himalayan jungles, be it the wild life sanctuaries. We're sitting at a height of seven and a half thousand feet surrounded by dense forests and doing a live session from here. Maya is doing this work also...it enters the mobile...the wi-fi maya. The wi-fi maya is here and this session is happening with that. Maya has become the great deceiver with so many different kinds of forms that it is taking. There's not much difficulty in keeping and handling the maya now. It stays in the mobile. Whether it's a meal in a hotel or travelling in an aircraft, payments are just a click away, "did you receive the maya?" you ask and the response, "yes, we did" is prompt.

Sadhaka: Swamiji, it's because of maya that sitting here in the U.S. and Europe we are connected to you and listening to you.

Sadhaka: Swamiji, it is because of this Maya that we are able to be in your presence while sitting here in the U.S. This is also a form of maya.

Swamiji: Maya is a great deceiver in both cases. Without two, balance isn't maintained, so it walks on two feet. Paramatma never makes one-legged things. He makes one-legged human beings but such things he doesn't make one-legged. Now, both things are there in this, so make good use of maya. Remember this well that maya has ninety-nine percent garbage in it. Ninety-nine percent garbage is being given in the name of spirituality. There are some people who listen to me also and take in garbage also. 'Prem gali ati saankri,tame dui na samaye', the lane of love is very narrow, it cannot hold two. Two cannot fit in it. But in the case of people who are listening to me as well as taking in garbage, it is garbage which will enter them. The sadhana is all about getting rid of the garbage. The influencers are impacting people with their speech. It means they are also listening to us.

We must make good use of this, since the esoteric group is activated with its wonderful support along with the divine cosmic energy support system. This means that if we are cleansing ourselves properly, the blessings and grace get showered on us. The showering of blessings is what the divine cosmic energy support system means. If you make use of the methods for meditation, the support system immediately co-operates with you; the instant an experience happens, that very instant the blessings come. The shower of blessings come in very fast and that is the reason why serious sadhakas whose sadhanas from past lives are good and who are worthy and deserving, are made to reach the right place and their resonance set well. This is also a result of the esoteric group and the divine cosmic energy support group's activation. Here you have a little free will. If you decide to take the spiritual garbage also along with what you're taking from here, then it's like consuming alcohol and milk. You consuming two sips of milk and one sip of alcohol consecutively is going to create problems for you. It will lead to digestive issues and illnesses, and your system will get spoilt. Either you consume alcohol or you consume only milk. You'll have to make a choice of only one if you want it to work for you. The support systems are active, the golden era is here. Now it's up to you how much you are able to make use of these.

Chapter 10

Conversation with Sadhakas from U.S. and Europe; Database Is Ego – 3

HOW CAN ONE ADVANCE IN SPIRITUALITY WHILE LIVING THE WORLDLY LIFE AND PURSUING A CAREER

Sadhaka: In one of your videos, you had said that the sadhaka has to make a jump, especially in cases where the sadhana of the sadhaka is successful. For instance, me and my wife are ready to make that jump but how should we take care that those who are dependent on us don't suffer?

Swamiji: This calculative mind, this matrix involving calculations is what doesn't allow the jump to happen plus we don't have faith in Astitva; we don't have faith in Astitva. If there's faith in Astitva, the jump happens; we make that jump. There's no break after that and whatever is our responsibility is then Astitva's responsibility because we ourselves are Astitva now. What happened after the jump – Existence and 'I' don't remain two after that, Astitva is 'I'. Having faith in Him means we are ready to merge in Him.

The jump has been made means the merging has happened. Merging means 'I-The Existence' has happened. The separation is gone and when I am Astitva, then is there anyone dependent on a separate me? Everyone is dependent on Astitva, on Existence. Everyone's feeding happens through us; are we the ones protecting everyone? Those who are dependent on you won't remain unprotected, unsafe. You'll be living in that body itself, which will help in better care being taken of your people, in a very natural way. When 'I am Existence', two doesn't exist. What do you mean by 'what will happen to our dependents'? Everything is Astitva, Existence. This entire creation is My (Existence) way of happening. I am the play and I am the goal. Why get into any mathematics or matrix! I am the play, the game, then what is the worry!? There are no children…it is I, the Astitva. They are My way of playing, My Leela. The entire creation is My Leela. It is Me happening, Me happening as the divine play, then what is the cause of worry?

'Shraddha', Faith – this word has a little depth to it. Talking of faith, either it is there or it isn't. The jump doesn't happen when you have faith…faith is the jump. It's not like you have faith and the jump will happen. Faith happens means jump has happened. Faith 'happens', jump 'happens'. It is in faith that surrender happens. Either surrender happens or it doesn't. Faith means jump and jump means merging. Whom did you have faith in? In Astitva. Where will the jump happen? In Astitva. The jump happens in Astitva and jump means merging. The meaning of merging is to be Astitva and you as a separate entity then exists no more. That is it, what else? When duality goes, the separation is just seen as a play, a divine play. Whose leela is it? My leela; it is I alone and everything is My way of happening, My way of expression – this entire creation and separation. Two has ended…Shivoham! Shivoham!

WHAT IS SIDDHA KUTUMBAKAM?

HOW CAN A FAMILY BE CARED FOR IF ONE LEAVES A CAREER FOR SADHANA?

Sadhaka: Guruji, we have our jobs and our family responsibilities as well. We leave in the mornings and come back in the evenings which leaves us with little time for sadhana. Making a jump means we must give up our jobs and devote all our time to spirituality which will put us all in trouble with no income in hand. This is my question.

Sadhaka: Another thing is, the weather here in the U.S. is very harsh and it becomes difficult to do sadhana. This being a capitalist country, if we don't earn money then the next month gets imbalanced and every time this happens, one has to go through a grind. One option is leaving the job and the other thing which can be given a thought, like you said, is to relocate to a place which has a more conducive environment for sadhana, where the weather is calmer and we can be in the company and presence of nature. The children are growing up and are already so connected to the environment here that it will become very difficult for them. What should we do?

Swamiji: Question is that you want to make a move, but how can it be done in the best possible way? There is an attraction for sadhana but you're not being able to spread it in your life because you don't have the pertinent circumstances for it. Influences are so many that despite having a desire and intention to spread sadhana in your life, you are not able to do it. You want to make a move towards it but circumstances don't allow, so how can the jump be made is your question.

First thing is to organize your daily routine. I have heard that people from your country i.e. America and other European countries party a lot. I'm not talking about you. They do jobs, they party and they take care of their families as well. From where do they remove time for the parties? The Hindus living there remove time to celebrate their festivals. They have maintained groups that they are part of. How do they remove time for all this? The time for all this is being made from the daily schedule that is being followed. There may be many more such things, although I have highlighted just two. If those things are cut out from your schedules, you'll have the time for sadhana. Even if it's not much, you'll be able to make some time for it.

This was one thing. Other thing is about making a move, so one has to ask oneself as to what their top priority is. Is sadhana really our top priority and what kind of sadhana is the true sadhana? Is the sadhana which liberates us from the school bag our top priority? If the sadhana which liberates us from the school bag is our top priority, then no mathematics, no calculations will work there. The move will be made. Now let us understand from the physical world perspective. You dilute everything that you've earned and shift to a place where the expenses are very less and you keep your living standard little simple. You invest your savings in the right way, in good investment products so that you get a fairly good income from there. You may have to do some research pertaining to where the money can be best invested so that you get a good return to live a moderate life. The life style doesn't have to be brought down too much nor does it have to be too extravagant. In this way the income will be more than required and you can save as well. This will be like a cost recovery in these times of high inflation.

As far as children are concerned, they will get used to the new place in the same way they had gotten used to the previous one. It may take some time but they'll get used to the place. If they find it very difficult to adjust, you can always give them the option of going back to the previous place or wheresoever they wish to, once they're capable themselves and start earning. They can be explained to, that you're doing the best you can under the circumstances to provide for them. They can be told about your own struggle period, when you shifted there from India and that they may probably have to do the same which will make them stronger and better. Nobody gets spoilt with struggle. If they understand they'll do so or else they'll adjust with the new place. This is how chances are taken and moves are made. If you think you will make the move only when everything is working in your favour or with this thought that everything should happen as you want it to, it won't happen. It doesn't happen like that.

Everyone has come with their karma-prarabdh. Everyone will keep getting what is meant for them. You should not get into anyone else's matrix. Everything is a chance happening, just like the coming together of a river and a boat. No one is anybody's son, father, mother, brother or sister. These are useless talks, the primary level talks for a sadhaka which should be understood before, isn't it. For a non-sadhaka, this kind of talk is a notch up for him to understand. He may understand after ten years or else while dying...just an hour or two before his death, he starts to understand somewhat that no one belongs to anyone. A common man doesn't understand this before, but a sadhaka has to understand it beforehand. Something that a common man understands at the time of his death, the sadhaka has to understand much before - only then he becomes a sadhaka. At the time of death, the desire to become a sadhaka is born in every common man. He wishes in those last moments, "I wish I had done sadhana and not got entangled in this worldly mess." On his deathbed does he realize that this was all a drama, an illusion. Before that he doesn't. They've heard the word 'prapanch' which is the maya, illusion, drama, but they understand it only when it's time for the body to leave.

Atal Bihari Vajpayee had written some poetries. Have you heard them? He has used some words time and again in them, 'beet gaya, reet gaya, beet gaya, reet gaya'. This is what he wrote in some of his poems. He became the Prime Minister and got famous, but his poems sang of how life has flown by and hands are still empty. I could not understand this earlier because I was quite small or else I would have asked him about it when he had come over to our house. I must have sat in his lap. But I was still small and didn't have the understanding, or else I would have asked him to recite the poems. I don't know whether he had this particular one written at the time or not. By the time I heard his poems, I had already lost interest in politics. Since I belonged to a political family, some interest had been there, but by the time I heard this poem, it had gone. A few years ago, I heard his poems which, if I'm not mistaken, were sung by Jagjit Singh. Holding a top ranked post in the country, post of the Prime Minister and writing such poems shows where this race takes one. After listening to his poems, one understands that this race takes us nowhere. This race takes us only till 'beet gaya, reet gaya', (life has flown by and one is left empty handed and exhausted), even if one becomes the world's richest person.

A friend once asked Albert Eistein before his death whether he wanted to become Albert Einstein in his next life i.e. a scientist in his next life. Einstein responded in the negative saying he did not want to do this madness in his next life. He said the best job to do was that of a plumber since there was no mathematics involved. He felt that being a plumber you just do your work and go home without worrying about 'what next'. People find you when they need you and the choice lies with you, whether you want to do it or not, whether you wish to take the next project or not. You know that whenever you want, you'll get a project in hand. You earn as much as is required to live. There's no need in this profession to get into calculations, and so you're away from getting involved in any matrix. If Einstein spoke about 'plumber' being the best profession, it surely wasn't random. This attraction must have been there since long. He must have observed that plumbers live happily. Whenever they want some work, it arrives. They don't need to open a shop or an office. Everyone is looking for one, was his observation. Look, what this means is that becoming Albert Einstein doesn't take you anywhere nor does becoming Atal Bihari Vajpayee (beet gaya, reet gaya), so wake up. Which race are you running? Wake up!

Shake and wake yourself up. You will have to make a move in this game and I'm not saying you have to settle in India. You can settle anywhere. It could be a country better than India or there must be other countries where the atmosphere would be very good, where the natural calamities would be less, the weather would be good along with the location and demography. Take care of the demography, that should be good. Population density in that place should be low, the quality of water along with its availability must be good. The place one looks for must also be less prone to tsunami and earthquakes etc.; a place which may not get as adversely affected during times of natural calamities which are foreseeable in the near future. There will be many such calamities that will happen like earthquakes, storms, cloud bursts, heavy rains in some places and very less rain in some. One must check all these things and then look for a place to relocate.

Actually, the sadhakas should collectively do some research, find a land and develop a township there. A sustainable model must be developed where there will be less attractions and interests to run behind, so that all tensions are over. With the recession that is happening in America, living costs have gone up. This will keep happening everywhere, in all countries. These games will be played everywhere. A sustainable model must be created where we'll have our own agriculture system, cowsheds, our own forest from where the medicinal herbs can be collected and brought to use. A wellness center can be opened. Solar power and wind power can be harnessed there. There should be engineers amongst us or people with such skills. We will not be slaves of the slaves. With no servants, we will do our work ourselves. Expenses will reduce. Whatever is required, we can grow ourselves. We'll maintain everything ourselves, so the maintenance costs won't be there. With no overheads, the money can be invested to receive interests as funds. We can live well with those funds.

This is a concept. My job is to give a concept. To work on the concept is others' job. My job is to give the concept and I have given one of 'Siddha Kutumbakam'. I've asked for a suitable place to be found for this. It doesn't necessarily have to be in India. It could be Russia or Vietnam or some other place where a big land can be bought, some forest area can be bought. Governments can be approached for certain schemes, even the World Bank. We will protect the forests - they can be told and given the design of the model being developed. They can be asked to give a grant, an aid – no loans, only contribution. Design the model in such a way that the world contributes towards it and donates. People will donate towards a sustainable model where the forests are being protected, conserved and nurtured. Such a model will be a success and others will follow suit. All such models that will come up will be good for everyone, so it's a good model that we're creating for the world and a good example which others will follow. All of you can start researching on the same. Do it in Vietnam, do it in Russia…demographically, they are safe zones.

This concept of Siddha Kutumbakam is all about simplicity. There will be simple huts and simple things for living, nothing big like huge homes. The group energy is going to work there i.e. the energy of the sadhakas will work, and in between the sessions will keep happening and techniques will be provided. It is going to be all about 'work meditation'. You must have heard about Osho's concept of 'work meditation'!? How will this work meditation happen? The work in itself will be meditation, as in, how can it be done in the 'here and now.' This project is not going to take years. Within one year it will be worth living and in a span of three years, it'll get complete because they are going to be simple and sturdy huts, not anything big and palatial. The concept includes a mix of simple and modern. The huts will be conducive to nature and certain elements will be made use of to keep the heating and cooling systems within them natural. Something on these lines needs to be designed. They will be cost effective and low on maintenance. I have shared the thoughts with you. In case you want to make a switch either to India or anywhere else, you can think about it.

WHO AM I?

Sadhaka: Guruji pranaam! During sadhana, we ask ourselves, "who am I?" When this desire and question to know who I am arises, then at times we ourselves say, "I am a soul – pure and holy". Please explain. There is one more thing I don't understand - to a question related to the birth of the soul, you had said it takes birth because of its attractions. Now, my question is whether the soul takes birth due to its attractions or does it take birth to go through its karma? What is it?

Swamiji: First of all, when we ask ourselves, 'who am I?', whatever the answer you receive is a lie. Who answers that question? It's the mind that gives the answer. What is the value of the answer that the mind gives? Less than two pennies. There is no value of the answer that the mind gives. Whatever the mind says, whether it is, 'I am pure, I am holy, I am Buddha, I am this or that', however big it talks, its value is less than two pennies. You have to condense the question 'who am I, who am I' and not look for an answer to that. As per Maharshi Ramana Ji's method of 'who am I, who am I', the question has to be intensified so that it has a penetrating effect, without seeking an answer to it. The question should get so sharp and penetrating that the question and I become one. Then, only the question must remain and nothing else. The 'I' should also get dropped. Only the question must remain and as that happens, everything will vanish. Then the question will arise; I myself will become the question 'who am I, who am I' and rest everything will drop. A solution will then fructify. There won't come any answer even then. Answer won't come, not in the beginning, not in the middle, not in the end. Answer will not come at all. What will come? A solution will come! What is the solution that will come? When the 'I' arises as a complete question, a burning question, it will burn down to ashes and vanish. This vanishing of the 'I' is the solution, the death of the 'I' is the solution. The answer to 'I' is less than two pennies…the mind speaks all nonsense, 'I am pure, I am holy, I am Buddha, I am this, I am that'. Only the mind talks such rubbish. There's only one donkey that talks nonsense like 'I am this and I am that', and that is the mind.

Your second question was whether the soul takes birth according to its attractions or it takes birth to experience its karmas. Now tell me, there was some action that was done but it did not happen properly and you could not do it the way it should have been done. What had to be attained from that action was not attained. You feel that it did not happen properly, but since you still want to attain what you wished to, you'll want to do it again. What is getting created here? Attraction! Attraction because what you wanted to get, you failed to get.

You make a girlfriend, a boyfriend with the desire of getting happiness or some other expectations but you did not get it. Your expectations did not get fulfilled despite having a girlfriend or boyfriend. Now what! It has to be found again – the happiness. The expectations need to be fulfilled again. Now supposing the girlfriend or the boyfriend gets old and dies. You could not have him or her in your life but you want to make them yours again, so won't you need a body again? If you want a girlfriend, you will need to become a boy first, isn't it? You will need to take another body, take birth as a boy and come again or take birth as a girl to have a boyfriend. You will take birth, grow up and start looking for the girlfriend or boyfriend who can satisfy you fully. If you don't find one this time, you'll carry a school bag again, you'll study 'A for apple and B for boy' again till the lesson is complete.

What is the lesson? Lesson is that you don't gain anything in this world even after getting it and you don't lose anything despite losing everything. Everything is a lesson which you have to learn. Till you learn it, you'll be handed over a school bag and asked to study 'A for apple and B for boy'. You'll have to go through it again and again till you complete the lesson. The attractions are there, for example, you earned money, made wealth which was all left behind, but the attachment remained and the feeling that you did not enjoy that wealth stayed as a desire. The thought that you earned less than you wanted to also takes over. Like in the case of, if I'm not mistaken, the founder and owner of 'Ford' whose financial worth at the time of his death was ten million dollars which was a huge number for those times. When he was dying, his PA asked him if he was satisfied with his life and he said he wasn't since he had not met his target of a hundred million dollars. He said he had achieved only ten percent of his desired target and now it was too late. The owner must be putting efforts again and maybe he has earned those hundred million dollars by now, only to have a next target of a thousand million dollars or a crore million dollars probably. He must be struggling somewhere and laboring hard. This is what attractions are and they keep travelling...it's a journey of attractions. This collection of attractions is what separation is and that is what I'm making you understand.

Now, if someone steals, it means he has an attraction for money. If someone murders, he has an attraction for dominion or supremacy. An attraction for supremacy or dominion means the person feels he is special, he feels he won't die but he can kill someone. This will bring him back in another life. What was the sentiment behind Hitler killing so many people? The thing was, he felt he was immortal and that nobody could kill him, although he could...he would live forever. But he too had to die finally. This illusion breaks one day but not entirely so...one takes birth again and gets attracted again. What is karma prarabdha? The looking out for another trick is karma prarabdha. The attractions will take birth again and for those attractions to be lived and desires to be fulfilled, a body form will have to be taken, through which efforts for the same can be put in. Meanwhile, if the give and take of any pending old karmas is there, they will be dealt with and completed under the blow of a cane, ending that karma prarabdha. If you had snatched something from someone, he'll snatch it back from you. It will happen in this interim phase. These are the karma prarabdha and the attractions that survive. Attractions in themselves are the motivation. The soul has to take birth to fulfill its desires but till it takes birth, it keeps experimenting. It enters other bodies who are afflicted with the impulse of the same attraction as its own. If somebody is greedy, this attraction group/soul will enter that body and try experiencing great contentment, although it doesn't get content, but it still tries. This is a vicious cycle. In the end, one has to understand that contentment doesn't happen like this, this is not the way. You will never succeed till you understand this thing.

Chapter 11

What Is Mind? Is It Possible to Be Free from the Mind? Can the Mind Be Used Constructively in Sadhana?

Sadhaka: Pranaam Swamiji! What is 'mind'? What is the role of the mind in this entire journey of liberation? Do any feelings or experiences of the mind remain after leaving the body? Where are the mind and consciousness during sleep?

Swamiji: What is mind? Mind is the most mysterious puzzle – most mysterious! There are many things that come up with this. When we talk of the Supreme Essence, the Shiv Tattva, we are talking of the 'No Mind' state (Amani dasha) i.e. where the mind doesn't exist. The state opposite to this is a state which is ordinarily understood as the language of relativity. In the language of relativity, we use opposites to understand things, like there is a rock and a stone and they both are beyond mind. Neither the rock has a mind, nor the stone but the Supreme Essence is there. They both are beyond the mind. The mind taking birth amidst the 'no mind' is the divine play, the leela…the happening of the meta-physical as the physical is an Existential Expression.

There is one theory spoken of, that a thought arose in Paramatma's mind and the creation emerged. In other words, a mind took birth in Paramatma and from that mind, a universe was born. This is kind of a myth. This creation is an Existential happening…a way of the Supreme Essence itself happening. This is a movement, a dance of that Still and Unmoving Essence…a dance from which the creation is happening. No creator has created the universe – it is just a happening, an Existential Happening, a Self-Expression.

The quantum theory says the same thing that Shankaracharya says – everything is an illusion/maya. Things seem substantial but they are not 'substance'. The quantum theory also says that the molecular structures are not actually made of any molecules, they are only vibrations of a special wavelength moving under a certain principle and 'The Law' is in-built in them. There's no one separately making 'The Law'. The frequency and wavelength of the vibrations is fixed in its own way based on 'The Law' which is in-built. It is following a certain principle on which the molecular and atomic structures are functioning. It is due to this dance that the creation is happening. The dance is going on and the creation is happening. It's not as if there is a wall – the wall is happening. It's a lie when we say there's a mountain…the mountain is happening. Similarly, the earth, sun, moon, stars, everything is happening. Everything is happening and there 'is' nothing. There's nothing like 'is'. 'Is' means duality…yes, 'is' means duality.

There is duality when we say, there 'is' a mountain, there 'is' a river, there 'is' a tree. Duality becomes the truth when it is there and when duality is taken as truth, one has to live it. For living the duality, one has to interact. There are so many things to interact with, and for an interaction to happen there has to be a separate 'me' and a separate 'you'. Now, if an interaction has to happen with you, how will it happen? There must be some process for the interaction to take place. That process is the mind. For living a duality, one has to connect with others in some way to interact with them. The mind is born out of interaction. If you look very carefully, you'll notice a mild trace of mind even in the stone. Otherwise, I have told you that the stone and Paramatma are the same...they both are an Existential Happening if we go into their molecular structure and vibrations and also their frequency and wavelength in which 'The Law' is in-built. 'The Law' itself is the mind. Upon closer observation, you'll see that there's a principle and it is in-built. Nobody is making it. It's just the way in which it is happening, just like Anahad Naad is in-built in the Shiv Tattva, in the formless, infinite and limitless 'One'. Anahad Naad is the way Shiv Tattva is happening. It is not that there is a Shiv Tattva and some Anahad Naad stays in it. Shiv Tattva is happening as Anahad Naad.

Similarly, in the creation also 'The Law' is in-built. This principle is also called 'Rit'. Rit is the way of the creation happening. Rigveda is also coined from the word 'Rit' and 'Rit' is The Law. There was a Chinese saint called Lao Tse. He was the legendary founder of Taoism. Tao, it is said is the 'Rit'. It is 'The Law'. The principle is inbuilt in it. Creation is the way this principle, this Rit is happening. The mind is also merged in it. The unmoving, unshakeable, infinite is the metaphysical and when it gets expressed as movements and vibrational dance, it is then the physical.

The creation is the physical world and it is merged in 'The Law'. Looking deeply, you'll see there is a mind even in the stone; it experiences and is also living the duality. When the breeze hits it, it experiences something. It has a centre. It experiences something with the heat and cold. The experience is less because it is gross matter. Gross matter means the consciousness is in less measure in it. It doesn't mean there is no consciousness at all. Everything is consciousness and has emerged from consciousness. It is a dance of consciousness which means consciousness is present as everything. As the stone, consciousness is happening slowly and softly. The density of consciousness is less in it, so we say the density of the gross matter is more. The fluidity of consciousness is less and so the density of the gross matter is more but it is not devoid of consciousness. The development is happening and the development is of consciousness. When the stone breaks and splits into two, it lands up having two centres, two souls...one in each split part. They have some common shared experiences from when they were one.

We have some common shared experiences with the Sun because at some point, we were one. Later there was a huge blast which led to it breaking and shattering. All the planets went separate ways, yet a whole lot of pieces even today move around its orbit. Of the remaining, some of them went out of its orbit, so the relationship with them ended. But we all have shared experiences as a collective, with the Sun. With the earth separating from it, few experiences have shifted and changed. Two centres, two souls happened...one of the Earth and one of the Sun. Everything that exists will have a soul...it will have a centre. Centre means soul, soul means centre. An alliance of too many motions, too many movements, become dense and a centre gets formed. That centre is what organizes all that is dense...it is the centre that holds all the atoms and the entire structure together. If there was no centre, the stone would have broken into pieces. Why isn't it disintegrating? Reason is the centre and the gravitational force in it. There is a gravitational force of the earth but there's one of the stone as well. That is the reason it is held together. All substances will have a centre and the centre will have a gravitational force which is why the substance remains held together as one. The mind is inbuilt in 'The Law'. The mind is present as a separation and that is the leela. The stone is living its separation because of its one centre. This one centre is what is holding the limited area of the stone together and that's where its separation got decided. The centre keeps the limited substance in place and holds it together which leads to that substance having a mind and soul. 'There is a soul' means there's infinity and because of the centre there are experiences. Paramatma is infinity without a centre and Atma (soul) is the same infinity with a centre. This centre is interacting with the movements created by other centres and having experiences. These experiences are the reason for the mind's birth which in turn is leading to the separation getting stronger. Akashic records are being made because of continuous reflection that is happening on the 'separation' that is being lived. There are akashic records of the stones too. It's not just you, but stones also who have their akashic records. They also experience heat, cold, sunlight, shade, storms, breaking, disintegrating, everything because they have a centre in them. Where there's a centre, there are experiences. These experiences, these interactions will give birth to a mind in them. It is living a separation because of a centre and interactions that take place with other centres which gives birth to a mind. The akashic records will give birth to a mind. There will be comparative situations in them and the movements will adjust them well…they won't organize or arrange them but will adjust them properly. This adjusting gives rise to the mind. Akashic records are a lot and they keep getting updated and along with that the mind keeps getting updated because of loads of movements and loads of interactions that happen. You're sitting here and the five senses are bringing in some information or the other, isn't it? Something or the other is going on, movements are happening and so the mind is also getting updated. When that happens, the awareness of separation happens along with it.

An illusionary identity is born as 'I am something' because of the centre which is nothing but a collection of or a coming together of a whole lot of movements/vibrations. There is no centre as such but to take care of so many apparent movements, a centre happens under 'The Law'. There is literally no centre, but there is something like it that happens...it is there despite not being there, and this is the foundation of the leela that happens. This is the maya; that it is there despite not actually being there and is playing itself out. The illusionary identity thinks he is playing, whereas actually the play is happening and this is what one has to understand. He is deluded that he is doing it and that he is something. It is not so...it is the thousands of movements which are updating each other and in all this, he thinks he is doing something. Listen, the movements are getting updated on their own but within him, he feels he is doing something. This illusion that 'I am doing something' must get immersed and that is what sadhana is all about.

The fluidity of movements reaches this state, a state where it's now possible to understand it; the play has reached a stage where it can now be understood, the leela can be understood. This is the development and this is what being human is. Human being means the mind has reached its full potential, it's wholeness. When it reaches its state of wholeness and full potential, it means it can now get liberated. Freedom is of the mind. It can get liberated from itself, from its illusion, from its falsity, from the false identity that got created. That centre can get immersed and the play will get over. An illusory centre had got created and the play went on and now when the illusory centre gets immersed, the play will get over. That what was 'complete' had got deluded of being 'incomplete' and of being separate. It got deluded that it was small and wanted to protect its limitation. Isn't it funny? We fight for our pettiness and limitation; all our struggles happening for protecting the limitation that we ourselves are. How intelligent of us!! All the wisdom, all the exercises to protect our limitation and pettiness, to indicate that we are small!

Someone says, "don't you know who I am?" Okay, who are you or rather what are you? You have become a minister, fine, but you aren't Paramatma. You are a minister, not Paramatma. You say you're a minister and you're special. Does this indicate your rising or downfall? You are not Paramatma but an ordinary minister living in one dimension of the infinite. In the infinity of that dimension, you are living in one 'verse' which has another smaller 'verse' and within that, you then hold on to one small 'verse' and call it multiverse where you live. The multiverse has many small verses and you live in one small universe. This small universe has many galaxies and you stay in one small galaxy called the 'milky way'. Finding your details in this milky way is very difficult. With great difficulty, one locates that you stay in a small solar system and upon looking again, one finds that you live on a small planet called earth which is ten crore times smaller than the sun. If you break the sun into ten crore pieces, every piece will be found to be bigger than the earth. The distance between other planets is so huge that eleven thousand earths can fit within that distance, within that gap. In that small solar-system you live on a small planet called earth. Eighty percent of the earth is covered in water. The remaining twenty percent is land and of that land area, you live in one small country and you are a minister of some small state of that country. This is all imaginary. In that infinity, even the multiverse holds no value and the universe certainly has no value. In relation to the infinite, the value of multiverse is zero.

Let's consider that in relation to the multiverse, the value of the universe will be very less and in relation to universe, the value of the galaxy will be less and then the value of the milky way will be lesser than that, leading then to the value of the solar system to be lesser than the milky way. In the solar system the value of earth will be less and the country's value in which you live will be very less in comparison to the earth. Within that, the value of your state and your designation as a minister holds negligible value. Then to look for you in this country! Even if one tries to find you with a telescope, you won't be seen. If you are such a big minister, why aren't you seen? You are such a big minister, thousands of kilometers long and thousands of kilometers wide is your size, still you're not visible!?To this, they'll say, 'no, no, the minister doesn't stay in the entire area covering the country. He stays in one city.' Oh! So, he stays in a city. You go and look for him in the city, you'll come to know that he stays in one particular area of the city. You go to that area and find out that he stays in a small house. Look for him in the house and he's found in one room sitting on a small chair. Such a great minister sitting on a small chair in a corner of a small room in a small house situated in a small area of a city. How shameful is that! Come on! Wake up! Be aware! The mind is not giving birth to separation – the mind is separation. The mind is separation and this is the divine play. The mind is born because that's a part of the play, so what is the harm in playing the game! A game is going on and what is bad about a game?

There is a game going on; is there anything wrong in that? Answer comes as a 'no, there's nothing wrong' but they don't want to play because they get tired playing football. Listen, playing is joyful and there's a joy even in that tiredness. Play, play the game, there's no harm in playing provided you take the game as a game and play. You play the game believing it to be real. Today the games that are played involve a lot of mathematics. It's a matrix. It is all about how much profit is going to be made, building a team accordingly, winning etc. The players are given money, that's why they play. Playing games has become a career now. If it's a career, then there's ambition involved and if there's ambition then where's the game? It's a matrix, a calculative mindset there. A game should be treated like a game, for what it's worth – playing, but we make everything serious. Hello! It's a game, so just take it as a game and when you do that, the mathematics of it will get dissolved and the seriousness will end.

Seriousness is your belief that all the data, information and urges that you have are true, but actually they are not. There is no truth to anything! There are many games which children play like the one where one touches the other and that other is considered dead in the game. He is asked to sit out after that, "you're dead, you're dead, I touched you, you're dead...look everyone, he's dead, I touched him...you go out and sit now." Is that other fellow actually dead? He knows that being called out dead doesn't actually mean he's dead. It just means he has to leave the game for now and sit out. Then when the game begins all over again, he comes back to participate in the game and starts playing again...he's alive again. It's a game and if you take the game very seriously, you'll suffer a lot...you'll be in great trouble. Now, the child in the game went aside and sat calmly after being proclaimed dead in the game. Then something happens and he's called back again, "come, come, join the game… you're alive again." He gets back into the game and starts playing. You see the games children play!? If you take the game just as a game, then there's no problem.

Now, to answer your question about the mind – what is mind and why? Mind is a 'problem', that's the reason you're chasing it. Mind is a problem. Who is the mind? You are the mind! Who is asking the question? Mind is asking the question. Who wants to understand? It is the mind again who wants to understand. Whom does the mind want to understand? The mind wants to understand the mind. If the mind wants to understand the mind, then what is the mind? Mind is the base of a game, for example, in the game of cricket, there's a bat, ball, stumps, umpire, batsman and a baller. Similarly, the mind is akin to a playground where this system, this game is being played. If you take the game as just a game, you will then be the knower of the game. You have become so involved in the game that you aren't able to witness the game.

What is the problem? You not being able to see the game is the problem and that's the reason you are the mind. The reason behind saying, 'you are the mind' is that you are so serious in the game that for you the game is not happening as a game. For you, the game is real. it is true for you. You taking the game to be true gives birth to a player and the player goes through emotions of sadness, happiness. You see how the players become sad when they lose. That's because they have taken the game too seriously. There are matches of cricket and volleyball that are going on. The team that lost was pelted with stones when they reached their country. They become serious and take the game so seriously that winning and losing stands true for them. The team that loses and comes, faces the wrath of the people and the team that wins and comes is adorned with garlands of flowers. If a team faces defeat and comes, it has to hide when it reaches the country, players need security to protect them or else people will hit them and break their legs. What did they do? They took the game too seriously and that became a big problem.

If the game is taken seriously by a player, then calling him a player won't be right. A player is one who stays present in the game for the fun of the game and not as a professional. They are called professional players. A new word should be coined in place of 'player', to be used along with professional. Instead of professional player…it should be professional 'something else'! They should not be called players. Player is someone who doesn't take anything seriously. He takes the game as a game. Those little innocent kids playing in the lanes of the villages are players…here they play and there they forget! They don't carry any burden of the game and move around. There's no record maintained of that game. It is these professional games for which the records are maintained…this year, this date, this stadium, these teams played against each other, this player made these many runs etc. The entire record is maintained. You are distressed because of the records that have been maintained! You play the game and keep the records and that is what I call the subconscious mind. You are playing the game and playing it seriously, then the records have to be maintained. The records of wins and losses have to be maintained. These records are what I call the subconscious mind, patterns, sanskaras and they are the problem.

The mind comprises of conscious mind and unconscious mind. Conscious mind is one that doesn't keep any records. If you're fully conscious and playing a game, no records are made. Look at children. They are so alive. How wonderfully they play in the village lanes, and look at those professional players who are playing only to maintain records…these many runs should be made, a goal has to be hit, I should hit a goal etc. They have the money in mind – the money they will earn from playing. Haven't you seen how angry they get when they lose? They hit the bat on the ground and look so remorseful. They are completely stressed after the loss. Hence, if you play seriously, it will land you in a messy situation.

Subconscious mind is the bondage. It is the obstacle and a loop. It is the bondage we have created. If you play like those village children who are absolutely alive and conscious when playing, then you'll be happy if you lose and happy if you win. A game is for enjoying and they're playing for enjoyment. If a game is played seriously which creates tension, that's not a game. This is the illusion that has been created. You're playing seriously and the mind is getting created. A game is joy in itself and it will be a joy if it's not taken seriously.

Why is this divine play happening? What was the need for Paramatma to create the universe, do this play and entangle us in it? Paramatma is playing, he is not serious, the play is happening. It's an eternal game. He is enjoying the seriousness and the separation. Take the game as nothing other than a game. When you take the game as a game, what will happen? You will awaken, you will be a witness. A witness is always conscious...is there anything like a sleeping witness? No, there is nothing like a sleeping witness. Just witness the play and your jump has happened! The game is for enjoying, the creation is for enjoying and the separation is also for enjoying. You took it seriously and that's the reason you got entangled. All this entanglement is of seriousness.

You've got entangled because you are serious. If you stop being serious, the world cannot have a hold over you, you won't get caught up in it. When no world exists, then it's a game. It's because of your seriousness that the world has happened. The world is your imagination, and your seriousness creates the world. Your seriousness creates the mind...what is the world? Your mind, your matrix, your mental mathematics, your data, your akashic records is the world. If you drop the seriousness in one shot, the play will be over and you won't be left with any records. You won't have to run around unnecessarily keeping records. There won't remain any need to be active as a doer. Where there's calculations and records to be maintained, doer is needed. If the seriousness is immersed, then there's no need for any calculations or records. There is no need for a doer then. The seat is empty, there is nobody, there is no need for anybody. Why will you pay a salary for him to sit then? Why will you nurture him? There is no work left, so bid it adieu, remove him from the job, there is no vacancy, there is absolutely no need left. You are the problem who keeps calculating…you are the doer. You are the problem. If you stop the mental mathematics, you'll dissolve. Who then remains? That which is ever present eternally remains. It doesn't have to come from anywhere. It just is, forever. That which is an eternal witness keeps knowing the game, rather the knowing keeps happening. He is the play as well as the knowing of the play Himself. He is not two, although He is the play and the seer, that is the reason I say that the 'witness' must also go. With 'witness' it seems as if there's a witness who is watching the play, so the witness (sakshi) must also go. There is a game and it is being known or seen. This emits a smell of duality, of conflict. It may not be serious, it may be neutral, yet it is there. Why should it be there? 'Being there' is the problem, it contracts you making you smaller plus 'being there' means there is a centre and centre is a problem.

'There is a centre' means there will be other centres as well, which further means that there will be interactions between the centres. There will be some problems and issues with this. Hence the 'witness' must go for the Supreme Essence to shine through…once the knots in the consciousness and in the mind open, what remains is the Supreme Essence. When there are knots in consciousness, there is mind, there is mathematics and there are records. When the knots open, only consciousness shines. There is nothing separate as the mind; mind is the knots on the surface of consciousness. It is the waves on the ocean and irrespective of what we think or say, the waves are the ocean itself. Waves are not separate from the ocean, how much ever we may delude ourselves. The waves move, whatever the speed maybe, but everything is still in the depths of the ocean. In the depths of the ocean everything is absolutely still and that is the play of the ocean. This game is a play of the ocean itself. Waves are a play of the ocean happening on the surface; in the depths, the ocean itself is happening as the stillness. When you dive deep within yourself, the realization of the True Self, the realization of the Essential Nature happens…'Nishchal Tattvam, Jeevan Mukti'.

Sadhaka: Does the mind experience anything after leaving the body?

Swamiji: Why will the mind not have experiences when the body alone has left without the mind dissolving? If the body has left and the mind hasn't, then the mind will go through experiences. The mind also should withdraw. The withdrawal of mind means the opening of the knots. When those open, the mind remains no more. That is the state of 'no mind', the 'amani dasha'. Mind is nothing but the conjoining of the knots - urges, obstinacy, should and should nots, I am this, I am that, don't you know who I am and so on. What is all this? Association with names and forms, desires, being pertinacious etc. – are these true or false? All these conflicts belong to duality. The thread is one in which the knots have come and that makes one believe that knots are separate from the thread. You can tie as many knots in the same thread and every knot feels it is separate. It doesn't consider itself to be the thread but takes itself to be a knot and when the knots open, they vanish…the thread comes back to its natural state.

Mind is there even when the body leaves and it is the mind which travels. It is these insistences which travel and because of the separation and seriousness, these insistences and urges have become serious. This is right, this is wrong, this is true, this is false, like this, not like this…things have become very serious. The knots are there because of seriousness. You become simple and the knots will open on their own. They'll open in such a way that you won't even come to know. It is in being simple and natural that the knots open on their own. Seriousness is the problem and the journey is of the knots. The insistences, urges and obstinacies are what take birth again. They have to prove themselves again and again, and for that they have to do something. Whether it's for things to happen a certain way or for things not to happen a certain way, they'll have to do something. For doing things, the separation will have to be strengthened. A body is also needed for 'doing'. You will take another body and stay stuck in the loop of coming and going. Who takes birth? Fools! Who are we? Fools! That is the reason we are sitting here.

I remember Ramanand Ji Maharaj from Omkareshwar for this reason. He had come to the sacred place of the Amarkantak pilgrimage and I was also staying there. We met there and during some discussions he said to me, "Maharaj ji, you are also a fool and I am also a fool." I asked him to open this up a bit more. Ramanand Maharaj ji said, "Look, you are also present and I am also present. Our presence is the result of our foolishness. We are living the separation, that is the reason we are here. Why did we take birth? We are fools, that's why we have taken birth. If we weren't fools, wouldn't we be liberated? Why have we worn this body? Because we are fools!" So, what is it that takes birth? Foolishness! What is foolishness? Seriousness, insistence, stubbornness, these are all foolishness. That is why it has been said that knowledge liberates. Now, in the name of knowledge, there is information that is given out after rote learning... will you call it knowledge? This is a huge knot in the name of knowledge. It is such a knot that will make the school bag really fat. One will have to do 'A for apple, B for boy' repeatedly. Knowledge is that where the knots open. That which opens the knots is knowledge, wisdom and that which tightens the knots is ignorance.

Sadhaka: Where are the mind and consciousness during sleep state and dream state?

Swamiji: Look, it is the mind that becomes the dream. Mind is all the desires, insistences, urges, obstinacy and all that you want to do in the practical life but are not able to. All of what you aren't able to do in your practical life, you start doing in your dreams. The insistence to do is so fierce that if you have an issue with a person you want to break his legs, but he is so strong that you might land up with broken legs in his place. You are so filled with aversion and anger towards him and your insistence is so strong that you wind up doing so in your dream. You become a super power and a super man in your dream and break his legs and beat him up thoroughly. There are lakhs of things which you want to do in your practical life but you can't and so you keep doing them in your dream state. You are the mind and you want to do. The insistence to 'do' is the mind and you doing it is the dream. Dream is the mind and mind is the dream!

Where is consciousness? It is upon waking up that you know dreams had come, it is upon waking up that you know you slept well, it is upon waking up that you know you did not sleep well. But is it 'you' who comes to know all this? The knower is that consciousness which knows everything. It knows your seriousness, it knows your simplicity, it knows all your good and all of your bad! When it comes to consciousness, knowing is a happening...it just happens to know. To know is the nature of consciousness. It is neutral so it can't do anything, but 'to know' is its nature. It doesn't do anything - in fact it cannot do anything but knowing is its nature. It knows not through effort but without effort. Its nature is 'effortless knowing'. It has been knowing everything since eternity. Consciousness is forever knowing and dream is the mind. Mind is actually nothing, it transforms into your dream and when you wake up, it becomes your thoughts.

When you wake up, it turns into your thought and 'you' then happen to be a dream. Sometimes it is the dreams of sleep state and sometimes it is dreams of 'you'. You are living in a dream and flowing in its current. Dream is a current and you are something that flows and continuously changes. You feel, that what is changing is the authority and you believe that to be yourself – an illusory authority at that! What is your true authority, true power? 'Nishchal Tattvam, Jeeven mukti' is your being! But your identity has become a separate 'I' with your flowing. You say that the flowing river is 'you'. Do you understand?

To sleep is to become serious towards the play of consciousness. When consciousness gets involved and entangled in the play, it arrives at a particular state where sleep happens to take over. You say you are awake. It is utter rubbish...you and awake!? You are either sleeping on the bed or you get off the bed and start walking in your sleep. It is in your sleep that you go and do your job, in your sleep you get married and in your sleep itself you give birth to children. The confused state of consciousness is 'sleep' which is the result of consciousness getting entangled in the play.

Do not think that you are awake. You, who are doing all your tasks in sleep, are not awake. You spend a portion of your sleep time on bed and the rest of it moving around, eating and drinking. You spend it doing something and that is why I say that sadhana should be of twenty-four hours. Be aware while eating. You eat in your sleep - your mind is somewhere else, thinking of something else. You are not in the 'here and now'. You live either in the past or the future and that is what sleep is – swinging back and forth from past to future is 'sleep'. Being in the 'here and now' is being awake. Awakening is to 'be' here and now and that is why I say while eating food, be the food, be the 'eating' of the food. Leave all the mental activities and become one with the food. Food will then be Paramatma. It is 'Him' alone, there is no second, no other. You 'be' one with the food and all duality, all of the matrix will drop. When duality drops, then we are eating Paramatma as no difference then remains between us, food and Paramatma. Paramatma is merging in Paramatma; duality ends and you are one. Sleep is the matrix. The immersion of all matrix is to awaken and awakening is liberation. Awakening means 'Supreme Consciousness". Wake up so that the lamp of consciousness can burn. Sadhana is of Supreme Consciousness but you are still in sleep. Here too, you are sitting half asleep and I'm trying to break your sleep. I'm trying to wake you up, 'Jaago Mohana pyaare!' I'm trying to shake you out of your sleep and you say, 'wait, it's a beautiful dream I'm seeing'. You say something is going to work out for you from the dream, so you want it to continue and that you'll wake up later. You postpone your waking up from the dream, you've been postponing it for so many lifetimes on the pretext of seeing this dream wherein something is going to work out for you.

Osho used to tell this story with Mulla Nasruddin as the character of the story. Mulla Nasruddin was sleeping, with his wife sleeping beside him. Mulla Nasruddin was talking as if speaking to someone, "no, no, I won't agree on this much. I will take a hundred gold coins and not ninety-nine. One more gold coin, I won't agree on ninety-nine, I won't", he was lying on his bed and screaming in his sleep. The wife shakes him up from sleep and he gets very upset with her and tells her that she has made him lose a big deal that he was on the verge of finalizing. The deal had reached its final stage of negotiation when she intervened. He calls her foolish for having harmed the business negotiation that was about to close. He then goes and lies down on the bed and closes his eyes, trying to get the dream to come back. When that didn't happen, he started screaming, "okay fine, I agree. You can give me ninety-nine, I don't want hundred. Ninety-nine will do, you can give me ninety-nine gold coins" and he started moving his hands and legs vigorously. Then he said, "he's not even giving me ninety-nine. You spoilt the deal. You always spoil things for me. This is such a huge damage. I was going to receive a hundred gold coins but have lost out on the ninety-nine also that was being agreed upon. I wish something had come my way. If not hundred, at least the ninety-nine should have come."

You dream catchers! Do you go and put the money you earn in your dreams in the bank or not? Does the banker accept it? Which banks do you visit? The government banks, the private banks, do they accept that money? If you earn money in your dream and you go and tell the banks that you have earned one crore rupees and that they should deposit that money in their bank, will they agree? Obviously not! What kind of a matrix are you in? What do you want to achieve in the dream? Where will you invest the profit from what you've earned in your dream? You are so involved in your dream. Your whole life is a dream and you on the other hand are exercising towards achieving something. In this dream life of yours, whatever you earn, be it money, status, knowledge, where are you going to save it? Do you have any such bank which is going to remain permanently with you? Where has all that you had earned in your past life gone? Why don't you disclose those records? Do you have the earnings from the past life with you? Is there anything from the past life? All this hard work, effort and energy to earn is ultimately for what? Look at your whole life – it is nothing more than a dream. Look at it carefully. It is a dream and there's no truth to it. Everything is connected to each other just like a boat and the river come together. Everything gets separated ultimately, whether its people, relationships, wealth, properties, investments, bodies, assets, everything.

Chapter 12

This World Is a Dream: Science of Dreams and Their Importance in Psychology and Spiritual Practices

Sadhaka: Gurudev namaskar! Not only sadhakas but a lot many people want to know about dreams since everyone gets dreams. There are different types of dreams and today we want to know what dreams are. What is the mystery behind dreams and what is their importance in our life? Is there any connection of the dreams to our past, our past lives or future?

Here I would like to share one or two dreams that I had. One dream is about me visiting some place and when I come out, I realize my footwear has gone missing. It seems as if I get this dream often although I'm not sure of it. There's another dream where I see myself having gotten off a train on a platform to get water but I miss the train and I see myself running to catch the train.

What is the mystery behind the dreams that we see? Do they hold any meaning for a meditator or indicate towards something?

Swamiji: The science of dreams is very vast and one session will prove short for it. We'll take some key points related to this topic. Even animals dream and it has been proved through experiments. Human beings get more dreams because the mind has merged in them. The meaning of mind is calculations and mathematics – how it tries to adjust the circumstances and situations to suit itself, the mind's planning to modify them so that they fit well according to what it wants, it even tries to manipulate circumstances which are beyond its control in its own favor. Time along with a future is born for these adaptations and adjustments to take place. Past memories are required for these to take place because for any kind of planning, past data and information is needed. There's a lot of madness in this era of data and information. This technology of information and data is growing at a fast pace and since the mind is also full of data, that's the reason I say that mind's presence itself is nothing short of madness. Which mind should we talk of? The mind which runs automated?

One is the conscious mind which we make use of when need be and make use of the available data. Actually, the meaning of mind that has been established now is based on the subconscious mind, for example when we say 'my mind is like this, my mind is like that, my mind has become like this' etc. these are all related to the subconscious mind. We talk only of the subconscious mind and nothing of the conscious mind. There's very little conscious mind present and I say that ninety percent is the subconscious mind and just ten percent of conscious mind is present in individuals. What is happening now is that there is an increase in zombies with ninety-two, ninety-three, ninety-four percent of subconscious mind operating and only five or six percent of the conscious mind functioning. Zombies means that the conscious mind is reducing.

One thing for sure is that the subconscious mind is perfect in executing the tasks once it has been trained and programmed. This program works well every time it's needed for execution of the task, just like a software works perfectly every time it is used because it has already been made once. Similarly, the patterns of the subconscious mind keep working once they have been made. But in this case the patterns keep getting updated for example when some other patterns come to support a particular pattern when needed, it gets updated. This keeps getting updated automatically, unlike other software which you need to update. The data and information in the subconscious mind is present since lifetimes. Whatever has happened ever since the separation began has left impressions. All those impressions on every centre of every unit that you were ever present as, have become memories and are present as akashic records...each and every one of them, whatever unit you were ever present as, be it a stone or anything else. These akashic records have been there and continue to be there with every split. There have been too many births and too much of information. Now, talking of sadhana, the data which is useless gets deleted automatically and that which is important remains, with the understanding that this is stored and this isn't you, nor are they your experiences. This information is available for use as and when you need it, and that it is not in any way relate to the 'I', to the pure being that I am. The understanding that this is related to the external superficiality, to the physical reality and not to the Supreme Truth is sadhana. As this sadhana progresses, dreams will keep getting lesser and their complexity will keep reducing. When we are going into sadhana, what happens is that we get more dreams or so it seems. It seems that the dreams have increased, we're getting more disturbed and the restlessness is increasing. One could sleep well earlier but with the disturbance due to the dreams, one isn't able to go into deep sleep. Certain dreams are coming repeatedly which means that awareness is increasing and you're getting to know the dreams. Everyone gets dreams and zombies and buddhas use the same language. I don't get any dreams but a sadhaka who is on a journey from being a zombie to being a buddha says that his dreams have increased because of which he is getting restless, with some dreams coming repeatedly. To be free from dreams, one has to re-live them consciously, with full awareness and once so done, the lesson gets complete. The lesson gets over once the dream is re-lived with full awareness and full acceptance.

Let the shoes get stolen, just accept it. It is only in the dream that they have got stolen, accept it and let it go. It's not necessary that it has to do anything with this life. It hasn't happened in this reality, it probably is coming from some past life where shoes must have been very important and to buy shoes again must not have been that easy. These days if you lose your shoes, you just have to order them online and they're arranged for within a couple of hours or a temporary arrangement can be made within no time. This incident you see in your dream belongs to a time when shoes must have been important and to arrange for them must be difficult. It must be those times where you had to travel fifty or a hundred kilometers far and the thought of losing the shoes in case you removed them must be playing in your mind because if that happened, then to arrange for a pair must be very difficult for you. Even if you ordered, the shoemaker would probably ask you to wait for a few days till he made them. Whatever it was, you have to relive it or else you won't be free from it. Hence, the dreams that sadhakas see have to be relived with full awareness and a state of mind which is fully accepting of them.

What can a sadhaka do for this? Make use of the methods for cleansing that have been provided. They must be applied in the daytime as well as the nights so that the dreams reduce. It's important to live with awareness throughout the day, whether one is eating, drinking, working, dealing with people or doing any other activity in daily life. As of now, we're living unconsciously like zombies. Everything is just happening unconsciously and so the more we live consciously through the day, our awareness extends into the night and we're conscious even at night, so night meditations must also happen. Even Osho has emphasized on this because the nights are long. If you manage the initial stage of the night, come into a meditative state and then leave yourself and your body completely, the entire night can be meditative. Even after lying down, sleep comes in layers and not at once. The first layer comes, then the second, the third followed by a fourth one and you have to be aware towards them. One layer comes and the body at that level sleeps but 'you' are awake. The second layer comes and you might get lost with it but with repeated practice, there'll come a time when the second layer comes and you'll be awake, knowing the second layer of sleep. Slowly, it will so happen that you'll be aware and awake when the third layer of sleep visits, and finally when you're aware with the coming of the fourth layer of sleep, it's done. If you're awake when the fourth layer of sleep comes, the jump is made.

This is what Patanjali says about the consciousness being awake; the body is asleep but you are awake. Krishna also says, 'The whole world sleeps but the yogi stays awake'. Since even Shri Krishna says the same thing, it's worth experimenting. But you don't have to be tense or take any stress, nor do you have to get disturbed since this is also a part of cleansing. When there is sadhana in a sadhaka's life, the dreams perform the act of cleansing for him. For an ordinary man, dreams act as a catharsis; whatever incidents he has gone through during the day and hasn't been able to speak about or speak up for himself, get released as dreams. The emotions like anger that he's held onto and doesn't know where to remove them, they get released as dreams and those incidents get a closure. But dreams come repeatedly if the closure doesn't happen.

There are many incidents from past lives, therefore remembering past lives helps. I have shared the technique for this where you keep going back daily. Going back and reliving the incidents brings about a closure to things. You have to start the technique from where you are right now and inching backwards scene by scene, as in, if you're in your bed at night and doing this, you'll travel backwards from where you are now, going back towards morning, recollecting every scene like pulling the quilt, lying on the bed etc. You will fall asleep within fifteen to twenty minutes once you begin doing it. Within a week you'll realize you're going back five-six hours and within a month's practice, you'll be able to reach backwards till that morning easily. Then one day, it will so happen that you will enter your dreams. Once you enter the dream, the next day you'll realize your speed has increased. Then a time will come when you'll remember a month's incidents in one hour. Later this will increase to recalling incidents of one whole year in one hour and then incidents of ten-twenty years in an hour. If you're seventy years of age, you'll go back recalling your full seventy years in half an hour or one hour. Whatever your age maybe, whether sixty-five, sixty-eight or seventy, you'll relive your full life backwards in one hour. If you're reliving your experiences with full awareness, your speed of seeing increases because whatever is being relived, its sting gets over and the obstacle gets cleared. Once the blockage gets cleared, it doesn't keep you stuck there anymore. When you're not stuck anymore, you travel back in speed. Travelling fast, one reaches one's childhood and your life starts feeling lighter, you become lighter. After this, dreams become very less and you'll enter your mother's womb and then the past lives appear close to you and things become very light. You may find it difficult in the beginning. You may have to observe silence to settle down with all that's going on. You'll have to let it settle down. A whole lot of new data will come in; going on reliving them constantly, much of it will get cleared. Reliving is important because it is through reliving that blockages get cleared. The memories also get cleared and they don't become dreams.

If you don't live something properly, you'll have to live it again. You'll have to live it again, be it in dreams or in some other way. That's why it is said that life should be lived authentically. There are no memories or records made if life is lived authentically. If any record is made, it is bound to come through using dreams as the medium. Sadhana is the sadhana of cleansing and clearing. Lord Buddha made people do vipassana which is being carried forward by Satyanarayan Goenka Ji who is not physically present anymore but he has given the world a very well-established system that he put in place before leaving the body. In vipassana also you'll see that a tool was first created for paying attention. That tool is not dhyana. Ana pana sati yog is not dhyana but a tool. A tool was developed for attention and not for concentration. It seems like concentration. A tool for paying attention was created and using this attention, a journey is made in the body. With the journey being made in the body, the sanskaras start getting excited and show up as sensations. The sensations are happening and once they're witnessed, you move on. Where there are no sensations felt, one stops there, which means there is something over there that is keeping you stuck and the moment sensations are felt you move on again. This is the sanskaras coming up. Initially when we do this, it's like a rotation. In a one-hour session, we may find that just half a round has happened whereas for some, four or five rounds would have happened. Ten rounds happen in some cases. With consistent practice, it so happens that one round gets completed in two-three minutes and then it comes down to one minute...one round of the entire body happening in one minute.

This includes going into each and every finger, finger nails and tips, not excluding any part of the body. There should be movement in the entire body with complete awareness and it does start happening in one minute. Then it starts happening a hundred times in one minute. Soon it starts vibrating in one second just like lakhs of vibrations that happen in a molecular structure with which maya gets created, but this happens at a speed leading to the understanding that 'I am not this substance'. When it starts happening at that speed, then all mysteries unfold. This process is similar...the vibrations become absolutely clear and you can then unfold this science beautifully.

It is in this way that this journey towards liberation happens. Reliving and cleansing are the only two options. To be free from dreams, one has to relive them. Today there is a term coined for this and has become a big business known as 'past life regression'. Why has this taken the form of a business? You are taken back in time and made to relive things where you're stuck but this technique is being misused a lot. Ninety-nine percent of individuals who are involved in this business of past life regression are not worthy of this nor capable enough. There's a lot of damage happening because of the way it is being done. Imagination is being used whereas there is no role that imagination can play in this process. I heard that people are asked to imagine things like mountains etc. and are asked to feel things. They are going the wrong way with this. They are going into imagination. I'm talking of reliving and reliving is no imagination. Reliving is the bitter truth being presented back to you as it is. If I see myself being murdered during the reliving, I'm going to live that murder all over again. Whether it's anything disturbing, be it an accident or a rape that a lady has gone through, one has to live it again with full awareness and not try to save oneself. If it's a murder, you have to live it fully all over again with the body writhing in pain, whether the incident has happened in this life or a past life. You will have to live the incidents one hundred percent. Only then will those incidents dissolve and get cleared, with no impressions left behind. The impressions have to be made zero so that you aren't stuck with them for lifetimes. Impressions are very strong so they must go completely since they're capable of holding you back. They're not just any floppy, they're akashic records and any amount of data can get added to them, so we have to clear all records, all data. We have to clear the more obvious ones which are keeping us stuck. We now realize that data will be there and will keep getting fed but the wisdom has to get developed that 'I am not this data', and this doesn't happen easily. This wisdom isn't born easily.

That is the reason 'neti-neti' is a great mantra. My family, my country, my caste, my religion, my party etc. are the very obvious identifications one lives with. You keep unfolding and so many more folders will come out, folders after folders. Hence, the importance of 'neti-neti', 'I am not this, I am not this'. The connection between name and form is just like the chance meeting or a happening between a river and a boat. With this understanding that 'I'm not this name and form', a sadhaka is born. As the identification with the name and form keeps breaking, the sadhaka keeps growing in wisdom and intelligence. It is only after this happens that the sadhaka's journey of Buddhatva, of wisdom, of liberation, of final emancipation, of Supreme state begins.

Paltu says, 'Ajhun chet ganvaar, sapna yeh sansaar', which means the whole world is a dream. You are living a dream, aren't you? What else are you doing? Why talk of only the dreams that come when asleep? What you're living is the dreams...you are living the dreams; all of the relative truth and apparent reality you're living is related to dreams, so live them like an artist, a performer. Whatever you do in this world, whether it is work related to dealing with people, relations, education, career, are all dreams. What else are they? They are dreams, dreams within the dreams, dreams ahead of dreams and dreams behind dreams...like that riddle, 'teetar ke do aage teetar, teetar ke do peeche teetar, aage teetar, peeche teetar, bolo kitne teetar?' We can say so about dreams too, but just that they aren't only two-three in number...two dreams ahead of the dreams and two behind, two on the left and two on the right, It's dreams and dreams all the way.

Therefore, witnessing everything as if a dream is going on is the greatest method. Witnessing the eating of a meal with complete awareness that it's a dream, going to work being conscious that it is a dream, going for a wedding knowing it's a dream; all of it with the knowing that a theatrical play is going on, a drama is happening, drama of a job, drama of marriage, drama of all that is going on. Everything is a dream and know the dreams as dreams. When you know the dreams as dreams, you'll be free from them. Remembering this one precept is enough that when a dream is recognized to be a dream, the dream shatters. For example, you're regular with the sadhana of awareness like a night meditation or some other methods, then while asleep if a dream comes and is recognized as a dream, it will not continue any further. Dream will then just be a utilitarian tool. All the physical experiences of this world are a dream. We don't have to take dreams so seriously.

Sadhaka: Swamiji, many people say that dreams come of use for cutting karmas. Does it happen that we go through the suffering of a karma in the dream? Are dreams helpful in dissolving the karmas of past lives?

Swamiji: I have said it innumerable times that karmic bonds can break with dreams provided awareness is maintained. Those who get connected to the dreams more and are troubled by them, it means karmic ties are breaking in those cases. But karmic ties do not break in cases where the individual doesn't even come to know of them and the dreams just pass away. Something does break though with the dreams, however unconscious an individual may be. Some kind of a reliving of the karmic ties does happen. One cannot see dreams in a state of one hundred percent unconsciousness. Some level of consciousness is there but it is so slow paced that nothing is really going to happen in that case. The other thing is that one must never open their eyes or move even slightly when the dream breaks. The sleep state of the body must continue. Although you have woken up and have come to know that it's a dream which results in the breaking of the dream, let the body continue sleeping, as in, do not associate with the body immediately upon waking up. You are there and you know there was a dream which has broken, which means there is a you and there is a body which is asleep. The breaking of the dream means that the flow of the mind has broken, the chain of the mind has broken. With the mind not being there, your body lying somewhere and you being present and aware, experiences of beyond the mind and body then happen. The 'no-mind' and 'no-body' leaves only the witness consciousness which is aware of the body; rather the knowing of the body is happening, to put it correctly. There is no effort in this knowing, the body is just being known. This is a very beautiful happening.

Sadhaka: I don't get many dreams, I rarely do. If at all they come, I don't remember them. Why is that so?

Swamiji: You must increase your sadhana so that the frequency of dreams increases. By increasing I mean you should be able to see them. Dreams come throughout the night but you aren't able to see them because of lack of awareness which is why they do not become a memory. Increase your sadhana so that there remains memory of them and you realise that a dream is going on.

Sadhaka: Guruji, for the past five-six years I've been seeing snakes a lot in my dreams. What does this mean?

Swamiji: If this is happening, you must find that video where I have spoken on this and have mentioned that snakes are not harmful. Snakes are lovely beings and you must go and live in places where they exist. You must live in such places and make friends with them. Stay with the snake friends and caress them, stroke them gently and slowly learn to take them in your hands. As you do this and your friendship with them grows, a lot of dreams related to snakes will stop. This is a very easy way because this problem is actually not a very big problem. In addition, you'll benefit a lot from making friends with a lovely being of nature. You caressing them and holding them in your hands may seem difficult in the beginning, but a whole lot of cleansing will happen with it. When I was small, a lot of fear was instilled in me with regards to ghosts. There were a lot of lions where I lived and the number of tigers was huge, maximum in the whole world. Leopards were there too. I was fed a lot of fear in the name of leopards and tigers because of which I had difficulties in the beginning since I was still small. But I would be there in the jungle with the mountains and river with this thought that even if a tiger comes in front what can I possibly do? I would sit quietly...there's the tiger and knowing of the tiger as the tiger is happening. Whatever happens will be seen then! What will it do? Now, the tiger was watching me and I was watching the tiger. I wasn't doing anything to the tiger, neither was the tiger doing anything to me. 'Why am I scared?' and when I stopped fearing, I relaxed completely. Once relaxed, I thought why am I standing, I should sit and whatever has to happen will be seen when it happens. That was when I realized that the tiger has nothing to do with me. It just wants to drink water and go somewhere. Slowly, such things started taking leave from my mind. What is really harmful is the fear. Post this incident, I kept sitting in the jungles till late at nights. During dhyana, there would be a leopard sitting close by at times and sometimes it would be a tiger. When I would be adjusting myself, it would do the same. We would sit next to each other casually even in the middle of the night, at about one or one thirty. I would get up for a stroll and they would walk as well. Living with the wild life made me understand that the fears have all been unnecessarily and consciously created.

One is a suspension in the vehicles which helps them to run smoothly and the other is the axle which is used to run the bullock cart. Fear is that axle which balances that vehicle in totality. You keep fearing, fear of this and fear of that. Dreams related to excitement are more than others, with lust and desires falling under this category.

Being wealthy is a kind of excitement and being poor is a kind of fear. Dreams are mainly created out of these two emotions of excitement and fear, which play a role in keeping the dreams alive and maintaining them.

Chapter 13

Can One Guru Be Replaced for Another? Is There Any Harm in Changing Gurus?

Sadhaka: Pranaam Swamiji, can we get associated or connected to another guru when we already have one? A feeling of guilt arises in people who want to go under the guidance of another guru. Why does this pull or attraction happen towards another guru? Kindly explain.

Swamiji: A guru may or may not be perfect and it could be that he is not in resonance with you, but it could also be that you are not entirely in resonance with him. Your way of flowering may be different and it's possible that the guru is not able to help you reach there. In the olden times, there used to be Zen masters. If the masters noticed that some of the disciples had stopped progressing beyond a point, they would send those disciples to another master or guru. They would provide the name of the master to the disciple and send him off, saying that he had progressed as far as he could with him and that it was time for him to move on to another master who can help him further. Wishing him well, the guru would divert him elsewhere so that he wouldn't waste his time with no further progress happening.

The reason for the attraction building up towards another guru could be because of the energies of the esoteric system or even the energy of the guru himself pushing you towards another guru since your growth is meant to happen there now. Hence you must first express gratitude to him, express immense gratitude to the guru you are currently connected with. Thank him for helping you reach this stage you are at, and for being open and encouraging towards your attraction for another guru where your sadhana will progress.

What is important is that sadhana has to be taken forward and complete liberation must happen, enlightenment must happen. If you see, more than ninety percent of people coming to me already have a guru but they are coming here and there's nothing wrong in it. The one and only important thing is that enlightenment must happen at the end of the day. One must be free from all defilements because it is the defilements that give rise to the chain of cause and effect, so wherever there is the possibility of dissolving the causal series of these defilements, one has to go there. They must have had experiences and benefited where they were connected earlier but the progress had stopped and to move ahead, another engine was needed. These shifts have to be made sometimes and there's nothing wrong in it.

There's certainly nothing wrong in it although there are certain foolish things that are said, like a guru and disciple relationship is like that of a husband and wife. They are inseparable and one should not betray or abandon the guru. But there is nothing like that, in fact some sadgurus push their disciples out themselves when they realise that he is not going to progress any further while staying with them. They ask them to leave and wander elsewhere. Wherever he's meant to progress, he'll reach there existentially, naturally. Whatever level they are meant to reach, they will reach. When the guru sees that the individual is not going to benefit further with him, he pushes the disciple out so that he doesn't waste his life there. This body is an opportunity and the flowering must happen within this opportunity. If that is not happening with a disciple and if the soil and water of that place aren't proving suitable and beneficial for him, he is asked to leave and find another piece of land where the soil and water will suit him and benefit him. His life shouldn't go waste. It doesn't make a difference to the sadguru when this happens, he doesn't have a problem. The sadhakas will have a problem when this happens with them because of the influence they are under. These things keep happening and you don't have to worry so much about it.

If an attraction is happening, reach there and your journey will progress from there. It must progress. One has to dissolve completely; enlightenment has to happen and there's still a long way to go. Don't get fooled by the mind and its commentary...this has happened in this place, now that has happened etc...lots of 'ifs' and 'buts' will raise their heads, but you don't fall for them. These things happen a lot. Your own relatives, your guru brothers and sisters, those following the same guru or for that matter, even the common man might say that you're wrong and will question your actions, but remember there is nothing like wrong and right. Who decides what is right and what is wrong? One has to see and decide for oneself whether your journey is on track or not. Living somewhere, if one is not progressing on the journey, then they need to move on. The previous guru also needs to be thanked and a feeling of absolute gratitude expressed before him. Being in his presence, one has certainly gained something and inner development has happened. One has progressed on the path but now one needs to move on since the growth seems to have stopped. Life is an invaluable opportunity which need not be wasted at all. Maya has a thousand ways and methods to keep you entangled but beware of them all. Don't get stuck anywhere and don't waste your life.

KEEPING THE MIND CALM

Sadhaka: Namaste Guruji! How can the mind be made calm and peaceful?

Swamiji: The mind cannot be calmed down. Nobody has ever been able to calm the mind, at least I haven't heard so. Neither was Buddha able to do so nor were Krishna and Mahavir. When Buddha, Krishna and Mahavir were not able to calm the mind, who do you think can? When such great beings were not able to do it, then surely nobody in the world could have done it. The mind cannot be relaxed but how we make the mind restless can be seen. We create our restlessness and we need to see the practices that we engage in, which lead to this restlessness. We need to understand these practices and the madness of these practices. Once they are understood, the practices will withdraw and as they withdraw, we will stop creating restlessness. How we react needs to be seen. Something happens in the house and we immediately react as to why it happened or why did anyone do what they did, following which we get into unnecessary arguments trying to remind others of the instructions we had given which weren't followed. These are our practices and the practices are making the mind restless. We need to see this madness, these practices as to how they're bringing about the agitation. Once you understand the practices for what they are, they will withdraw and their withdrawal is presence of peace...peace which was always there, peace which had never left. Agitation and restlessness of the mind is our own creation. We create it continuously and then we ask why the lake isn't calm. How can the lake be calm if we keep throwing stones in it continuously? Do you now understand that no one has ever been able to bring the mind to rest or calm it down.

Lord (Bhagwan) Buddha was once travelling with Bhikku Ananda who used to stay with Bhagwan. While on their way, Bhagwan asked Ananda to get water to drink as he was thirsty. His vessel was totally empty. He told Ananda that there was a flowing river which they had crossed two miles behind. He reminisced that streams were flowing from the close by mountains over there and some bushes were there too. In the midst of all this was a track for travelers from where pure and fresh water was flowing and He asked Ananda to get water from there. Ananda went back and upon reaching the place he saw a lot of bullock carts crossing that track. They were loaded with goods and belonged to a businessman who was traveling for business. As the bullock carts crossed that track, the water flowing from there got dirty. Ananda, for a minute or two got thinking as to what he could do about it before wading into the water which was probably knee deep. He tried to tap the water with his hands gently so that the water would calm down somehow and the dirt would settle down, leaving the water clean again. The more he tried to do this, the dirtier the water got. When he couldn't understand how to solve the issue, he came out of the water and walked back to where Bhagwan was. He reached back absolutely tired and sat down. He then told Bhagwan what had happened and apologized for not getting the water as it had become very dirty and wasn't worth drinking. He suggested they should move ahead where they might find something. But Lord Buddha insisted he was very thirsty and that it was very difficult for him to walk ahead... he told Ananda that they wouldn't find water ahead and he was aware of this because he had been on this track before. Bhagwan asked Ananda to go back once again to the same place and get the water. Ananda tried to convince him that the water had become so dirty that it wasn't worth drinking. But Buddha pressed him to go back. Ananda went back all the way thinking of why Bhagwan had persuaded him to go back to the same place.

Ananda walked back to the place, murmuring to himself. When he reached there, he found the water clean to a great extent. He was surprised to see that. When he was leaving, Buddha had said, "Ananda, be a little patient, the work will happen", and so Ananda thought of waiting a while longer. He sat down under a tree watching the water closely. Slowly the water became crystal clear. He got up, drank some water himself and took some to his venerable master. He gave the water to Bhagwan and touching his feet said, "I know why you sent me back again. You sent me back so I could see how foolish I had been to have done what I did earlier. The water was getting dirtier with me trying to do something, but when I left from there it calmed on its own. I realized this when you sent me back. Following your advice, I sat down patiently this time. I did not do anything. I just watched. Things just settled down and the water became absolutely clear."

That's the reason I say that the 'doers' spoil everything and without doing everything becomes alright. The practices which involve 'doing', like 'why this, why that, it should be like this and not like that', make the mind restless and agitated. When you don't 'do' anything but just sit peacefully, the mind becomes calm and peaceful. Things get ruined by 'doing'. Immense stubbornness and persistence that lies within needs constant observing. There's too much of 'this should and that should not' in the mind...so much stress and restlessness for these things! No one has been able to calm their minds, not Buddha, not Mahavir, not Krishna. Whatever is happening is being known just as it is. Things fall in place when one sits peacefully and patiently. Doers spoil everything, without doing everything becomes alright.

Chapter 14

Miracles of Saints: Reason Behind Saints Not Using the Powers, Siddhis and Accomplishments for Themselves or in Their Own Interest

Sadhaka: Pranaam Gurudev! There's a question which repeatedly comes in the mind. It's about the great siddhas, saints and yogis who would heal people suffering from diseases just with their blessing, but it's been heard and read as well that these great souls themselves also suffered from some disease or the other, for example Swami Ramakrishna Paramhansa Ji had a serious ailment. Why is it that those who were/are equipped to heal themselves with a single thought or intention never did/do so and lived/live their life with the disease? This question arises as to why someone whose blessings alone can help make things better in the world, doesn't heal himself/herself?

Swamiji: This is an important question because more often than not it is seen that saints have serious health issues. If we look in the recent past, Osho had diabetes, some dental health problems and some other issues as well. Paramhamsa Yogananda had very high diabetes and Ramakrishna Paramahansa had cancer of the throat. Ramana Maharshi too had cancer and Mahavir had died of a disease called sangrahani rog which is the irritable bowel syndrome. He died due to loose motions. There are different diseases seen in practically all saints.

These saints don't really cure the health problems of other people but they are so compassionate that when someone comes in contact with them or tells them of their problem, compassion just flows through them whether they say it or not, and health of a lot many people starts improving on its own. If medicines aren't suiting someone and haven't really been working for them, they start working and the patient gets cured. They don't cure anyone, rather their presence and compassion is what heals people, whether they exhibit it or not. They don't apply this on themselves though, nor do they ask Astitva anything for themselves. Instead, they ask Astitva to send them their remaining karmas, sanskaras, patterns in bulk, so that they can get over with them. To get over all the karmas, they ask Astitva to send them some serious illness which is a source of continuous pain and suffering, so that all the sanskaras keep getting dissolved. They invite it upon themselves.

Tell me, what is the reason for diabetes to happen? Diabetes has increased now but it wasn't so prevalent when it happened to Osho. Yogananda Paramhansa and Neem Karoli Baba also had diabetes although they were present years before Osho. Similarly, you'll find majority of saints to be diabetic if you try finding out. Why is it that they are diabetic? They shouldn't have stress, right? But they have stress of a different kind…stress related to cosmic arrangements plus they're a medium for auspiciousness and wellness to spread and that has some impact on them. What happens when people come with a lot of stress to the master and a method is being taught and applied for the stress to get released? The stress of so many people that is getting released circulates and somewhere or the other impacts the saint. Saints do not have stress otherwise and yet they are stressed. They are stressed when the arrangements are happening – those arrangements which are happening out of compassion. They do not want anybody to feel uncomfortable or face any difficulty when they come. In order to help alleviate others' suffering, they listen, they try to make others understand and in doing so they take the stress upon themselves. They do so knowingly and with awareness that they are not the body, they are not the mind, they are not the stress, but the impact comes on their body and mind i.e. on a psychosomatic level when there's many people around. They do not resist any of it coming towards them out of sheer compassion for the people in front of them because they want their suffering to end. What happens with this is that the psychosomatic body gets affected because the rules of the physical world will be applicable on them too. There are four bodies of the physical world – physical body, etheric body, causal body and mental body and the psychosomatic effects happen on these bodies. The body comes under the rules of the physical world, so the external impacts will affect it. When Krishna was hit by a poison laden arrow on his toe, he did die, didn't he? The arrow worked on his body just like the rules applicable in the physical world normally work on any other individual.

The body is a part of this world with the exception of the level of consciousness which is different in the saints, but their four bodies come under the laws of the physical world and because they do not resist it in anyway, they are great. There are the siddhas who keep themselves fit and keep doing miracles etc. but they aren't considered great. Why aren't they considered great? With the kind of prowess they exhibit, they should be considered great, but they're not. Look at Buddha, Krishna, Mahavir, Ramana Maharshi, how great they are considered. Even Osho, look at him although he isn't being considered that great because he did not go against the common laws and rules. If we look at Buddha, he never exhibited any miracles but his disciples did and he criticized their doing so. He was totally against miracles although miracles would happen around him. He always remained against miracles...he was not in favour of any such thing like miracles. He wanted that the common rules of nature should be accepted by all. If we're not accepting the common laws of nature, it means we're struggling. Who struggles? The 'I', the 'Ego' struggles. To resist anything, ego is required, a self-centre is required and that is the ego. This self-centre is what we have to be free from. We have to be free from this separation that we're living. Now, if someone is struggling and resisting, going against the laws of nature, it means he's standing in opposition...there is someone separate who is standing in opposition of what is. When separation is being lived, how is liberation possible? How will he be great? Great is someone who is one with everything...whatever is happening is being known. He has merged with this oneness where the common laws of nature work, but his level of consciousness has reached its wholeness. He is now complete, infinite – he has merged into the endless and the unbounded because of absolute acceptance of all that is.

They are in a state of absolute acceptance and so their negative karmas show up very fast since there is no barrier now and no resistance from their end to face the prarabdha karma that is coming in front. They have to go through their prarabdha karma which come in bulk and get cut at great speed. They will appear as diseases and all the prarabdha karmas get over. This is what needs to be understood very well that there should be no resistance whatsoever for the prarabdha karmas to get dissolved. There should be no resistance when they show up so that they get dissolved and the accounts get closed. When it becomes zero, the separation gets dissolved. Till the time there are some accounts remaining, some kind of give and take that needs to get over, till then there is duality. Duality is there because any balance accounts, any give and take always happens between two people, ten people or thousand people. What accounts or records will remain for a person who stays alone? There is no account left... there's no money in the account!

Sadhaka: Guruji, the great saints, despite being liberated, would keep a desire alive to remain in the world and be involved in welfare work, for example, Swami Ramakrishna Paramhansa had kept his desire for food alive and Paramhansa Yogananda would consume jalebis (a sweet), sometimes as much as one kilogram since he loved them so much despite being diabetic. Is it that they keep their desire alive so that they can spend more time in this world? Is there any truth to this?

Swamiji: Yes, they have to do such odd things where some or the other desire acts as a medium to keep them tied to this world or keep their boat afloat in this worldly ocean. The boat can be kept afloat or made to last with the help of any one sense out of the five senses. There may be others who would be taking pleasure in music and that will become one medium of hold or tie. The sense of taste matters more because it is a gross sense and one can stay here longer with taste as a medium. There are various things which are there. Some or the other desire or aspiration is watered more out of compassion for all, so that the body survives longer. They have been made to practice this from past births itself which is why it happens this way. It's a different kind of a pattern that has been fed wherein all other patterns dissolve, barring this one. This pattern remains till that birth or till the time he doesn't accomplish the work he's here for and shares with people what he has to with absolute compassion. Till that time, it doesn't get dissolved and such things have been getting created in gurukuls along with the support of the esoteric support systems. The choice of people was based on their immensely good capabilities and their extremely good convincing powers. Such people are able to represent better and make others understand very well. They are able to present the truth in the most effective way with their ability to speak proficiently and effectively. They are intelligent in a different sense and are made to stay back and for them to stay, they are fed these things. The entire esoteric system works towards schooling them for that time, so that the individual takes another birth. The esoteric support system and Astitva works in such a way that this individual becomes a sakdagami, a 'once-returner', taking one more birth. It is made sure that his birth happens in a good era and till then he remains in the higher realms as a deity. Those who have done good sadhanas and got stuck in the higher realms because of some limitations are given an opportunity to come back here and cut their subtle remaining ties.

Chapter 15

Process of a Soul Choosing a Womb

REINCARNATION MEMORIES

CAN THE DOWNFALL OF A HUMAN BEING LEAD HIM TO BECOMING AN ANIMAL?

Sadhaka: Guruji Pranaam! How is the choice of a womb made? How does the one who dies make a choice of the womb he wants to enter and take birth from? What are the things he considers before choosing the womb and how long does it take for him to choose it? Does it all happen according to his karmas? How are all these things determined?

Swamiji: Choosing a womb is a big event. First of all, every soul cannot choose a womb for itself. It is pushed by its karma prarabdha and it takes birth unconsciously. It starts looking for the wombs though. A common man's soul can see the wombs generally after three days of its death. It takes three days to understand that it has left the body and died and starts craving deeply for another body. For the want of another body, it's race begins according to its karma prarabdha and it takes birth in the environment it was earlier in.

With the soul's limitations set in and around that area, it is there that it has to settle its accounts, and that is where its birth happens. There's nothing conscious about this entire event.

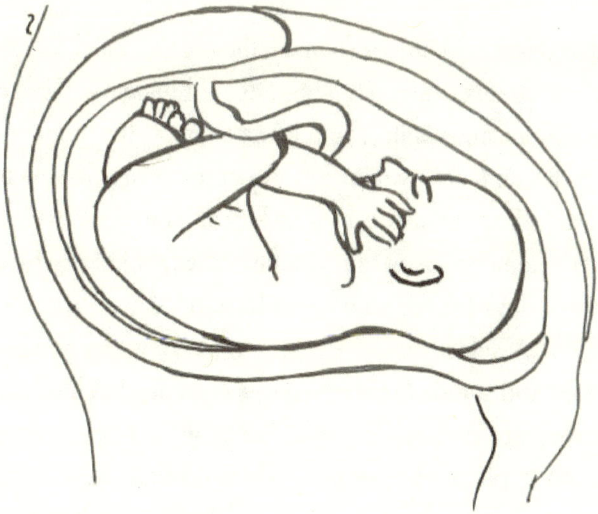

Taking birth consciously which means the soul choosing a womb for itself, is a big event. This is only possible for a soul who lived consciously and with full awareness when alive and was fully conscious while dying. Do you know that 99.99% people die unconsciously, so how do you think will be their next birth? It will happen in ignorance. The one who dies unconsciously will be born unconscious. One who dies consciously is born with awareness. That is why the sadhana of awareness, sadhana of being conscious is done.

All the practices including intense meditation are done so that awareness is maintained while leaving the body. The whole preparation is for the moment of death which can arrive any minute, and only the person who accepts the fact that death can happen any moment is capable of doing this sadhana of awareness. The next moment could be the moment of death and what is death? What is seen in the world has been determined and defined with the body being taken as a separate self...that event of separation is denoted as death.

What is death? There are so many theories, so much information on death but what is death actually? It is said that you'll find heaven when you die; means what! You'll come to know what death is only when you die and only when you die consciously. If you become unconscious before you die, even if its half an hour or an hour before, how will you come to know that you have died? That is why it takes at least three days for the soul to understand where it is and what it is doing. Their close and loved ones are crying and howling, and the soul goes and stands there trying to ask them what has happened and why they are crying. To avoid this from happening, a system has been put in place wherein the body is taken as early as possible for cremation. Why has cremation been chosen as a last rite? This is for some specific rituals attached with it, where the soul would be asked to leave post the burning of its body. It would be conveyed to the soul that there was nothing left of it and that it should leave. In this way, a conversation would be initiated with the soul through the rituals. Like the "bardo' meditation that happens in Tibet. Just like that, there were certain customs and practices over here also before the funeral. These days what is left of those customs is just a formality where some nonsense ritual of breaking the skull is being performed during cremation. All of it has boiled down to this alone now. Breaking the skull of a dead body!? How can anyone else do the 'kapal kriya?' (Breaking of the skull). You yourself have to do the kapal kriya...opening of the brahmarandra through sadhana. Somebody else doing the kapal kriya, be it the son or whoever... come on! What sense does it make to do this on a dead body? Yes, it used to be done in the olden times as an integral part of some rituals that were performed for the benefit of the soul who left the body and not as a formality. If the body is buried, it keeps roaming around the grave thinking it is still there. Liberation doesn't happen in the grave and that is why they don't have this concept of liberation. They say, when the doomsday comes, liberation will happen. They are being fed that there is no need for liberation and so, stay put. Then a concept was given that this journey is over and since you aren't liberated, why suffer; go back and take birth as soon as possible. There is a message being conveyed through all this.

The effort is put into reading out the Geeta to the dying person so that whatever little spirituality he has practiced in his life can be recalled and maintained, so that in his last moment some positivity takes over. But what I do is, sit with the dying person and converse with him regarding death – what death is, that there is nothing like death, death is a lie. I talk to him and tell him to see, and then ask him what is it that he's seeing. Then I ask him to continue seeing whatever it is, without forming an opinion about it and that there is nothing like death happening; he must continue seeing whatever it is that he is seeing. I then tell him that right now he is in the body, but later he will not remain in the body, and he must see that also. He must see his body from afar, he must see his mind from afar if it arises and not get associated with it. This is how I speak to a dying person.

I had a friend who passed away. I went for his funeral and asked his people to let me talk to him. I called upon his soul and said to him, "Look brother, you have left the body and we are going to cremate it. Your kids will be taken care of and will grow up just fine. Your wife too will lead her life. You aren't there anymore, so there's no wife that you have. This body will merge with the soil, so from which angle does she remain your wife anymore or your kids remain your kids anymore? What do you have to do with them? Just leave and go on your next journey." Since he was a friend, I spoke to him in a very informal way asking him to leave, for there was no need for him to get stuck here as there was no role he needed to play here anymore; that he should move on and find a good womb for himself. I told him, "If you're able to understand what I'm saying and if you're conscious, then remain conscious and choose a good womb for yourself. Take birth through such a womb that you can be on the path of sadhana in the next life. Be on the path of sadhana properly." This is how I conveyed the message and this is how it must be done.

A normal soul takes on the process of coming back in three days. If not in three days, then they take birth within ten days or thirteen days. Talking of sanyasis now (the hermits), they are not cremated because they are liberated. Their loved ones remember him and listen to his discourses or deshnas but the thing is that not all sanyasis are enlightened and so not cremating them is not right. Probably one in a thousand gets enlightened so even the sanyasis should be cremated. They should also be put on the funeral pyre and cremated just like Guru Nanak Dev Ji and Kabir Das ji. Later the remains of the dead body, the charred bones and ashes can be handled the way the disciples want or by following the instructions of what the sanyasi himself gave and went. In Kabir Das Ji's case, the remains of his cremated body were divided and of course, Osho who ensured beforehand that his body be cremated. Osho had given the option of making a memorial (also called samadhi) with the remains of his body but not with the body itself. He was clear that his body had to be cremated. He wanted to give a message by doing so. He said it was madness to keep the body of every sanyasi and sadhu that dies. Forget the sadhus, he had said, even he shouldn't be kept as a body but made into charred bones and ashes which should then be washed away into a river after keeping some, if at all anyone wished to. This kind of sincerity should be there. In Amarkantak, there was one Barfani Dada who had given instructions that his body should be burnt post his death and the remains of his body be put in the river Narmada. His instructions were followed with sincerity. There were talks of him being a thousand years old. I used to have fun with him and spend time with him alone. I would say in good humour, "Maharaj, so you are now a thousand years old?" He would say, "Maharaj, why are you making fun of me! I have turned eighty recently." He was an honest man. He would share a lot of things about himself when we would sit, just the two of us spending time together. He said this thing about his body; it should be cremated and immersed in Narmada Ji. He was very honest and sincere. He also mentioned that there was no need for his memorial or samadhi to be made. Now, there are others whose grave is turned into a memorial. What will that grave do? It will harm, isn't it! Will the energy of the grave of someone who was not liberated himself help in liberating people going there? Hence, one should not go to all samadhis, even if it's written 'samadhi' over there. You must go to rivers and try to understand the energies there. One who can do that should then go to such places.

Sadhaka: Guruji, oftentimes a death happens suddenly and the individual doesn't even get a second before leaving the body. An accident happens and the person is gone instantly. How do such souls choose their body again? How does their reel-revert happen?

Swamiji: In a case where death happens instantly and the reel-revert doesn't take place because there was no opportunity for it to happen due to the suddenness of death, the soul of the person remains stuck near and around the place. What happens is that when an accident takes place, the person becomes a little conscious and aware, with the unconsciousness reducing to quite an extent for a few moments. The soul misuses this consciousness by hovering around in that area. It hangs around in the neighbouring trees and looks relentlessly for a womb either in and around that area or in the close by villages. It wants to choose a womb with a desperation because he was conscious for some moments while dying, which happens in accidental and sudden deaths. Imagine if someone comes here now with a staff/stick or a snake comes in this place, will there not be a different kind of an awakening that will happen!? There will be a sensation in your navel; you'll become alert, isn't it? When an individual dies suddenly in an accident, the person becomes alert and aware for some time because of which the soul can choose a little, just that the quality of its choice will be different. Its choice will be to take birth in the same area or vicinity where its body had died and reconnect over there again. There are so many such examples in Haryana. There was a child who remembered his children from the past life, and landed up giving away his daughter's hand to her groom (Kanyadaan) during her wedding in the present life. He was a ten years old boy who did the main ritual of kanyadaan at his daughter's wedding. She was twenty-five and he was ten years of age. He said she was his daughter and he wanted to do this important ritual. He also made them spend a lot at the wedding, for those memories were there of when he was alive and must have wanted to do those expenses at her wedding. If a person dies with a lot of awareness, the memories remain. Some sleep at night and don't wake up in the morning. They die unconsciously in their sleep and take birth unconsciously.

Sadhaka: Guruji, some people love animals. There was a Rishi who loved a deer and it is said that at the time of his death, his love for the deer was alive within him because of which he had to come back as a deer in his next life.

Swamiji: This I have already mentioned about people who get too attached to animals, for example there are a lot of people who are dog lovers and are very attached to them; many of them come back in the form of a dog. Some people get so attached to them that it turns into an attraction towards them. That is why it is said that the sadhana should be of developing awareness and consciousness. The awareness must be there each moment. That is why the intense meditation is required; to boost your quality of awareness and apply it throughout the day. Your walking, sitting, getting up, eating, drinking, everything should happen consciously and not in ignorance or unconsciously. Every moment should be a moment of awareness because death can knock any moment, hence the importance of being conscious and equanimous each moment. Being equanimous is being conscious! Where there is equanimity, there is purity of awareness. Everything is happening and being known, we don't have to understand anything nor do anything. Why do I have to know anything? Why should I concentrate? If I'm concentrating to know things, it means the mind is involved in the knowing. I am using the mind then. Concentration means the mind has become active, and whatever is known by the mind is of no value. What is the mind worth? What is this head worth?

Don't do anything and just be in the knowing of whatever is happening as it is, with equanimity. Whose quality do you think this is? You can call this the quality of the Atma, Paramatma or quality of the Shiv Tattva. Depending on the purity of the soul, it is called 'Sakshi Atma' (witness consciousness or the witnessing soul), Paramatma (Supreme soul or supreme consciousness) and Shiv Tattva (Nishabd – that which is beyond words and cannot be spoken of), respectively. Arrival at Shiv Tattva means arrival in the Infinite...everything is happening and being known. 'Being known' means it is existentially, naturally being known. There is nobody to know anything – it is simply being known or in other words, the knowing is just happening naturally. It's not like there's someone who comes to know something, because 'someone' means there is a centre and centre is present till the level of Atma. It doesn't go beyond it. Therefore, if someone is present to know something, it means the play of the centre is happening; the individual will stay stuck and entangled in the loop of Atma.

Now, coming to how a womb is chosen. There are many factors involved in this process. How will the soul of a person who dies with awareness choose a womb? The soul will see where it's sadhana will receive help so that it can get upgraded, and whether the period will be suitable for taking birth. If at all someone dies with awareness, his soul will go to a higher realm and stay there as a higher being, waiting for a period to arrive when the situation and circumstances are conducive for sadhana. Then the soul looks for a womb and makes the choice of a place where taking birth will be appropriate, which mother and father will be appropriate, which planetary placements are conducive for its growth and liberation.

This is the Golden Era and if we come to look at it, astrology is not a complete waste in this era. It's a very miraculous thing that out of one or two lakhs of people, there may be one person whose astrological chart will have the planet Ketu placed in his twelfth house. Ketu in twelfth house means this will be that person's last birth. The soul decides the time period of his birth and the planetary positions, constellations, the house divisions and the condition of the houses. It makes sure that Ketu falls in the twelfth house and then takes birth. Choosing a womb is a big exercise for the soul although Astitva's support is there. The conception takes place under all such circumstances which will help the soul in taking birth and getting liberated; everything is aligned for all this to happen. It is then that the higher beings are given the opportunity to take birth. Everything is aligned in such a way that at the moment of birth Ketu falls in the twelfth house and this birth becomes the last birth for the soul.

A person who has lived consciously in his life and is dying consciously but has some attractions and karma prarabdha still left, will take birth again since he was not fully liberated. Such a person, when he comes back again, takes birth consciously. He will take one or two more births, or at the most seven. This happens with the srotapannas since they die with so much awareness that they can then choose their birth. Srotapannas are the ones who are in a constant state of reflecting upon sadhana. There is a continuous flow of conscious reflection on sadhana going on within them. Whatever a srotapanna may be doing, a contemplation of sadhana is happening simultaneously. Reflecting upon sadhana means the person is a srotapanna. It means he has gone into the source. Now whatever will flow, will flow in the direction of liberation for him. It may take maximum seven births for him to get fully liberated, if not one, two or three. People who are in resonance with me are all srotapannas. The ones who are not srotapannas can never be in resonance with me, it's impossible. Only those who are srotapannas from past lives can understand what I'm saying and can be in resonance with me. There is a possibility that people who are not srotapannas from a past life, but have reached here will become srotapannas. This is a possibility but there's not much that can happen with all of them. They will come in contact with me and will become srotapannas but this will happen with some, not with all. Those who were srotapannas in their past lives will resonate with me and their sadhana will complete. Among these sadhakas, for some three lives are left, for some four or maybe five or six. It could be that this life becomes the last birth for someone who otherwise was meant to take six more births. This is quite possible. Maximum number of births for these srotapannas from the past lives is six. It is not that they will become srotapannas after six births; they will take maximum six births to get fully liberated. Such sadhakas will come in contact with me and the possibility of this life being their last birth is very high. There is maximum possibility that this will be their last birth.

Chapter 16

Science Behind the Birth of a Soul and the Different Realms in Which It Wanders

WHAT IS ASTROLOGY AND HOW CORRECT IS IT?

Sadhaka: Pranam Swamiji! My question is, do the planetary placements decide where and how a person will take birth, how their life and death will be or is it their past life karmas that play a role in this? As per astrology which time is considered to be the time of birth – is it the time of conception or the time when the baby is born? These days, the child is brought into this world after deciding an auspicious time for his/her birth, so which time should be considered right astrologically?

Swamiji: Astrology has forever been attracting human beings because future is uncertain and uncertainty scares a lot. Uncertainty brings fear with it. There's a lot of uncertainty in this era, a kind which was never there before. There is an influx of resources and systems and as many uncertainties. What is instilling maximum fear in us is the economic uncertainties because of the rising inflation. Buying properties is considered a good investment but there are various kinds of challenges attached to it now. There is a rise in financial insecurities. There is a question mark on the security of the institutions one is investing in. The investments are getting affected by the global geo-political situations. Your income is also getting affected, your jobs are no longer secure, the recession may hit anytime, so these are times of extreme financial insecurities and uncertainties.

Whenever the fear of uncertainty arises, astrology starts attracting because people then want to know what the future holds for them. Why is the financial uncertainty affecting us so much? It is because there is no trust left in relationships. The support systems aren't the way they used to be anymore...relatives and close associates are no more as supportive as they used to be in earlier times. There is no guarantee that they will be supportive in times of need. It's also possible that they may withdraw their support or you may not get the support you expected. In fact, these days it is seen in some cases that even children are not supportive of their parents. Not all children are like that but there have been such instances, so we really don't know what's going to happen in the next moment.

India still sees the relatives and friends supporting each other, even though it has become a rarity. Other countries seem to have lost this entirely. In India, this arrangement, this structure of relatives and close ones helping and supporting each other was made so that a person would not live in any fear, even fear of the future. The assurance that basic requirements would be provided for in dire times kept them away from fearing, and not fearing meant that their mind would be at ease and not get active. The more one fears, the more the mind becomes active. What makes the mind voluble is fear. If you have a deeper look within, you'll see that the root cause which is responsible for the mind becoming very active, voluble and reactive is fear.

Money has become the symbol of abundance now. There is a feeling of safety and security that money brings. One knows that if you have money, a house can be bought anywhere, food can be bought anywhere. It is easy to liquidate as well as convert it into different currencies wherever you may be. Liquidity brings along a lot of security. But money also brings about a feeling of malaise, with thoughts like money getting taken away or the value of money going down taking precedence in the mind. In a society where money has become priority, relationships have taken a back seat and fear has increased extensively because one is only thinking of money and wealth. Look within and you'll find that you're constantly worrying about where your money is lying and what will happen to it, where should you invest it, whether your money is safe where it is, how is the property you're interested in, whether the property is safe or not, so on and so forth. Such a structure has been created and majority of your thoughts are related to all this.

The thing is that the population has also increased a lot and so have the struggles to live life, because of which the financial insecurities have increased taking up one's energy to a great extent. The worry of consequences if one falls sick has led to health insurance policies becoming popular. The fear of whether anyone from the family will support or not has led to people buying health insurance policies. The thought at the back of the mind is that if anything happens to them, the relatives will at least be willing to come forward and help when they know they don't have to pay for anything and that the insurance money will take care of the bills. Money has become a major decision maker as far as relationships are concerned now. With the rising fear, people are getting attracted towards astrology in the hope of finding some kind of certainty... questions like what will happen, how will it happen, why will it happen, then arise. There are other questions as well that come up;

how is our birth decided and how is our future based on the birth. The attraction for astrology is increasing by the day in this era. One has to be careful though. I had a cousin whom I met once when he visited us. I was small then. He asked to see my palm and seeing it he mentioned how my personality was and some other things. He told the others also about their future. We were influenced to some degree by what he said. I asked him when had he learnt astrology. He said he hadn't. Then how was he telling things about us was our next question. He said he was doing so only to impress us and that he was telling some common things that fit and apply on everyone based on psychological facts. He said it had nothing to do with our future. We did get impressed by even the common things he spoke, so astrology, you see has mostly become like this. But does astrology work? Yes, it does. Astrology is a great science. I have spoken about 'naadi jyotish' (palm-leaf based astrological system) where your thumb impression is taken and an astrologer then, without asking you anything, gives you information about yourself. With your thumb impression, he'll first locate a specific leaf on which your entire past, present and future is written. These are believed to have been written by sage Agastya Muni along with others. The astrologer will then tell your name, the names of your parents, children, about your relatives, how many girlfriends or boyfriends you have, their names, your occupation, your date of birth, your city of birth, how and where you will die, where you will make your home, which year what car will be bought, the colour of the car, the model too even if it hasn't yet been launched. It is possible that even the car company doesn't exist and may be launched after ten years and you may buy that car after twenty years according to naadi astrology. He might even give you the name of the yet unborn company. All this, provided the astrologer is one of the ten percent of the best naadi astrologers that are now left. Ninety percent of them are corrupt, so one must look for someone who belongs to the remaining ten percent.

So much is already decided for us, which leaves us wondering what the meaning of this life is. When everything is absolutely predestined, then what is the reason for us to be here. We are no more than puppets in that case. Then people say all kinds of things like, "We are puppets, we are dancing to someone's tunes, we're like toys with winding keys...the toy that works as long as the key unwinds, after being wound up to its maximum limit or to a certain chosen limit." After all this one wonders about the meaning of this life. Astrology is all about the life lived in ignorance. It is for a life which is lived unconsciously. Everything can be told about that person or that life because it is an unconscious one. Astrologically, a full prediction can be done in this case. Astrology fails where a person has gone deep into sadhana. This person decides his own future. Astrology doesn't work on him.

How is it decided as to how this life and this birth will be is the question? When the birth takes place, a lot of things will impact you based on your birth. A whole lot of energies influence you, so how must your life be? Some births will be ordinary and unconscious where one cannot decide one's future; in that case some of their past merits will fructify. A merit fructifying has its importance and this is very clear from Buddha's discourses. Suppose nothing been cooked somewhere and you go and donate a little, feed someone hungry or do some odd jobs; all this counts as merits. What will one benefit from these merits? Sometimes it is money in return for money, more food in return for food and likewise. But sometimes a very different merit unfolds for example, you may land up helping a person who is ill or someone falls and you pick him up; you may end up serving a saint or you land up where Buddha's discourses are being read or it could also be that you land up serving an enlightened being. Many people do that. They have something within them which they're not even aware of but they say they want to do seva, they want to serve. Why do they want to do that? There's something clear within them from past lives which tells them that by doing so, something will happen. What will happen, they don't know but they just serve. Their serving the saints, siddhas and sadgurus may lead to something special happening. This merit of serving the Sadguru brings him the Master's grace and blessing, and he will be benefitted not just then but in future also. He will get refuge of the Sadguru and be under his guidance time and again. This is an extremely good fortune. From a population of eight hundred crores, how many are sitting here…it's not by chance that this happens. There are five-six hundred more like me and if one goes to count the people sitting with all of them, how many will you find? You won't find more than 0.1% people with them. How did 0.1% get decided? It got decided by the people who reached there and upon being asked they said they had reached somehow although they were not planning to. Then they say, they were not going to stay in the retreat for long but landed up extending their trip despite the mind saying otherwise and confusing them with all kinds of chatter. The mind uses its full power but despite that, some people stay back and some leave.

Why did the ones who stayed back do so? Why did the ones who came here, actually come? That is because of the merits emerging and people using the free will that they have. This free will is the point, the source, with which we can change our destiny. It is with this free will that you do charities and selflessly give without expecting anything in return. That is why charity has been considered important and special. It does work at times. It has its importance although I do criticize it at times due to specific reasons in some places. Charity, virtuous deeds, serving the saints, all this has its value but see to it that you don't fall into a loop of influences because of this. If an influence gets embedded within you, you will land up being operated by the influence and that will be a cause for disaster. There is great importance of serving the saints. You have the benefit of the master's company and the energy that you receive from him even if you're able to understand little of what he says. It is said that out of the lakhs of sentences spoken by the saints, even if one or two go and strike a chord within, they will act as a catalyst. They will act as a virus bringing about a change in your life.

Now, understand this well. There is a bindu (point) and from this point, you either go in a straightforward direction or you go in endless directions. You'll pick up one direction and go straight on that track. Suppose you're working on something in a particular place at a particular time, then understand that where you are at a given point in time becomes a bindu for that time. It was on the basis of the past bindu that you had travelled ahead. The work that you are doing at a specific time is your centre point or the bindu. If you can understand this, well and good, otherwise you can reflect upon it and it will unfold at some point in time for you. The work that you do at a certain place at a certain time becomes your centre point. That is the centre point of that time since you are living in that time. The bindu is endless, but you are living in time and space, which means you have a centre and vice versa. If you do some service, some charity or a virtuous deed at any point, you get the result immediately and there's a flowering that happens within you. There's something that strikes you somewhere.

Sadguru says lakhs of things out of which one strikes a chord with you and there's a positive shift that happens within you. What happens is that your direction shifts by one, two or three degrees. If you've done something good, it may shift by three degrees. Now, you were supposed to go on a particular straight line before this three-degree shift took place. Look, examples are never complete and can't do justice but I'll try to explain nonetheless. So, the straight line that you are on now is three degrees apart from the one that you were supposed to be on before this shift happened. Consider these straight lines as we draw them in mathematics. One straight line is going in one direction and the other straight line is travelling three degrees apart from the other one. Both these straight lines are being drawn from one point, so what will be the distance between these two lines? Initially they'll be really close but then the distance will keep increasing as you keep moving ahead and there will come a time when the other straight line will not be seen at all. You have now gone in a very different direction but wherever you are at whatever point in time, there is your bindu. You try to improve that bindu by doing something, and in the process of 'doing' you bring about a shift of a degree or so again. This improvising on the bindu and bringing about a shift of one or two degrees happens due to the free will that you have.

Your karma decides your destiny and even if you don't understand anything about karma, just understand that you must serve the saints. You must not serve the influencers but the saints. Being in the presence of saints and the satsangs will take you forward. How will you be in the presence of a saint? Is just staying with a saint enough to feel his presence? No, staying with a saint doesn't mean you're near him although his fragrance will get absorbed within you to some extent and something from the wisdom he imparts will definitely strike a chord in you. Even if you're not in resonance with the saint but are in his presence, the resonance will happen at some point in time. It's tough for the resonance to happen specially when it comes to the saints. Resonance happens easily with the influencers but it's not easy to resonate with a saint.

Saints are unpredictable and weird, absurd and irrational. They don't fit into any structure. They go against your mental propositions and keep acting in a way that creates a negative image in front of you. They'll keep going with, "This is wrong, this is not in order, that is a mess...", but this is their leela. This performance they put up is their play, a trick to clean up, to sort out, to filter out, as in, whoever can be filtered out, gets filtered. After all this, if some stay back with the saint and some of the master's words happen to strike a chord with them, bringing about a shift of one or two degrees, then they will experience profound changes in the long run. Then the next births you take happen with a changed destiny...the destiny changes in the future lives. Destiny will change and whatever was written for you earlier will stop working. What will work in the next birth is the 'Samudra Shastra' because in the next birth, the lines on your palms will change. They will not stay the same because they keep changing. If observed carefully, you'll find they change. You can experiment by taking a photograph of your palm and check again after one or two years, you'll find they would have changed. The astrology based on samudra shastra keeps changing. The other astrology based on the time and place of birth will only highlight about that much, and proves wrong at times. But the samudra shastra astrologer will tell you that things change. Two years later you go to the samudra shastra astrologer, he'll say things have changed, this should have happened but now this will happen. Why so? It is because the lines on your palms have changed.

Sai Baba used to say repeatedly not to trust the lines on the palms, rather he would ask people to keep observing them and see for themselves that the lines keep changing. He would also say that if we want, we can change the lines on our hands, so you see, this astrology can be changed. Certain things have been decided at the time of birth, yet it can be changed. If there was no possibility to change, then this life would hold no value and suicide would be the most beautiful thing. Talking of suicide, suicide is also cutting the flow of life since we are 'committing' suicide. In doing so, we are changing the course of life and destiny, if at all there is a pre-decided destiny. For that, free will is required somewhat but yes, destiny can be changed. Only then this life is meaningful otherwise this birth and life is meaningless. If you cannot decide your own destiny and change it, then this life is worthless, it is of no use...where is it valuable then! You can change your life. Serving the saints will get you a good next birth where you'll get an opportunity to be in the presence of a sadguru again and receive his blessings. The virtues and merits will arise again.

Lord Buddha says in one of his tales that in one of his lives he was an ordinary person, a woodcutter and he had no understanding whatsoever of sadhana. It so happened once that an enlightened being was coming but he wasn't aware of the term 'enlightened being' (buddha purush) or 'gyani'. That being who was approaching just seemed very special to him. There was a group of people coming along with him and when they were approaching, he saw a resplendence which brought feelings of respect and admiration. He did not understand anything at the time. He was just an illiterate woodcutter. He just thought he should do something for them but what could he do, he wondered. He saw that this resplendent being would have to cross a narrow path which had a big ditch and it was filled with muddy water. Since the ditch was big, it would be difficult for the group to jump over it. He just went and lay down in the ditch quietly in such a way that they wouldn't come to know that he was lying there, or else they would hesitate to walk over him. The resplendent being walked along with everyone else over his body and crossed without coming to know that he was lying underneath. They faced no difficulty whatsoever. He says he did not know what else he could have done at that time for them, but he just wanted to do something. He as a woodcutter did not recognize who the special person was. After many lives he came to know that the person who seemed special to him was an enlightened being.

Lord Buddha as a woodcutter in that life did this much, and the merit that got accumulated from this deed became the cause of him getting blessed by a Sadguru in his next birth where his sadhana began. The sadhana was profound and within a few lifetimes he arrived at Buddhahood.

After he got into sadhana, he took refuge in different Buddhas, one of whom was Virochana. He saw Virochana and got very impressed by him. He didn't know what to do but felt like touching his feet and so he went and fell at his feet. Virochana got up and in return touched his feet. Buddha mentions that he got nervous and panicked when this happened and he asked Virochana, "Maharaj, I know why I touched your feet but I'm unable to understand why you touched my feet." Virochana said, "You don't know that you are also going to be a Buddha in the near future. Your simplicity and naturalness are such that you are going to be a Buddha soon." Within two-three lives, Buddha happened.

The next birth saw him living on a mountain in Maharashtra. He was called Sugat in this life. On that mountain was a cave which he made livable and stayed there. He did sadhana there and that mountain later was called Sugatgiri (giri means mountain). Later, the name got distorted and was called Igatpuri. This is the same Igatpuri where the biggest center of vippasana in the world is situated. It is situated right in front of that mountain. This center is the global head quarter of vippasana institutes all over the world. You can see that mountain across from there and it looks very attractive. All the sadhakas who go there spend hours looking at it. That mountain attracts so much. Serving the saints and attending satsangs become the cause of changes in your life and I have seen how small changes work.

One decides one's destiny for the next life. There are those who are influenced by politics and enjoy political conversations. They are also deciding their destiny for the next life. If you're too interested in politics, you'll become a politician in this life or the next one. This is like falling in a ditch. If you're attracted to wealthy and rich people and talk of money all the time, you'll work very hard and earn a lot of money in this life or the next one which means your enlightenment has got postponed. You'll first have to earn money or become a politician, enjoy it and only when you get disinterested in it, is liberation possible. In case your interest in politics increases more, you'll have to take one more life and when you finally develop a disinterest in it, you'll start walking on the path of freedom. Similarly, you're earning money but if your attraction towards money is immense and you feel that you haven't earned enough, you will take birth again to satisfy that urge of earning enough. 'Enough' means till the time you're disinterested in earning more it will never be enough, whether you're earning a hundred crores, thousand crores or one lakh crores. The point is whether you have become disinterested or not. If you have an amount of one lakh with you and your disinterest has developed, then you have become free from it. Whether it's one lakh or ten thousand is not the concern, if you've developed a disinterest, you're free from it completely. The money will then be there and it will be made use of as and when required without any attachment to it.

King Janaka stayed in the palace, in the midst of riches and wealth and got disinterested in it. He kept using the wealth as and when required. His disinterest in the riches did not make him leave the palace or run away. Kabirdas Ji was small when this feeling of detachment and indifference towards things happened. He remained indifferent even if he had food only for that day and no assurance of whether he would have something to eat the next day. You are being pushed around by the influences around you, creating immense vibrations of anxiety and restlessness in the mind and moving your centre point, your bindu. If your centre point is still and not getting affected or impressed by any influence, that is the 'amani dasha', a no-mind state. If the bindu is getting affected by the influences and is moving, that is the mind. No-mind state is when the bindu becomes still, although there is nothing like a still bindu. Remember this, for you may not understand it now but you will at some point in the future. These are aphorisms you must keep in mind and you'll understand at some point in time that there is nothing like a motionless bindu, and that it is with movement and motion that a bindu is created. Bindu is influenced by the influences and when many influences collide in a place, a bindu is created. You'll understand, when you understand that there is actually no bindu! What is a bindu then? The collision of too many influences and movements at some place (they will collide somewhere) creates an impression of a bindu. Every bindu is a result of continuous collision and keeps getting updated. Everywhere there are collisions happening in endless circular motions.

This creation, this universe is nothing but an integration of movements and there are endless movements and vibrations happening. This is a continuous, eternal play, a leela. There are endless vibrations continuously colliding everywhere. There is a bindu being created everywhere. The birth of a bindu is happening everywhere, some in the form of human beings, some as living organisms, some as stones, some in the form of particles, some appearing as atoms...everything is bindu – small bindus, big bindus, bindus of different kinds. It's all bindus and bindus. Movements and vibrations are happening, leaving an impression in places with their collisions. It is with these collisions that some consciousness emerges.

What is consciousness? See, the collision of the continuous movements or influences creates a bindu and when that happens, consciousness appears or is born in that bindu. This consciousness then survives while moving ahead and all the collisions that happen afterwards are the experiences of this consciousness that survived, which is us. They are our experiences. As the consciousness emerges, the separation is born simultaneously. The consciousness is the consciousness of separation. Wherever a collision happens, there the birth of a bindu happens, consciousness appears, experiences are born, and from all of this the akashic records are created. It is because of these akashic records that the separation is surviving and the continuum is maintained. What is maintained? A continuum is maintained and in the continuity of this bindu, the akashic record gets created. If there is no continuity of the bindu taking place, where will the akashic records come from? Akashic records get made because of the continuity of the bindu. Creation of a consciousness has happened in this bindu, a circle has taken birth and this circle is being pushed, being updated, being increased and decreased. Who is increasing and decreasing it? The other movements, the influences are increasing and decreasing it and this is all a play. The influences are a leela and since there are influences and influences everywhere, collisions are bound to happen and they'll continue happening. Put these things in your mind even if you don't understand. Never mind if you don't understand these things now. Just keep them in your mind like a seed which may sprout, and flowering will happen at some point even if it takes one, two or five lifetimes. They can flower anytime, so bindus i.e. the centre points do get created.

Where does the soul come from? Population has increased so much. It wasn't like this before, so where do these new souls come from? The bindus keep getting created by the collision of the moving influences, and a circle of consciousness keeps getting formed. The consciousness is circular and if it keeps getting updated, that means it's motion and speed is maintained. The Cosmic Consciousness is different. We are not talking about that here. Here we are talking of the consciousness which creates the web of illusion. This consciousness comes into a cycle which keeps getting updated because of which a whole lot of influences keep impacting it, and influences are a continuous affair.

What are all these influences? It is that which is updating your separation and the collective influences of your consciousness. If you're getting influenced by it, then the cycle will catch more speed and the bindu will get stronger. Any influences that push you bring about a change in your motion. It brings about a shift in degrees, thus changing the course of your path, resulting in your journey taking a different direction. Your attractions acting as the influences decide what has to happen and where, according to which the bindu then gets created in that place at that time. A kind of a zig-zag goes on with this; if the bindu in a particular place gets impacted by an influence, then how many degrees of a shift will that influence bring on it with its impact and things like this is the zig-zag I'm talking of.

Understanding that zig-zag and underlining it is astrology. How do the planets and constellations work in the understanding of the zig-zag and underlining it? Look, energy gets released from the planets and constellations and there are various kinds of gravitational forces in them. The gravitational forces and planets are bound to each other with energies. It is with the gravitational force of the sun that all the planets of the solar system are bound. That is why they have a fixed orbital speed at which they orbit around the earth, with the hours and minutes in three hundred sixty-five days already fixed. Hours and minutes are all fixed but the difference that is seen not only in seconds but even nano seconds, helps in predicting the changes coming in the orbit. There's a one nano second difference that happens in the entire year. The solar system is our own and these movements, speed, the gravitational forces of the sun, energies of other planets and us, we are all relatives, with mostly everything being a play of energies.

Like I said, all the planets are our relatives and they leave an impression on us, with some planet being our mother, some planet our father, some father's sister, another being father's brother. There was only one star, the sun which was actually a 'black hole'. It exploded and with this explosion, its pieces scattered far and wide and it became flammable. Some pieces of this were left behind which led to it becoming inflammable and that which was in a slumber so far got ignited and became active. A dormant planet became a star, the sun. The pieces that were left close by became the planets. We are that...we are made from the mud of the earth. This mud is of the planet earth which was earlier there. The journey of the mud goes along with time and such has been the case since eons. Who knows from where this journey is happening, who knows from where we have come...we are going along with the flowing wind, we don't have a say in the direction the journey takes. One line from Nida Fazli's ghazal, sung by Jagjit Singh goes, "Apni marzi se kahan apne safar ke hum hain, rukh hawaon ka jidhar ka hai udhar ke hum hain."

We were there and got separated from there. If someone from a joint-family shifts somewhere else or maybe abroad, does the relationship end with them? The relationship continues even if one has shifted far. The earth is our mother which makes the sun our grandfather. Does the relationship with the maternal family end if the daughter (earth) shifts somewhere? Our relationship with our grandfather, the sun will never end, however far it may be. It is eight minutes and sixteen seconds away from us in light-time. Light travels at a speed of three lakh kilometers per hour. You can calculate how far our maternal home is! It's not just the grandfather but other relatives as well over there and they too have an impact on us because we are connected. We don't get entirely disconnected from those who've left and gone very far from the grandfather, just that they don't have too much of an impact on us as they are out of our radar. They may be very far from the grandfather but they'll still remain our relatives, like saturn, jupiter, venus, mars...their movements and speed impact us. They are all connected to each other and they attract the earth which means they attract us as well. We are also the earth, made from the soil. The moon has a major impact on us and we call it our mamu (uncle-mother's brother). Mamu is a fairly close relative and since it is a part of the earth and has separated from the earth, it has a greater impact on the bindu and on this psychosomatic body. They all impact us, leave an impression on us in their own distinctive ways.

This is why they count a lot in astrology as this is a relationship of day and night. We are absolutely tied in relation to the solar system and planets. This energy works continuously and we are pulled towards each other. Hence these calculations work in astrology, for instance, at the moment of your birth which influences have an impact and how much - which bindu is getting created at that time, how many influences are impacting it and how many energies are working at the time. All these things along with what you have brought with you from the past decides what the journey of the bindu will be from there. The combination of these two aspects makes the destiny.

When a person who is not into sadhana dies, the bindu is pushed into taking birth because taking birth is not in his hands. But a sadhaka on the other hand decides which bindu he wants, through his free will. It is because of the sadhana and accumulated merits that the level of his consciousness is raised and so the level of the free will is also high. Our free will decides the simplicity and spontaneity of our consciousness. Simplicity of consciousness is that which gets less affected by influences. The lesser one gets impacted by influences, the higher the level of consciousness is. A simple and spontaneous individual doesn't get caught up in influences. He doesn't watch all the nonsense being served on social media, television and internet, as his level of consciousness is high. He doesn't get attracted or influenced by any of it. That one line from the ghazal, 'apni marzi se kahan apne safar ke hum hain!', which means 'we are not on this journey with our own free will!' It shows that influences control the consciousness which is at a lower level.

The level of consciousness being high means, we bypass the approaching influences and don't get affected by them. Our level of consciousness for this reason is high and so the sadhana happens with better awareness. This is the sadhana, where we are able to bypass some influences and some we are not. How can we bypass the ones that aren't getting bypassed? We are attracting them; why are we attracting them? There are certainly some attractions within us. I call them sanskaras, I call them patterns. Attraction being present means there exists a bindu of attraction within us which is why the influence is affecting us. Sadhana is where the guru tells you, "Child, dissolve it. If that's not happening, go through it, experience it and see, but experience it with awareness. Remain conscious when experiencing it and it will get dissolved. Dissolve it or else it will become the cause of another birth and the cause lies within you."

Why is the influence impressing upon you? If the influence is pushing you towards something, it means there is some attraction within you which is pulling the influence towards you. Dissolve the centre within you and the influence will go elsewhere. It will stop pushing you and go towards someone who is attracting it. Why will it then come towards you? It comes towards you because you have some attraction for it within you. Accept that you have attractions inside, accept there's disease within you, only then will you be able to cure the disease. The cause of the disease is within you. You'll find it if you look for it. When you find the cause, dissolve it, go through it with awareness. When you go through it consciously, it will get dissolved and you'll make the jump. Then see the next pattern and so on. Initially there's attraction for excellence and beauty and an aversion towards that which is abominable. Stay indifferent towards both so that it doesn't come towards you but if it does, remember the cause is within you and experience it with awareness so that it gets completely destroyed. If you are truly able to remain equanimous, patterns will dissolve.

The importance of satsang is there because it allows a sudden detachment to arise, and without any process, the cleaning of patterns and sanskaras happens altogether. That is why the 'Grace of the Guru' is so important since without really experiencing the patterns, most of them get washed away. You are not aware of how things happen when you are with a guru. To you, the work going on in these sessions may either seem to be more or at times less, but while you're staying here, the Supreme alone knows the amount and the kind of work that is going on inside you. So many patterns have got dissolved which otherwise wouldn't have happened even in lifetimes to come. That is why the retreat has been kept and those who will stay long enough, those who are capable of staying for a longer duration and those who are patient, are being chosen. Their reservation for the next retreat is certain, while the possibility of others getting a chance will reduce. Seats will be limited. Cleansing happens for those who come here, a whole lot of cleansing. In fact, it happens without even going through or experiencing things. Sadguru and his aura are a protective shield. Being in the presence of a Sadguru and satsang is very important because he is a shield of protection. When you stay under his wings, influences don't come towards you. There are lots of influences that stay away from you, they just can't come close. In this way you'll stay protected from influences for a long time. Meanwhile your sadhana will start deepening and you'll get many glimpses. There will be lots going on which you won't understand, a kind of chaos. There will be many dreams and thoughts while in meditation. This is the work that is going on, work of removing the garbage stored inside. You were not even aware that so much filth was lying within you and which is now coming to light. So many thoughts and dreams have taken over, you can't even make out whether you slept or not. What is all this? A lot of work is going on and hence staying under the shelter of a Sadguru is a truly auspicious happening. Auspicious because it is beyond destiny. Lots is going on, and what is going on is the essence, rest is all useless.

Astrology does work, but there is a solution to come out of it. How can the bindu be protected from the influences? With this sadhana! Take the bindu to a place where the influences don't work. Take it to that point, take it in the presence of the Sadguru and the influences get bypassed. They leave the bindu, and the attraction prone bindus lying within fall asleep. Then at an opportune moment, they get destroyed. Everything starts boiling, all kinds of thoughts suddenly bubble up and get cleansed. Life is valuable because of this. If the entire system was robotic and systematic, life would be meaningless. There was no meaning to life so far, and sadhaka is one who takes refuge in a Sadguru. This is also an influence but a right one. It is then that everything else stops working for him and in the next birth, he is himself able to decide under which constellation, at what time, where and how he will take birth. A common man dies and takes birth, dies again and takes birth again with his school bag. A sadhaka dies, looks for a womb and when he doesn't find one, he waits and the esoteric system works for him. The support system makes him wait till an appropriate, suitable womb is found for him. By the time a womb is found for the soul of a sadhaka, ten or twenty or even fifty years could have passed. Finally, when a situation works out where the right womb for the soul is located, the soul enters the womb. Ninety percent of the soul's syllabus is complete, only ten percent remains. It takes birth with a very light bag and with the intention of completing its journey for good. The esoteric system helps the soul in this way and doesn't let it take birth immediately wherein the school bag is very fat and heavy. It looks for a situation where the books become less and the bag lighter. Sadhana means how many books are lessened. The soul is guided to go and live with complete awareness, reduce the books and if possible, burn the school bag completely and return. He'll be asked to go and live in the Himalayas, sit and burn all patterns up in black smoke, burn his school bag completely and merge all the black smoke in ether. Situations work out for a sadhaka wherein he can change his destiny. Your questions on astrology were aplenty but I took them up in a way where I gave what was needed and left out some things which weren't important. I have left those for the scientists. Whatever was important for sadhakas to know, that I have taken up.

Chapter 17

Humans Turning Into Machines? Effects of Reactions and Involvement

Sadhaka: Pranaam Guruji! My question is about the mind getting involved in thoughts, situations, what we see, what we hear, what we read etc. It's not just about getting involved, it is also that we react to those situations. What should we do about this? What effects does this have on us?

Swamiji: Involvement still happens! Association still happens! Reaction to situations still happens! Involvement happens the instant we react. The first condition to getting involved in a situation is giving a reaction. The moment we react to something, we get associated with it and the moment we get associated, the series begins – the series of analyzing, categorizing and defining the situation, of forming opinions and deciding whether we favour it or oppose it, whether we want to side it or not. Then we speculate how the situation can be turned in our favour and hence, the entire process is a process of adjustments. Understand carefully as to what it means when you say that a situation should be favourable for you. It means it should be compatible with your concepts. Who are you? A coming together of concepts is who you are! We have to go deep into the root cause to see this. Who are we? We are concepts conjoined together and we feel that situations should be according to our concepts. This means that things and situations are not acceptable to us the way they are.

What does concept mean? Standing in opposition to Astitva when we want things to happen our way is what a concept is. We are not agreeable to things as they are and we want to change them, manipulate them to suit us. Whenever this is the case, cleansing is required. If concepts exist, one needs to increase the cleansing and how can one increase the cleansing process? There are many methods that have been given for cleansing and you will have to make use of them. There are more than seventy-eighty methods that have already been given. Another thing that needs to be done for cleansing is to live consciously. With cleansing, awareness increases and with conscious living, the need for cleansing reduces. When we live with awareness, equanimity gets established. This needs to be understood again and again that equanimity gets firmly established when we live consciously, and that is why I have to repeatedly say this. Firmness of equanimity means awareness will increase. We will then stay equanimous, accepting everything as it is. The way things happen will be acceptable to us. When we accept everything as it is and do not react, new patterns will not get created and the old ones won't get updated. The sanskaras, the patterns of the sub-conscious mind are coming up all the time and you are getting associated with them by reacting towards them. The patterns keep coming up but you do not react - this is very important. What do you think is required for non-reaction? Consciousness, awareness is required and so, we are clear of this concept now that awareness needs to be maintained at all times and there is absolutely no need to intervene or try to improve anything. We don't have to be reformers trying to improve things. We only need to accept everything that's happening as it is. What happens with this is, the pattern that's rising up will play its part in the drama but will not receive any feeding from our side. What will happen when the pattern doesn't get fed? It will dissolve completely and as the dissolution of patterns will happen, liberation will happen.

Our habit of reacting is not from now but from lifetimes. If one cannot recollect the lifetimes, one can go back to one's childhood and see how we've been doing it since then. The training one has received is a training of reactions, as in, how to react immediately. One thing is 'reacting' and the other is 'knowing what's going on' - knowing whatever is happening means things are happening and being known. What happens by a continuous knowing is that the awareness grows and we don't get associated to anything. It is the body and mind that gets associated, but in the 'knowing' even the body and mind is getting known. We will stand behind and just know the reaction, knowing the mind and also knowing the body's involvement...we are aware towards all that is going on. We stand back knowing the reaction of the body and the mind; we see the entire process of the body and mind. We stand behind which means we are the witness to all that is going on which is a very good state. We are a witness to all that is happening, as it is. We just let the body do what it's doing and we let the mind do what it's doing – I am not this body, I am not this mind, I am the knower. 'I am the knower' is being said for the sake of understanding here... you don't have to actually say it, it is being known on its own. Where does the need to say anything arise or the need to even concentrate? Where does the need to take any decision arise when equanimity gets established?

If you watch deeply, you'll realize that when you're seeing things you feel you are watching without 'doing' anything, but you are actually doing. You see a web and deep within you go, 'yeah, web' or 'yeah, pole'. This happens with such speed that you can't hear the arising thought but reactions keep happening within. You see a tower on a mountain and you go deep inside, 'tower' or 'temple', 'grass', 'tree' and so on. This happens with such great speed that we can't even label it as a reaction. As you continue to see, there's fog, clouds, sun, sunlight, rain, etc. and we're so used to reacting. It is a major habit we are in because of which the separation continues as it is. What does reaction mean? It means 'I am separate'. Reaction is an announcement of you being separate from the 'whole'. Reacting means there are two, "I am reacting and there is another who I am reacting towards". We are creating duality. Just stand behind and watch this reaction also...the mind is reacting and the reaction is being known. Everything is being known. Reactions are a practice since too long which will continue to happen and won't go easily.

Sadhaka: Like you said that while the 'seeing' is happening, reactions are happening simultaneously. Do the reactions happen even when we are listening?

Swamiji: Look, this is called 'right listening'. When the 'right listening' is happening, it shows there is complete acceptance towards what is being heard and there won't be any reactions. When there is the 'right seeing' or 'right viewing', there is no reaction but if the seeing is not the 'right seeing', reactions happen. Reaction means we don't want things the way they are. We are not accepting them the way they are and are invariably giving some reaction or the other for example, "tower shouldn't be there, it's a wrong thing to be". Now, this reaction happened so quick that you couldn't even catch hold of it but it did happen. All the concepts related to a tower – a mobile tower, working of a T.V. etc. everything crossed your mind so fast that you just couldn't catch it. "Oh! There's a mesh. I hope it doesn't fall down. There are poles attached to it so that the mesh is held together." All this happens so fast that you can't catch it. When the awareness grows, you start catching on to these reactions completely and allow them to happen. Let whatever is happening, happen. Do not interfere with it. Thoughts like "why is this happening" shouldn't be paid heed to. Do not get entangled in such thoughts. Whatever is happening, is happening and it is being known. What is it that we have with us? We have consciousness which needs to be strengthened. Equanimity will get established when awareness grows and things will be known from somewhere far behind. Whatever is, will just be seen for what it is!

Concepts are involved in the reactions that take place. It is with reference or in relation to concepts that reactions happen. Concept is a mental pattern and when it gets activated, it sucks our vital energy. It sucks our energy anyways but when it gets activated, it sucks more than usual. It hacks the energy a lot and then some patterns start coming up. All patterns are taking up the energy but some show up which means that they need more energy than they already are receiving. Therefore, it comes up and takes up more energy. It hacks more energy and with that energy as a medium, it manipulates its reactions.

The Amazon Rain Forests lie directly on the equator and the trees there are extremely tall. Why is it that the trees are of such height over there? It is because of the high humidity there. The rains and humidity are ideal for those trees. There's a lot of shade because sunlight doesn't reach and to get the sunlight, the trees grow taller and taller using full force only to catch a glimpse of the sunlight, to hack that energy, to steal their portion of the sunlight from all that it has to offer. Similarly, a concept, a pattern comes on the surface to stay on a larger surface area, hack the available energy and play its game. Since it needs energy to play its game, it raises its head and comes up. Why do the mental defilements surface and the sensations intensify? It happens because they need energy to play themselves out, so they hack whatever energy they get hold of. If it's not sufficient then the breathing is hacked and once the breathing is hacked, it's the turn of the conscious mind to get hacked...all this, so that it can play its game. But if we are aware, we can stop all this energy from getting usurped and block the feeding process. We don't have to 'do' anything for this to happen. We only need to remain conscious and aware and the feeding gets blocked on its own for good. It can never happen again because once we are aware, the conscious mind cannot be hacked. It will not get any energy from the conscious mind and simultaneously, a stop has also been put to the hacking of the vital energy, which now gets diverted to the conscious mind. The concept, the pattern has no more vital energy left with it. The breath is also free now and not getting hacked of its energy anymore, but the play of the pattern still continues because it can stay alive only by its excitation. There is no such thing as a still or stationary pattern - patterns play themselves out continuously.

You may think that there's one thought at a time that shows up before the next one comes but that's not true. There are lakhs of thoughts going on within you simultaneously. You can only see the ones that come on the surface. All the patterns are active simultaneously but the ones which get more energy are more active and the ones that don't have that kind of energy available to them are slow in speed and they play out in a feel-dead manner. That play is so slow and seemingly remote that one can't really hear it or see it. It's important to have the 'right view' where the 'seeing' is happening without any involvement. Not getting involved means one is equanimous, which in turn means one is conscious and when one is conscious there is no defining anything. When there is no 'doing' involved, then 'only seeing' is happening. When this happens, no pattern gets made and none of the old patterns get fed either and therefore no reaction happens. We move towards the 'no-mind' state when reactions stop. If we find the right perception through any one of the five senses, there comes a stillness in that mode of perception and no reactions happen after that. The witness gets strengthened and everything keeps getting known. Where there is the presence of witness consciousness, the energy cannot get hacked, no thief can enter where the witness is awake. With no hackers getting an entry, the energy comes back in its natural flow. It rises up naturally through the spinal cord in the form of the 'sushumna naadi' and travels up to the sahastrara, the brahmkshetra. It goes to the brahmkshetra and gradually the speed of the energy flow increases to the point where it makes a hole (randra) in the brahmakshetra leading to the opening of the brahmarandra. The hole in the brahmakshetra is known as brahmarandra. The energy has now found a way and it starts flowing there. With this, the hacking of energy comes to an end and the activation of the brahmarandra is regularized and maintained. Once the brahmarandra opens, it should stay active for forty-eight minutes at a stretch, without any obstructions. If the energy continues to flow through it for forty-eight minutes without any defilements arising, without any other hacking or influence obstructing it, then it will never get blocked again. But in some cases where sadhana is the priority, it so happens that even if some hacking has taken place, that hacking breaks very soon. What is the reason for this 'breaking of obstruction' to happen? Definitely, the sadhaka would be connected to a Sadguru and must be a recipient of his live deshana. He must have invested his energy in the Sadguru's deshana and the Sadguru's energy must be integrated in it, that's why this 'breaking of obstruction' happens. Whenever you experience a downfall, the Sadguru will take your hand and lift you with the live desahna, the vital energy, the divine energy which is now within you. Wherever you miss a step or wander, you'll be pulled up. That is the reason deshanas of a living Sadguru and satsang are needed. After that, what the Sadguru gives and you receive is your identification. Stay in his company and remain in his presence. You ask me how many sessions will be done. Look, sessions are not so important but taking refuge in a Sadguru is…it's important to be in the Sadguru's presence. It's not important whether five sessions or seven sessions happen in a day. What is important is to stay in that energy field. Sessions are a happening – they happen when they happen. Sessions that are not a 'happening' are not sessions at all, they are just a drill. There is a difference between a drill and a session.

When people say 'so many sessions happened', you must understand that they were not sessions, they were a drill. Sessions are a happening and they happen when they happen, not otherwise. When they happen, the esoteric support system and the cosmic divine energy support system are involved. It's a big event and the divine energy is getting transferred in it. Sadguru is a medium, he is a cathartic agent. The 'Great Energy' passes through him and enters you and this work cannot happen without him. The energy is passing through him and that's the only way. If not for him, it won't pass. It passes through him, so his presence is very important and whenever you wander from the path, you'll be pulled up. That is why there is importance of 'diksha', initiation; but I do not give diksha. Neither do I give diksha nor do I promote asceticism. Diksha should happen on its own. I say that real diksha must 'happen'. What people of the olden times did, was it wrong? No, they were right in their own way. They did what was right according to them. I have been assigned work to deal with limited people who will arrive here. There won't be too much of a crowd here and for those who come, their diksha will happen on its own. It will be the real, true diksha – a happening! Earlier, masters would still give diksha;

why so? They would give diksha with the intent that it will happen sooner or later, but then they did get involved in some way because some kind of a ritual did take place. The sadhaka would follow the ritual and keep doing something. In such cases, the memory of that diksha keeps coming and they know it will happen sooner or later since a great Sadguru has given it to them. The diksha has not yet happened but still some support system has got connected to him if the master is a true Sadguru. Diksha is given by thousands of people but many of them are influencers.

There happened to be some Sadgurus like Osho, Lahiri Mahashaya, Yukteshwar Giri Ji, Ramakrishna Paramhansa and maybe one or two more. These were the rare Sadgurus. Influencers give diksha to lakhs of people but that is not the true diksha and it has no value. The diksha given by those rare Sadgurus I have named has some value, but they did some other experiments too. They gave some energy through the diksha which would help the sadhaka's journey to continue slowly and steadily, and in case he wandered in the middle, he would be supported. If not this, then he would be connected elsewhere, connected somewhere according to his worthiness.

There is something about diksha for sure, but what I have been assigned is to stay away from giving diksha. I don't have to give diksha. Diksha will happen to those whom it has to and the jump will be made. There is no turning back for those whom it happens to, because they have now reached a higher state from where there's no looking back. I don't say that this individual's mahaparinirvan or supreme liberation is fixed or guaranteed, but he has definitely reached a state from where his liberation cannot be stopped from happening either. There is no way his liberation can be stopped. If a lot of force is applied to hold him back from getting liberated for some reason, he can be held back for only one more life, not more than that. He cannot be kept stuck more than that. This is how it is. You must remain thankful that you get lifted up when needed but if you fall back, do not take this as negative like most people do. They feel they tasted a little peace but then they went back to where they were. Look at it this way that even if you wander away after diksha has happened, you are brought back and lifted up. You see there is such a huge support system working along with you. You have been wandering since eons and your sadhana is a relatively recent development. Ever since this real sadhana began, the progress has been so fast that you get it and it happens to you, but you fall back again and again and the moment you wander, you are lifted up. Who else can be as fortunate as you are!? You are fortunate. Your 'arrival' has happened so far; what has to happen further will also happen. It's all about priorities as to what is at the top of the list. You have the free will; it's just about playing the card! Everyone has a free will; how much are you able to make use of it? Grace will happen depending on how much free will is made use of, since the showers of grace are eternal.

WHAT IS SHAKTIPAT? CAN A GURU MAKE SHAKTIPAT HAPPEN FOR A SADHAKA?

Sadhaka: Guruji, namaskar! I have heard a lot about shaktipat. What is the importance of a shaktipat? Is it necessary for a sadhaka to get initiated with a shaktipat diksha? Can a guru give shaktipat? What does the sadhaka benefit from it?

Swamiji: There is a lot of attraction towards shaktipat which these days has turned into a business. It is being sold to people, "Come for getting initiated; pay this much and shaktipat will be done". So, you see, there is a business also going on. Shaktipat cannot be done; people are mistaken that a guru can give them a shaktipat or initiate them. Having said that, one needs to know that shaktipat does happen; it happens and it happens only through the guru as the medium. No guru has ever done an initiation but almost all shaktipat's have happened with the guru as the channel. Shaktipat is a happening which cannot happen without the guru but the guru does not do the shaktipat. It happens in the guru's presence; it cannot happen in the guru's absence, although the guru does not do it. It is an existential happening, a natural event but happens through the guru. Shaktipat happening without a guru is a very rare occurrence, probably one in lakhs. The individual must be blessed with some very special qualities for shaktipat to happen in the absence of a guru. Shaktipat, when it happens, it happens below the navel. Two, two and a half inches below the navel is the hara centre where you feel a current and the current is a perfect current, just like the current from a naked wire. It is literally like the current from a naked wire and nothing less than that; if you've ever touched a live wire, you'll understand. The experience does not happen any other way, it is exactly like a current from a live wire, as if a naked wire has been touched there for a moment or two with the current flowing. Post that, the state of the sadhaka changes. He should then pay more attention to the sadhana and must not wander here and there; neither must he collect garbage nor spend time in wrong company.

After shaktipat has occurred, one must exclusively be in sadhana as the possibility of his kundalini rising soon is there. The possibility of the kundalini rising increases after the shaktipat; it can happen anytime. This has a lot of benefits. What one needs to be aware of is that during the period when it happens, one must stop doing anything and everything. One must be involved in sadhana alone during that period. After that, sadhana should be a way of life.

WHAT IS INTUITION AND WHERE DOES IT COME FROM?

Sadhaka: Pranaam Guruji! Are the intuitions that come to a human being generated through the patterns or is it the support of the higher dimensions at play? Can intuition be used for spiritual growth?

Swamiji: Intuition does not come from a pattern; it cannot come from a pattern. Intuition comes from a higher dimension. It is an extra-sensory ability, an ability beyond the senses also called as the sixth-sense. This does not fall under the five senses of perception and is known as the sixth-sense. They are the signs that come from the higher dimensions, for example, it could be a warning before something is about to happen, a warning as well as a solution as to what should be done. It always comes from a higher dimension and this is what I call 'the esoteric support system'. This system supports, as well as, gives intuitions. There is the esoteric support system which is always providing support for sadhana to the sadhakas. In that support, the intuition is also included, as in, what should be done and what shouldn't, what to stay away from and what to go along with.

You must have heard about the 'inner voice', 'antaratma ki awaz'. What is that? It is the intuition. Why does the higher dimension support you? I have tried to explain this many times that the deities are cursed to do good; doing good for this one, doing good for that one, holding someone back from going astray, stopping someone from harming or spoiling things, protecting people, warning sadhakas from going astray, giving guidance to them so they can make the jump. They are cursed to do good. They'll come and disturb the sleep of the sadhakas; those sadhakas who they know can get up and do sadhana in the morning. They'll do something to wake them up – give them a dream which will wake them up, flash a torchlight or something of the sort so that they wake up for sadhana. The deities of higher dimensions put in all efforts to support. It is their job to support.

One more thing is that many of the sadhakas are deities themselves. Sadhaka means deities who have taken birth as humans again and now being the golden era, deities from higher dimensions have taken birth and got entangled in maya. Before taking birth, they had asked their friends, the other deities in their realm, to take care of them and keep nudging them because they knew after taking birth, they would get entangled in maya. They ask their own support system to alert them if they go astray at any point as humans. They themselves ask for the support before taking birth and they are assured by the other deities, their friends, who are going to stay back there, that they will provide the required support to these deities so that they get liberated. But when the time comes, they are deceived and taken to the higher realms again. They are then stuck there as a sakdagami which means they will have to take one more birth and become a guru. This happens so that when the fellow deities take birth, those who haven't yet had a chance to be born, these gurus can then support them. They are asked to support these fellow deities in return for the help they had given before. This kind of transference has to remain somewhat, for the Astitva's play to go on. Just think, if this sort of a thing wouldn't happen and all the sadgurus would quietly leave after liberation, what would you all do? If they said, "no support", what would you do? You would listen to the influencers who are serving all kinds of garbage!? Sometimes, deities don't become sadgurus. Taking birth here, making the jump and leaving without looking back, with no baggage left...this is impossible without the sadguru's support and this is an existential arrangement. It is the work of the higher dimensions to create a balance in the world. This is their work and they keep doing it. What they are doing is not wrong and because they are doing all this, you all are receiving the support. How else do you think you are being supported? It is possible that someone sitting here had me entangled and that is the reason I am here!

THE ENERGY FIELD SUPPORTS THE SADHAKAS DURING SADHANA

Sadhaka: Guruji, the holy places like Kedarnath, Amarkantak, the banks of River Narmada etc. are considered to be places where shakti resides even today. It is said that some siddha beings, in their subtle forms have been living in these places for years and that is why those shaktis are there. A lot of places are considered to be places with a divine energy field. What is all this?

Swamiji: Higher beings stay there in the subtle form. Any sacred place where the energy is very good will have the presence of higher beings there. There's a group of higher beings which resides in places which are big. There's no individual higher being present in a place. It's always a group which is working there and maintaining it. Even the Perfected Beings visit these sacred places. They visit these places and do their work that they go there for. When the Enlightened Ones reach these places, the higher beings get a lot of support from them. The divine cosmic energy support system gets energized when these beings visit these sacred sites. They recharge the idols in these places along with the entire sacred site. Just like you need something to recharge the gadgets…what is it called? Adapter, charger, connecter? What is that called? Yeah, so you need that to recharge, without which the instrument will not work. The perfected beings are like that; they reach there and the work gets done through them. They keep visiting these places as and when appropriate. When they visit, these places get charged with energy and the energy support system over there becomes very strong. The divine esoteric support system working there also gets strengthened. It is they who arrange for these enlightened beings to come to those places and then try to align themselves with the energy of these enlightened ones so that they too reach perfection through them.

Sadhaka: Guruji, why do these places experience floods etc.?

Swamiji: Yes, the floods etc. in these places come because they must come. They should come, that is why they come. Is cleaning required or not? You sweep and mop the floors in your house but sometimes you even wash them with water. Once in a year, during diwali, don't you wash your house with water? That day you don't mop the floor but take a pipe and scrub the floors well and wash them off. This must happen once or twice a year; the house must get thoroughly washed with water for the accumulated dirt to get removed. This is required and so whatever is necessary, that alone happens.

Sadhaka: Guruji, where else are such pure and high energy sacred sites?

Swamiji: There are many such sacred places. Badrinath is a very good place. You can go to Tirupati Balaji which is another wonderful place. There are some small temples in the forests with good energies. Some remote places also have some small ordinary looking temples worth visiting. One must go and feel the energy there. It is really good. There are some very old temples in villages, check out the energies there. Circumambulating around the river Narmada is considered great. Many energy support systems have been built there, so much so, that the whole of Narmada has been made energetic.

The river Narmada is energetic as is river Ganga. A lot of work has happened on these two rivers. There are many rivers but these two are the main ones and immense work has been done on these two rivers. Narmada is called 'Siddhidatri'. One must do sadhana there in their youth and once perfection is attained, one must go and live at the banks of Ganga. During the period of sadhana, be near Narmada and later, live near Ganga and give discourses. All have stayed there, be it Shiva, Kapil, Kanaad, Bhrigu; they all have stayed there. Who hasn't been there! Osho had been there, Sai Baba, Guru Nanak Dev, Kabirdas Ji and Rahedas Ji also stayed there. One gains merit by bathing in the Ganga but one gains merits by merely seeing the Narmada. 'Seeing it' means when you go to see the Narmada, you enter the cosmic energy support system, that energy field present there, and being in that energy field is advantageous. Why one benefits from taking a dip in the Ganga is because the molecular structure of the water has been changed.

Now it is another matter that I also make fun of certain things people say, just like Ramakrishna Paramhansa would. When someone asked him if the sins get washed away by taking a dip in the Ganga, he would say, "Yes, when you take a dip in the Ganga, your sins leave you and enter the river, but when you come out of the river, the sins come back into you again." People think they can keep doing wrong and then go and wash off their sins by taking dips in the Ganga. They misuse it.

Sin is when we are too involved, attached and meshed up in the worldly affairs. By bathing in the Ganga, you think those attachments will reduce? What is meant by the word 'sin'? Sin doesn't mean that all your wrong actions will get washed away or your worldly attachments will reduce by bathing in the Ganga. It means that a sense of detachment slowly arises when you bathe in it, but when you are near Narmada, it just happens on its own. Staying near river Narmada, the sense of detachment keeps getting profound. I have stayed a lot near Narmada. My childhood and youth were spent at the banks of Narmada; I would go and live near the river time and again.

GIVING UP ON TEMPLES, PRAYERS, SCRIPTURES AND RITUALS

Sadhaka: Swamiji, does giving up on temples, prayers, scriptures and rituals have a negative impact in any way? There is haunting fear that something might happen or go wrong if we don't go to the temple and do the rituals. What should we do regarding this?

Swamiji: When we start resonating in one place and give up going to places which we were attracted to earlier, there is a feeling that we are disrespecting those places. This feeling is accompanied by a fear which says what if something goes wrong and a fear of a curse coming our way. All kinds of thoughts take over like, "I hope this doesn't happen or that doesn't happen". These are mind games and they will continue. Despite all this, if surrender is happening where we're currently resonating, then the wandering ceases once the surrender is complete. Even so, I do not stop anyone from visiting temples if they want to but the frequency of these visits naturally reduces. You will go when you feel like it and not go as a ritual. You'll make good use of the energies present there without getting entangled in any rituals. Now when you're in the temple, you will not ask for things in a ritualistic manner of "give me this, give me that". I say if you want to ask for something, you must ask directly, "Lord, I can't find anyone who can come and do the sweeping, mopping, wash vessels and cook food. I will make an offering of one kilogram of sweets. Do the household chores and since the office boy is also absent, do his work as well."

I don't oppose anything. Go and enjoy. In fact, I also take those who come here, to some of the temples myself; temples where the energy is good. I ask them to sit there in sadhana and let the meditation happen. If you feel disturbed about something, just observe the arising emotion or disturbance and face it. Face the fear and ask, "What will happen if I don't go there?" We are not disrespecting anybody by not going there anymore. Not going somewhere is not disrespecting the place...you're not a slave. What will happen if you don't go to a certain place? That fear will slowly dissolve. You have to face it yourself. Fear is the reason behind not facing the issue. Once you face it directly, the fear vanishes. Fear means you are not facing the arising emotion but once you face it, it goes.

Sadhaka: Guruji, does one attain liberation by doing good actions?

Swamiji: A good birth happens once again! By doing good actions, a good birth happens. How will liberation happen? Isn't karma a bondage? Liberation is a huge event. It is beyond good and bad, beyond holy and unholy. It is unmeasurable. If you live with a calculative mindset, how's liberation possible? You do good, you'll receive something good in return; you donate an amount and you'll get back accordingly. Where will liberation come from? You'll receive liberation in lieu of donation or charity!? Look, the thing is that these good deeds do become a stepping stone. It's good to feed the hungry, it's good to do charity. Good things must happen, but they must not be done with the thought, "what will happen with this or what will I get in return?" Something will happen with this also. I am not against it but it is good if it happens naturally, from within, and not with a calculative mind of receiving something in return. One must do it because it feels good to do so. One must do it because it brings joy. When something is a joy for us, then the joy goes on increasing till it reaches liberation and turns into supreme joy (paramanand). Supreme joy is liberation. That is why I say, do not go around announcing what you do, be it charity or supporting someone or some cause. The right hand should be unaware of what the left hand has done. One must never go around making announcements of any virtuous deeds done or acts of benefitting others.

– AUM

Gratitude

I bow down in gratitude to you, Sadgurudev, for giving this invaluable opportunity of translating 'Atmagyan ka Vigyan'. It has been a humbling and an extremely transformative experience. No words can ever thank you enough for the wisdom you unceasingly bestow upon us.

I seek forgiveness from you as well as the readers, for any errors or mistakes that may have gone unnoticed. I sincerely hope that each one who holds a copy of this work, this book, makes the jump. It was you, Astitva, who graced this 'happening', end to end.

May we all remain under the canopy of your love and benediction. May the Great Liberation happen under your refuge.

– Geeta

Follow & Subscribe:

WhatsApp:

Siddha Community

https://chat.whatsapp.com/FOKEBWK0JQQ8AFqLtdY6eA?mode=ac_t

YouTube Channel:

The Siddha Talks

Siddha Sangeet

Siddha Kriya

Divya Dhyanam

Website:

Siddha Kutumbakam

"https://siddhakutumbakam.com/"

siddhakutumbakam.org

Instagram:

Siddha Kutumbakam

Facebook:

Siddha Kutumbakam

www.ingramcontent.com/pod-product-compliance
Lightning Source LLC
LaVergne TN
LVHW090314210926
848480LV00001B/244
* 9 7 9 8 9 0 3 9 2 2 5 7 4 *

www.ingramcontent.com/pod-product-compliance
Lightning Source LLC
LaVergne TN
LVHW090318210926
848480LV00001B/285